STORM
from the
EAST

STORM FROM THE EAST

From Genghis Khan to Khubilai Khan

ROBERT MARSHALL

BBC BOOKS

TO THE MEMORY OF BRUCE NORMAN

Published by BBC Books,
a division of BBC Enterprises Limited,
Woodlands, 80 Wood Lane
London W12 0TT
First published 1993

ISBN 0 563 36338 X

Designed by Harry Green
Picture research by Paul Snelgrove
Maps by Technical Arts Services

Set in Plantin Light by Ace Filmsetting Ltd, Frome, Somerset
Printed and bound in England by Clays Ltd, St Ives plc
Colour separation by Technik Ltd, Berkhamsted
Jacket printed by Lawrence Allen Ltd, Weston-super-Mare

Frontispiece: Genghis Khan with his sons
Hulegu and Khubilai, after a hunt

CONTENTS

PICTURE CREDITS

MAPS

ACKNOWLEDGEMENTS

This book is largely a product of the work done by a great many people who came together to work on the television series *Storm from the East*, the inspiration for which came from my colleagues at NHK Television in Japan. Over the course of the last two years we have shared and learnt a great deal together, and I want to give credit to their contributions. First of all Mr Takashi Inoue whose determination ensured the project happened at all. I would also like to acknowledge the work of Hisashi Anzai, Sanji Eto and Nobuya Yamamoto. I especially want to thank my colleague and now friend, Tomohito Terai, for his dedication, enthusiasm and indomitable spirit of co-operation.

I am, of course, deeply indebted to everyone who worked on the series here in London. Their contribution has been enormous. I want to mention, in no particular order, John Slater, Vivianna Woodruff, Jo Langford, Susan Vogel, Angela Moonshine, John Adderley, Ron Brown, Paul Dawe, Mike Burton, Sheila Ableman, Martha Caute, Joanna Wiese, Paul Snelgrove, Harry Green, and, especially, Habie Schwarz for her invaluable scholarship and imagination.

Naturally I have relied a great deal on the contribution of our academic advisers, and their enthusiasm for the series has been a great encouragement. I want to acknowledge the work of James Chambers for his insight into Mongol military matters, Dr Morris Rossabi for his work on Khubilai, and Drs Reuven Amitai-Preiss, Peter Morgan and Judy Kolbas for their advice on the Mongols in the Middle East. My deepest gratitude goes to our series consultant, Dr David Morgan, author of *The Mongols*, for his guidance throughout and for patiently reading my manuscript.

Robert Marshall
London 1992

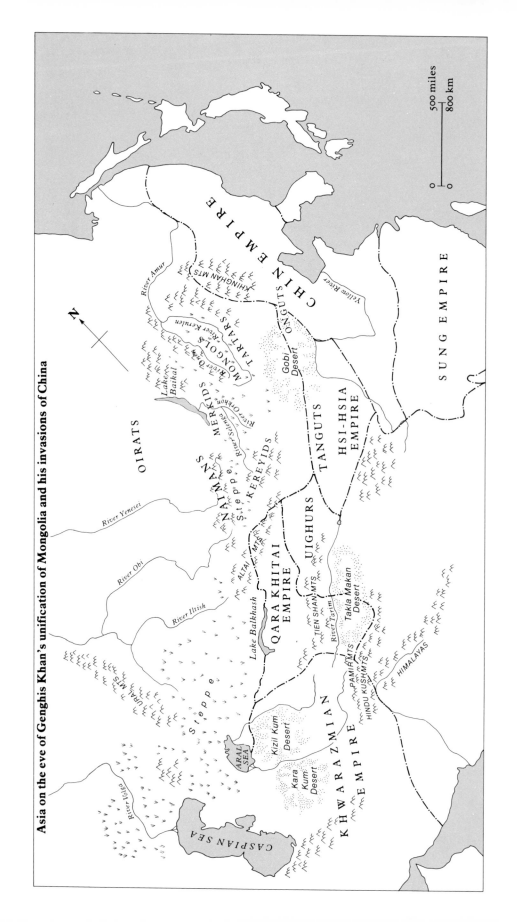

Asia on the eve of Genghis Khan's unification of Mongolia and his invasions of China

CHIN EMPIRE

SUNG EMPIRE

OIRATS

MERKIDS

NAIMANS

KEREYIDS

Steppe

MONGOLS

TARTARS

ONGUTS

Gobi Desert

TANGUTS

HSI-HSIA EMPIRE

UIGHURS

QARA KHITAI EMPIRE

Takla Makan Desert

Lake Baikal

River Selenga

River Orhon

River Kerulen

River Onon

River Amur

Yellow River

KHINGHAN MTS

River Yenesei

River Obi

River Iltish

Lake Balkhash

ALTAI MTS

TIEN SHAN MTS

River Tarim

PAMIR MTS

HINDU KUSH MTS

HIMALAYAS

URAL MTS

Steppe

Kizil Kum Desert

Kara Kum Desert

ARAL SEA

KHWARAZMIAN EMPIRE

CASPIAN SEA

River Volga

N

500 miles
800 km

1

BIRTH

OF A NATION

N THE CENTRE OF THE MAIN SQUARE in Cracow stands St Mary's church, considered one of the most important churches in Poland. Every hour on the hour, a trumpeter from the Cracow fire department presents himself at the balcony of the main tower and blows an alarm. This ceremony has taken place each day, almost continuously since the middle of the thirteenth century. It commemorates the destruction of the city, for the trumpeter is blowing a call to arms, a signal that the enemy has been sighted and is at the gates. As the trumpeter sounds his haunting melody he comes to an abrupt halt midway through the call – at precisely the moment, so legend has it, when the Mongol arrow struck.

When the alarm was being sounded on that first occasion, more than 700 years ago, the population of Cracow were already abandoning the city, making for the forests beyond the city walls. Some days before, the Polish ruler Duke Boleslaw the Chaste had sent his army out to meet the invaders; but they were ambushed and the small Polish force was decimated under a hail of arrows. When the news reached Cracow, Boleslaw and his family gathered up all the

Overleaf: The Onon River in north-eastern Mongolia, said to be
the birth place of the Mongols. According to legend, a blue wolf and his mate,
a fallow deer, settled here to raise their offspring, who became the tribe
known as the Mongols.

wealth they could carry. With the remaining contingent of soldiers they fled for Hungary, leaving the citizens to fend for themselves. When the main body of the invading army reached the city, they found the streets strangely quiet, and on 24 March 1241, Palm Sunday, Cracow was put to the torch.

THE FURY OF THE TARTARS

To the rest of Europe, the news of the sacking of Cracow seemed a terrible omen; an unearthly storm was sweeping away everything in its path. From Cracow the invader moved west to confront an allied European army of local mercenaries, Teutonic Knights, Knights Templars and Hospitallers – the very flower of Europe's chivalry. For the Europeans the battle was a complete disaster and within a few days a second great Christian army was destroyed. Bewildered medieval chroniclers could make no sense of it; confused by the lightning tactics of the invader, they consistently estimated his strength at four or five times their actual numbers. However, for the European commanders the experience had been a devastating lesson in warfare. At every major battle the invaders had been outnumbered and yet their generals constantly outmanoeuvred, out-thought and out-fought the Europeans. Their armies had operated like disciplined machines, co-ordinating a complex series of tactical moves with extraordinary precision. In the grand scheme of things, the Mongol armies had conducted a brilliantly complex campaign, carefully planned and executed from first to last – from Poland to the Hungarian prairies.

News of these disasters swept through the rest of Europe, bringing predictions of utter destruction and damnation. Rumours spread of diabolical atrocities committed by inhuman monsters, of creatures with the head of a horse that devoured their victims, possessed supernatural powers and had been unleashed to bring retribution upon an ungodly world. In Germany this superstitious hysteria generated stories that the Mongols were actually one of the lost tribes of Israel and that Jewish merchants were smuggling arms to them across the borders. As a result many innocent Jews were summarily and pointlessly executed at frontier posts. The Hungarians described the invaders as 'dog-faced Tartars', while a French monk living in Austria wrote that, after the Mongol soldiers had raped European women, they tore off their victim's breasts and delivered these 'delicacies' to their 'dog-headed' princes, who devoured them.

The Church was not above regurgitating ancient myths and legends in a vain attempt to explain the disaster. A Dominican monk, Ricoldo of Monte Croce, explained that the name Mongol was derived from Mogogoli, the sons

of the legendary Magog. Gog and Magog, so the legend goes, had been a pair of marauding giants who had terrorized Europe in ancient times. They had been defeated by Alexander the Great and locked away behind massive gates in the Caucasus Mountains. Now their descendants were loose and bent upon the destruction of civilization. Only by invoking the name of Alexander could these monsters be subdued. In packed churches across northern Europe sermons were being conducted before a terrified population, while prayers were offered up pleading: '. . . from the fury of the Tartars, oh Lord deliver us'. The only sizeable army that might stand in the path of the invader was that of the French King, who was prepared for the onslaught but expected martyrdom. To the Pope it seemed that all of Christendom would be destroyed: 'When we consider that through these Tartars the name of Christian might utterly perish, our bones shudder at the thought.'

Europe had been struck and left reeling by an alien force that might just as well have come from Mars. The Mongols, or Tartars as they called them, were a race that had emerged from a land which, to Europeans, was on no known map. Narrow and inward-looking Europe had no knowledge or experience of the territories beyond the Urals. Indeed, European ignorance of who the Mongols were or what they had accomplished persisted for centuries. This was not just because of the limits of European knowledge, but also because the sheer breadth and scope of the Mongol conquests beggared the imagination. Never had so much territory been conquered so quickly. The sudden and overwhelming devastation that shook Europe to its core had already been visited upon the entire expanse of Asia. From the Korean peninsula to the River Danube, nearly a third of the world's land surface lay under the command of one single family – and all this had been achieved in less than fifty years. Yet still they continued to expand. No more than thirty years after their armies had stood on the frontiers of Germany, the Mongols had completed the conquest of all of China and were launching invasions upon Japan and Java. By any standards it was a breathtaking achievement.

The storm that swept across the world during the thirteenth century changed the political boundaries of Asia and Europe, uprooted entire peoples and dispersed them across the continent. It transformed the ethnic character of many regions, while at the same time permanently changing the strength

Overleaf: The Mongolian plateau is subject to dramatic extremes of climate. From above 40°C (104°F) in the summer, the mercury plunges to −40°C (−40°F) in the winter, causing the lakes and rivers to remain frozen for nearly six months of the year.

and influence of the three major religions: Islam, Buddhism and Christianity. Most important, the Mongols opened up the East to the West, expanded our knowledge of the world and in so doing created for the first time one whole world.

MOUNTED HERDSMEN

All of this is remarkable enough, yet when one considers the Mongols' humble beginning it is almost beyond comprehension. At the end of the twelfth century, the Mongols were one of a number of small nomadic tribes that inhabited an isolated plateau in the heart of Central Asia. To the west lay two massive and converging chains of mountains, the Altai and the Tien Shan; to the north were the vast frozen Siberian forests; while the Gobi desert lay to the south and the Khinghan Mountains to the east. Though technically the Mongolian Plateau lies within that vast expanse known as the steppe which extends across the breadth of Asia from Manchuria to Hungary, in reality it is locked behind natural barriers that kept the inhabitants safe from invasion for centuries.

The plateau lies some 1200 m (4000 feet) above sea level and is subject to dramatic extremes of climate. In the summer the temperature often rises above 40°C (104°F) and in winter drops well below −40°C (−40°F). The soil itself varies from a loose gravel to a thin clay and is frozen hard during the winter. By November all the streams, rivers and lakes are also completely frozen and water has to be got by laboriously cutting and dragging large blocks of ice to the nearest fire. Nothing stirs until April. Add to the extreme climate a low rainfall, and it is clear that the steppe makes poor agricultural land. However, during the summer it is carpeted by a luxurious blanket of grass that gives the countryside the appearance of a gently undulating billiard table. Even during the winter months, the more sheltered valleys retain a hardy turf that provides reliable pasture for the herds of sheep, goats, cattle and horses that nomads have kept here for centuries.

The life of the Mongols is therefore a constant cycle of seasonal migrations from the flat open summer pastures to protected river valleys for the winter. These migrations are not arbitrary. Each tribe or clan would return to their traditional pastures year after year, and would only alter this pattern if the growing size of their flocks obliged them to search for more land, or if they were forced off their traditional territory by other nomads. Maintaining control of traditional pasture or seeking out better pastures was a common source of conflict between the Mongol tribes. The need for good grazing land for their herds was a primary preoccupation, for their survival depended on

it. Today, the life of the average Mongol herdsman has changed little in 800 years. Sheep still provide the main staples of life: meat, milk, cheese, leather and wool for clothing and the manufacture of felt from which they still build their tents. Cattle are also kept for meat, but are more commonly used as beasts of burden. During the autumn months each Mongol family slaughters a number of their sheep, prepares the mutton and then freezes it, usually by simply burying it in the ground before the snows arrive. Mutton is the major source of protein, and through the long winters it sustains the population on meals that are usually produced by melting a block of ice in a cauldron and then boiling frozen slabs of the stuff until it forms a thick stew. Another useful food during the long winters is *ayrag*, a mildly alcoholic and somewhat bitter fermentation made from mare's milk.

Today, extended nomadic families live on large collectives of land controlled by the state. Any number of families may share these tracts of land, herding their sheep or horses, which are bred both for riding and for their milk. Eight hundred years ago, the Mongols lived not on collectives but in loosely defined tribes or clans. They tended not to live together in a single large encampment; instead, the tribe would be scattered amongst any number of smaller encampments that might be spread across two or three different valleys. These encampments had to be mobile enough to be struck and loaded on to wagons for the annual migration. An essential aid to this mobility was the *ger* or *yurt*, the Mongol tent which is still made by stretching a piece of thick woollen felt across a squat cylindrical framework of thin wooden struts. The floor is usually covered by simple planking while beds, cupboards and chests containing the family heirlooms are arranged in a circle against the wall. Beside the centre pole stands a stove which is vented through a hole in the roof. Although the average *ger* can be dismantled and re-erected in under an hour, it was not uncommon for clans simply to lift the entire structure on to the back of an ox-cart. It must have been an extraordinary sight, the migration of vast herds of sheep and horses and, in their midst, three or four mobile *gers* sailing across the steppe.

The key to the nomads' dominion over the steppe was the horse. Since its domestication in southern Russia during the second millennium BC, the horse's remarkable speed and stamina has been exploited by steppe nomads. It became an essential element of daily life, the primary means of transport, an aid for tending the herds and of course an invaluable asset for the hunt. All steppe nomads were exceptional hunters. Their principal weapon was the compound bow, made from alternate sections of horn and bamboo, bonded together by silk and resin. They developed stirrups (perhaps borrowed from the Chinese), which enabled them to ride without using reins. As a result they

Most steppe nomads still live in the traditional *yurt* or *ger*. Made of felt
stretched across a wooden frame, it can be dismantled and loaded onto an
ox-cart in under an hour.

could fire arrows or use the lasso while at full gallop. It was these skills that were
to contribute to the emergence of a great military power from the heart of the
Asian grasslands.

From around 800 BC onwards, the settled societies to the south began
encountering nomadic horsemen who appeared periodically, sometimes
attacked and pillaged the towns and villages, and then disappeared again. But
what set these people apart from their predecessors was their exclusive use of
cavalry: a swift and lethal force of men on horseback, able to direct a withering
barrage of arrows at their enemies from a distance. They became the scourge
of most settled societies. Indeed, historians have recorded that wave upon
wave of nomadic horsemen have charged out of Asia through the low passes
of the Tien Shan and Altai Mountains into Europe or down into the Middle
East, from the days of the Scythians in the fifth and sixth centuries BC right up
to the Mongols.

The Mongols excelled at the hunt. This scene,
from a Persian manuscript *c.*1300, shows two horsemen
feasting on wild boar.

The relationship between the steppe nomads and settled societies was
never an easy one. Living in their pastoral wilderness for century upon
century, trapped within a perennial struggle against climate and the fluctuations of tribal power, the nomads developed no technologies, produced no
manufactures nor even learned simple mining. The demands of seasonal
migrations made this impossible. So the nomadic societies soon developed a
traditional dependency upon the settled societies that had developed in the
Middle East and China. Wrought metals and products such as swords,
armour, silks, gold and silver were bought, traded or stolen. In terms of the
exchange of materials it was a very one-sided relationship, for the nomads had
little to offer in return but woollen goods and animal skins.

Be that as it may, the nomadic horsemen never saw themselves as
inferior to the settled societies. Quite the opposite. For more than 2000 years
the people of the steppe confronted the largest agrarian society in the world,

19

China, without ever being politically or culturally absorbed by it. Indeed, these two societies surveyed one another with mutual arrogance. China's deeply rooted cultural traditions had led to a perception of itself as historically superior to all other societies and states. Its ancient name of Chung-kuo (Middle Kingdom) implied that it was the very heart of civilization, and because of the resilience of its cultural traditions the Chinese also have a long history of absorbing other civilizations that hovered along its border – or heavily influencing the more distant cultures of such fiercely independent societies as Korea, Japan and Vietnam. Virtually all of eastern Asia adopted Chinese calendars, cuisine and literacy. All, that is, except for the nomadic horsemen of the steppe.

They not only rejected Chinese culture and ideology, they also refused to see any value in it – except for the few material goods that it could provide. From their perspective the vast majority of the Chinese population spent their lives on their hands and knees scratching away at the soil. To the nomadic horseman, the peasant farmer was regarded with the utmost contempt, and was of less value than a horse. The contempt was mutual. Chinese government officials writing about how to deal with the bands of horsemen on their borders argued that it was impossible to have proper relations with people who migrated to and fro like birds and beasts. So the relationship between these two peoples developed along simple lines: the Chinese saw the periodic incursions as a blight, not unlike a natural disaster such as flood or famine, that had to be dealt with as and when it arose, usually by means of large bribes in return for being left unharmed; while the horsemen, on the other hand, saw the Chinese as little more than a resource to be plundered.

EARLY NOMADIC EMPIRES

The first major empire to be forged by nomadic horsemen was that of the Turks, the people who eventually colonized Anatolia. From around the sixth and seventh centuries AD they controlled an exclusively steppe empire that extended from the Chinese frontier to the Black Sea. After the collapse of the Turkish empire the eastern steppe came to be dominated by the Uighurs, a semi-nomadic people who had their capital in the Orkhon valley, in what is now Hentiy Province in modern-day Mongolia. The Uighurs were a cultured people, natural traders and sophisticated artists. After the collapse of their empire in the ninth century they migrated southwards and westwards to settle along the Tarim River, in what is now Sinkiang, at the most western extremity of modern China. Here the Uighurs established themselves and flourished for another 300 years. They adapted an alphabet from the people in eastern Persia

and were the first semi-nomadic people to become literate, going on to develop a sophisticated legal system and a civil service.

The Uighurs had been forced out of their original domain in western Mongolia by the Khitans, another semi-nomadic people who conquered most of Mongolia and northern China. In the tradition of all conquerors of China, the Khitans were soon tamed by the resilience of Chinese civilization and absorbed into the great Chinese melting pot. To assume control of China it was expected that the invader would adopt a Chinese name and establish a new dynasty; this the Khitans did, calling themselves Liao. With the Sinicization of the Khitans, their invasion actually became a reverse conquest, effectively extending Chinese control westwards into Mongolia. The Liao established a new frontier, forcing the remaining Turkish peoples and any others who would not submit further to the west. It was the Liao Dynasty's occupation of this part of the eastern steppe that provides historians with the first evidence of the appearance of a people that eventually became known as Mongols.

By the early twelfth century the Khitans themselves were forced out of northern China, displaced by yet another semi-nomadic invader, the Jurchen from Manchuria. These new people were less interested in the lands beyond the traditional Chinese frontier, and left the eastern steppe to the tribes that had traditionally inhabited them. The Jurchen were more concerned with securing control over China proper, which they managed to do far more successfully than had the Khitans. But the Khitans, like the Uighurs, didn't simply disappear. One of the Khitan princes, together with a large group of his followers who were unwilling to submit to Jurchen rule, migrated westwards deep into Central Asia to establish a new empire called Qara Khitai. They settled even further west than had the Uighurs, near Lake Balkhash close to the eastern frontiers of the great Persian empire. Meanwhile the Jurchen, having conquered northern China, adopted the dynastic name Chin and it was this dynasty that was fated to encounter the emerging Mongol empire.

SECRET HISTORY

However, at this time the Mongols were still an emerging people struggling along with other tribal groups for control of the eastern steppe. Historians find it impossible to account for Mongolian history before the thirteenth century. Most early descriptions of nomadic empires come from the literate civilizations like the Chinese or Persians, whose own histories describe the frequent encounters they had with nomadic invaders. Apart from the Uighurs, most nomadic groups, and certainly the Mongols, were illiterate. So, whether by design or circumstance, Mongol history begins with Genghis Khan, because

it was he who commanded that the Mongols adopt the Uighur script and adapt it to the Mongolian language. After Genghis's death his successor commissioned the famous *Secret History of the Mongols*. In a curious mixture of myth, legend and apparent fact it describes the rise of the Mongol people, the early life and struggles of Genghis Khan and his breathtaking world conquests. Scholarly opinion varies on whether it actually does provide a reliable account of Mongol history. For some it is no more reliable than the Nordic sagas, a collection of legends brought together to enhance the reputation of Genghis. But others disagree. There was once an official history kept at the Mongol court known as the *Altan Debter*. Substantial portions of it survive in Persian and Chinese histories, and these scraps make certain things clear. The *Altan Debter* and the *Secret History* are two completely separate works, compiled independently of each other; and yet they describe the same events in roughly the same way. So it is more than probable that at least some portions of the *Secret History* can be assumed to be fact.

It has to be said, however, that the *Secret History* begins quite solidly in the realms of myth, as it describes the genesis of the Mongols.

> There was a blue wolf which was born
> having [his] destiny from heaven above.
> His spouse was a fallow doe.
> They came, passing over the Sea.
> Batacaciqan was born when they camped
> at the head of the Onon River,
> at [Mount] Burkan Qaldun.

In the traditions of Old Testament genealogies, the *Secret History* then goes on to recount how Batacaciqan begat Tamaca and Tamaca begat Qoricar Mergan . . . and so on until it quickly arrives at the twelfth century, where at least some events can be corroborated by Chinese sources. The most important subject that the work covers is the early life and struggles of Temuchin, as Genghis was known before he assumed the title Great Khan. Here again historians speculate about its value as a reliable account. The description of his rise to power becomes something of a litany of betrayal and revenge, as one after another of the tribal rulers proves to be disloyal and the young Temuchin is forced to take reprisals. His motives are always above reproach, his methods ruthless but justified. Because of this repetitive cycle of events it is tempting to see the *Secret History* as merely a panegyric; a more sober view might suggest that it was Temuchin who had been less than straight with his rivals, and his struggle nothing more than the most ruthless scramble for absolute supremacy. But that is too simple, for the *Secret History* also produces at times

a very unflattering picture of Temuchin. Would a panegyric mention that the young Genghis Khan was afraid of dogs, or describe how he murdered his half-brother and was then bitterly rebuked by his mother? Although it is an extremely difficult work to classify, it is at least invaluable in one respect: it is a wholly Mongol account of Mongol history and life. It vividly presents a Mongol perspective of the importance of their conquests and their place in the world at that time. And whether it is historically accurate or not, it does present an extremely dramatic profile of one of the greatest generals of all time.

The political scene in Mongolia during the twelfth century was characterized by a struggle amongst all the tribes to fill the vacuum left by the defeat of the Khitan by the Jurchen. These tribes are perhaps more correctly described as Turko-Mongol, in that they all spoke either Turkish or Mongolian and intermarried. Indeed it was forbidden for any male to marry within his own tribe. The most powerful of the tribes during Temuchin's youth were the Tartars, who lived alongside the Mongols in eastern Mongolia. Other tribes that play a part in the saga are the Kereyids, who lived in the very centre of Mongolia, the Merkids who were to the north of them, and the Naimans, to the west. It is often confusing that the term 'Tartar' seems interchangeable with 'Mongol', when originally they were two separate tribes and in fact were sworn enemies. It is even more confusing since, during the early civil wars, the Mongols eventually exterminated virtually the entire Tartar tribe. The explanation lies in the fact that, up to the point when the Mongols gained supremacy, the Tartars had been the most prominent of all the steppe tribes; in addition, their name appears in Chinese registers dating back to the eighth century. Consequently, the name was employed by both Chinese and others to refer to all the steppe tribes of central Asia. The Tartars enjoyed this pre-eminence over the other tribes because they were supported by the Chin Chinese.

It was the traditional tactic of the Chinese, of whatever dynasty, to develop an alliance with one of the nomadic tribes on its frontier and encourage them to sow unrest amongst the remainder. Should another of the tribes appear to be gaining the upper hand, the Chinese would abandon their ally and take up with the emerging new tribe. The purpose was, of course, to foster internal strife, for as long as the tribes fought amongst themselves they were unlikely to pose a threat to anyone else. This was the background against which Temuchin rose to greatness. But the task of uniting the tribes under his leadership and maintaining that leadership against the usual fluctuations of steppe politics would be an extraordinary achievement. Temuchin emerged from an extremely marginal position within the clan hierarchy. Although born of a clan that had provided leaders in the past, there was no tradition of

leadership being passed on through a hereditary title. Mongol clan or tribal leaders were chosen because they had demonstrated particular qualities in battle or in some other field – and leaders were also as easily abandoned if they failed to maintain those leadership qualities. There were loose confederations of clans, structured around a unique Mongol concept known as the *anda*: a boon companion who has sworn his brotherhood to another. However, none of these confederations had ever succeeded in permanently dominating the others, and there was definitely no history of all the Mongol tribes ever having been united under a single leader in the past. Besides, the Chin were extremely successful at exploiting the enmity that arose towards of any leader of these confederations. If all this suggests that Temuchin had the odds strongly stacked against him, then it is hardly surprising that his conquest of the steppe tribes and the establishment of order consumed most of his adult life.

TEMUCHIN'S RISE TO POWER

Temuchin was probably born in 1167 of the Bjorjin clan. His father, Yesugei Bat'atur, was the leader of a small clan that had been caught up in the relentless feuding between the Mongol and Tartar tribes. Yesugei had arranged a marriage for his nine-year-old son Temuchin with a girl from his wife's tribe, the Unggirad. According to Mongol custom, he had left his son with his future in-laws. During the journey home he encountered some Tartars. Unaware of their identity, Yesugei asked them for a drink. The Tartars, on the other hand, recognized their old rival and gave him a draught of a slow-acting poison. By the time he reached his family *ger* his life was already slipping away, and he died before nightfall. Temuchin was summoned home. His mother, Ho'elun Ujin, attempted to keep her late husband's people together but a rival clan, the Tayichi'ud, incited them to desert the family. Ho'elun and her children were forced to migrate to the mountains near the River Onon where, friendless and in constant danger, they survived on wild berries and by hunting and fishing. In this harsh environment Temuchin grew into adolescence, during which time he befriended a boy named Jamukha, who came from another clan and who became his *anda*. Their lives would later become closely entwined.

It was in this period of harsh hand-to-mouth existence that Temuchin is known to have quarrelled with his half-brother over some birds they had shot, and in a moment of uncontrolled temper shot him 'as though at target practice'. It seems unlikely that they were merely arguing over the spoils from a hunt, but rather that Temuchin was already exercising the rudiments of clan politics by eliminating a potential rival for the head of the family. In any case,

according to the *Secret History*, Temuchin's mother recoiled in horror, branding him a murderer. She went on to lament:

> At the moment when you have no companion other than your shadow;
> At the moment when you have no whip other than your tail,
> At the moment when you are saying, 'By whom shall we take vengeance?' you
> do this to each other. Saying, 'How shall we live. . . .'

Soon his mother's distress turned to anguish as Temuchin was carried off by the Tayichi'ud clan, the people who had incited the late Yesugei's men to abandon the family. Some scholars claim it was in revenge for the murder of Temuchin's half-brother, who had been related to the Tayichi'ud. Others suggest it was simply a pre-emptive strike for fear the young Temuchin might later seek revenge for the hardship his mother and family had been forced to endure. According to the *Secret History*, Temuchin remained a captive for some months but managed to escape during the celebrations of a local festival. He was helped by a number of characters, all of whom are rewarded in later episodes of the *Secret History*. What seems to be emerging in these accounts of Temuchin's development is a picture of a young man who, although of noble birth, is familiar with the life of the peasantry, has learnt from his elders how capricious and faithless they could be, and how true loyalty was often found outside the clan or tribe. At the age of sixteen he returned to the Unggirad clan to marry his betrothed, Borte, as arranged by his father. Soon after the wedding, Temuchin, thinking he might need the help of a patron if he was ever to reclaim his birthright, sought out a friend and former *anda* of his father, To'oril, the leader of the Kereyids, a Turkic people living by the shores of the upper Onon River.

The Kereyids were nomadic horsemen, not unlike their Mongol neighbours except in one respect; they were Nestorian Christians. Christian communities were not uncommon, even this far east; they were the product of a great wave of evangelical monks that had spread from the Middle East during the eleventh century. When Temuchin arrived at To'oril's camp, he presented him with gifts and was repaid with To'oril's promise to support Temuchin in his struggle to recover his father's people. But before he could begin, Temuchin's camp was raided by a party of Merkid and his wife, Borte,

Overleaf: The Chin army in retreat, from a manuscript
of the famous history of the Mongol people,
Jami al-tawarikh, by the Persian scholar
Rashid al-Din.

carried off. To'oril responded to the news by immediately raising an army to attack the Merkid, which he placed under the command of Temuchin's childhood *anda*, Jamukha. The campaign was a complete success; Borte was rescued, and in the course of it Temuchin distinguished himself in battle. The only disappointment was that Borte returned pregnant; her first child, Jochi, was forever haunted by the stigma of possible illegitimacy.

For eighteen months after the successful campaign against the Merkid, Temuchin and his followers rode with Jamukha. Although both men had enjoyed good relations, an unspoken rivalry had developed between what were clearly two very ambitious young princes. One evening, sensing that they no longer saw eye to eye, Temuchin and his followers left Jamukha's camp and rode off into the night. In the morning they discovered that they had been followed by a detachment that had decided to change their allegiances – apparently because, of the two, Temuchin inspired greater loyalty and confidence. The generosity with which Temuchin treated his followers soon earned him high regard. According to the *Secret History*, the would-be converts declared, 'The Prince dresses his people in his own clothes, he permits them to ride his own horses; this person could truly bring peace to the tribe and rule the nation.' Soon afterwards, Temuchin was elected Khan of the Mongols, though this title had scant practical value as he had actual command over only a small fraction of the Mongol population. However, tales spread which were soon taken up and embellished by the shamans that held the Mongol audiences in such thrall, telling how Temuchin had received a heavenly mandate to rule the steppe. Temuchin certainly knew how to exploit these tales. He is said to have proclaimed, 'My strength was fortified by Heaven and earth. Foreordained [for this] by Mighty Heaven, I was brought here by Mother earth.' Soon the clans were flocking to his banner.

Temuchin's apparently effortless rise incited Jamukha's jealousy, and it was not long before he decided to confront Temuchin in battle. He launched a surprise attack against his childhood *anda*, from which Temuchin only just managed to escape. It was now Temuchin's turn to seek revenge, and his appetite was further whetted when he learned that the men that had been taken prisoner after the ambush had been executed by Jamukha, who had boiled them to death in seventy large vats. But before Temuchin could have satisfaction, his patron, To'oril, the leader of the Kereyids, called upon his vassal prince to come to his aid. A faction within the Kereyid confederation had risen up and deposed the old man, casting him out to wander the Gobi Desert with no protection. When Temuchin heard the news he raised an army and led it into battle against his patron's enemies. His stunning success only further enhanced his growing stature within the steppe tribes, and he soon

went on to further victories when he repelled an attack from the Merkid who had hoped to exploit the temporary instability within the Kereyid confederation.

Meanwhile, larger political moves were afoot. In typical Chinese fashion the Chin, having become irritated by their Tartar clients' growing insolence, enlisted the help of To'oril and Temuchin to act as mercenaries and remove the Tartar nuisance. The Mongols, eager to avenge themselves of their old enemy, threw themselves into the task. The subsequent defeat of the Tartars not only bathed Temuchin in further glory, but also dramatically altered the balance of power on the steppe. In gratitude for a job well done, the Chin honoured those responsible, bestowing a nominal title upon To'oril and renaming him Ong (Wang) Khan. (As the histories of this period of Mongol history were written and corrupted with stories from other cultures, Ong Khan soon became the best-known Christian prince of the East, and the name Ong or Wang later became confused with the word 'John', which helped nurture the seed of a great Christian myth.) Temuchin was also ennobled, receiving a minor title.

Although he was by now something of a military celebrity, he was content to remain in Ong Khan's service. Together they waged campaigns across the steppe, from the Altai to the Khinghan Mountains. But their growing power and influence soon attracted enemies, and Jamukha, whose enmity towards Temuchin had only intensified, was quick to exploit this. He gathered round him an alliance of discontents – the Merkids, the Naimans, what was left of the Tartars, the Tayichi'uds and even Temuchin's mother's tribe, the Unggirad. The war that followed, an apparently uneven match between the armies of the Ong Khan and virtually all the rest of the steppe tribes, was fought during the winter of 1201–2. Jamukha's confederation was badly organized, and sections were easily picked off and dispersed. The campaign came to a climax with the massacre of virtually the entire Tartar army in the foothills of the Khinghan Mountains, a revenge attack for the murder of Temuchin's father, Yesugei.

SUPREME COMMANDER

As a result of these wars Ong Khan's Kereyid confederacy, staunchly supported by Temuchin's Mongols, had successfully taken control of the eastern steppe. Yet as the campaign continued, the trust between the Ong Khan and his protégé began to disintegrate. After the elimination of the Tartars, Temuchin had felt the time was right to seek a marriage alliance with the Ong Khan: Temuchin's eldest son Jochi would receive the Ong Khan's daughter as wife. The Ong Khan, irritated by his vassal's impertinence, not to

say his ambition, dismissed the idea outright. But the old man had also begun to fear Temuchin's growing importance and it soon became apparent that, when on campaign, the two men no longer fought so well together. On more than one occasion Temuchin found himself almost overwhelmed by the enemy, with the expected relief from the Ong Khan's troops having failed to arrive.

Gradually the clans began to sense that Temuchin was no longer in favour, and they started to desert him. It was another painful lesson about the realities of steppe loyalty. After an appalling encounter with an overwhelmingly superior Kereyid force, in which Temuchin's second son Ogedei was badly wounded, they were forced to retreat with 4600 men and found refuge on the shores of Lake Baljuna. He tried to make contact with his former patron, but was rebuffed. This period in the wilderness, thought to have been around 1203, is regarded by the early chroniclers as the greatest test for both Temuchin and his followers. In the years to come, those who could claim to have been with Temuchin at Lake Baljuna were assured of high honour.

Eventually the Kereyid confederation, now under the inferior command of the Ong Khan's son, showed signs of fragmenting. More and more of the clans swung back to Temuchin's side and, when finally he felt his strength adequate, he struck back – catching the Kereyid unguarded. The ensuing battle against superior forces was apparently an epic engagement that continued for three days. Victory finally came to Temuchin; the elderly Ong Khan fled the field, but was captured by a neighbouring tribe and executed. Temuchin, keen to refocus the loyalties of the enemy commanders, ordered that they should not be punished; he even went so far as to praise their heroism in public. But now the Kereyid were defeated they had to be absorbed into the Mongol nation, and to encourage this he took a number of Kereyid princesses whom he gave as wives to his sons. One of the Ong Khan's youngest nieces, Sorghaghtani Beki, who was given to Temuchin's youngest son Tolui, later became one of the most powerful figures in the empire and the mother of some of the greatest khans.

It might be assumed that by now Temuchin enjoyed absolute supremacy throughout the eastern steppe, but in fact as a result of his victory over the Kereyid he now faced even more determined opposition. The last remaining significant power in the region was the Naiman, a tribe that lived

Temuchin proclaimed Genghis Khan, from
a manuscript of Rashid al-Din. He is attended by courtiers,
and his two eldest sons, Jochi and Ogedei,
who are standing on the right.

north-west of the traditional lands of the Kereyids – between the Selenga River and the Altai Mountains. It was here that an army of fugitives from the other defeated tribes had gathered. It was here, too, that Jamukha had sought refuge and was now plotting Temuchin's downfall.

Temuchin realized the inevitability of this final encounter and so he called a *quriltai*, a meeting of the tribal leaders in his command, to plan the campaign. He wanted it to be a decisive confrontation, a victory that would spell either the end of all tribal conflicts – or oblivion. In preparing for this encounter, Temuchin restructured his army into groups of thousands, hundreds and tens. He also reorganized the command structure. When all this was complete he consecrated his battle colours on the day of the Feast of the Moon, in the Year of the Rat (1204), and then began his march on the Naiman armies. By the time they encountered the enemy, an overwhelmingly superior force, the Mongol horses were exhausted. He decided to make camp and by lighting hundreds more fires than were necessary, successfully convinced the enemy scouts that his army was far greater than in fact it was. When the two armies finally stood before each other in the field, Jamukha studied Temuchin's new battle order and, perhaps because it confused his own calculations, slipped quietly from the field even before battle was joined. The Naiman marched forward to meet the Mongols, but as Jamukha's forces fell away behind their master the Naiman lost heart and were soundly crushed. The Naiman king died of his wounds, his son fled to the west and Jamukha, who had also taken flight, was finally captured and, according to the *Secret History*, was executed at his own request. Temuchin was now absolute master of all the tribes of Mongolia. At a *quriltai* in 1206 he was finally proclaimed as such, and invested with the title Genghis Khan.

THE NEW MONGOLIA

This account of Genghis Khan's epic rise to power describes a struggle through a seemingly endless nightmare of alliance and betrayal. For historians who have attempted to bring to life the personality of one of the most important figures in world history, these events seem to supply some insight. Certain facts are unique. He emerged from an extremely marginal position within steppe politics and therefore had no firm base of support from which to launch his bid for outright leadership. Moreover, that support which he was able to gather invariably slipped through his fingers at the first hint that the tide seemed to be turning against him. This fickleness, it is argued, shaped his ideas not only about military strategy, but also about how to organize the political structure of the newly united Mongolia. Bitter experience had taught him that

he could trust neither the individual clans nor even his close relatives, for even his uncles and brothers had at some time allied themselves with his enemies. They were just as likely to elect him khan one year and desert him the next. He understood that these ancient habits had to be broken and that the narrow interests of each tribal group had to be subsumed into the greater needs of the union. The traditional view is that Genghis Khan's ideas about the future political structure of Mongolia were part of some vision of a nation that would eventually begin a campaign of world conquest. But a more recent view suggests that this new structure was the only possible answer to the problem of maintaining control over an army of nomadic horsemen that in 1206 probably numbered less than a hundred thousand men.

The traditional loyalty to tribal lords, or *tus*, had always been conditional and unreliable. According to the *Secret History*, the most formative experience in Genghis Khan's early life was the period when he and his family were deserted by his father's men after his death. Left to fend for himself, Genghis learned that the only reliable support was that which grew out of his own personal following. This group became the backbone of the army command, and consequently of the political powerbase. There were two basic relationships that developed. The first was the *anda*, the sworn brotherhood, which was effectively an alliance between equals as the respective partners swore both loyalty and support in times of trouble; support that included the men and families under the command of the respective 'brothers'. This relationship withered somewhat under the new imperial structure, which replaced it with the *nokor*, someone who had sworn personal allegiance. Those who swore themselves as *nokors* were subservient to their patron and had proved themselves faithful in battle. A *nokor* could expect to be rewarded by being given command of a division of the new army which, apart from bestowing prestige, also entitled him to a larger proportion of booty. However, anyone who betrayed his *nokor* could expect no mercy. When Genghis Khan came to set up the command structure of his army, the most remarkable aspect was the absence of most of his family members. There were no uncles, cousins, brothers, nephews or sons – with the exception of Jochi. Later, when the Mongol army had grown, he grudgingly distributed small units amongst his family. But he was always reluctant to entrust important affairs to his family and extremely suspicious – one might even say paranoid – about family motives. Throughout his struggle for supremacy Genghis Khan executed or threatened to execute about a dozen members of his family because of plots, real or suspected, to overthrow him or exploit some influence over him. On the other hand he was extremely trusting and generous to those to whom he was not related and had proved themselves loyal in battle.

Genghis Khan also developed the *keshig*, or personal bodyguard, made up of seventy day guards and eighty night guards. As his power grew this expanded to some ten times its original size, and when finally he was proclaimed master of Mongolia it had expanded to about 10000, made up of ten units of a thousand. Its leaders were recruited from the sons or younger brothers of his divisional commanders, thus reinforcing the new imperial loyalty. The *keshig* also provided a group of young warriors whose advancement would be tied to the new imperial government, and not to traditional tribal loyalties. Their duties, apart from the protection of the sovereign, included providing units of hand-picked warriors and messengers for special imperial duties. The development of this new model army often meant removing the traditional commanders of tribal armies and replacing them with commanders from another tribe. Genghis was even prepared to break up and scatter entire tribal armies within the ranks of other units, especially if they had been particularly unreliable in the past. So effective was this strategy that, as time passed, the old tribal divisions gradually disappeared. No one was allowed to move from one unit to another, on pain of death, without explicit permission. Discipline was strict and subject to central authority, and the men were regularly trained to fight as a large unit and not as individuals. Those who broke rank to loot or who engaged in private feuds were severely punished. Genghis's aim was to make the army the focus of each individual Mongol warrior's loyalty – and he himself the focus of the army's loyalty. Hard experience had taught him that the empire would have to be founded upon a personal following. Absolute autocracy was the key.

The reputation that Genghis Khan earned as a great general was based upon the fact that he had always been prepared to take greater risks than his enemies. He did so because he had no choice, he had nowhere else to go, and he needed the victories because failure would have meant being abandoned again. Victory brought him loyalty. In 1206 the newly proclaimed Genghis Khan, now aged thirty-nine, was, in terms of the Middle Ages, past the prime of his life. Yet now he stood at the head of a nation that, just a few years before, had not even existed. More importantly, he stood at the head of an army that needed some greater purpose. But what that purpose might be was by no means immediately apparent. All that he could possibly have understood was that he had to go on from here.

Genghis adopted as his standard the 'Nine Bands' made from yak hair. It later became the imperial standard and even today stands as a symbol of Mongolia's past glories.

2

FROM CHINA
TO THE
CASPIAN SEA

THE LAW-GIVER

SOON AFTER GENGHIS KHAN WAS MADE master over all 'the people with felt tents', he is said to have set down his great *Yasa*, a promulgation of general laws. It was customary whenever a new steppe empire was inaugurated for the leader to 'mark the foundation of his polity' by establishing certain decrees. Genghis Khan's famous legal code came to be regarded so highly that it set him above any previous nomadic chiefs as a great administrator and law-giver.

The *Yasa* was supposed to have been set down soon after the *quriltai* of 1206, and entrusted to Genghis's adopted brother, an orphan of the Tartars, Shigi-Qutuqu, who was made a kind of chief justice. It enshrined Mongol attitudes towards religious toleration, exempted priests and religious institutions from taxation, prescribed the death penalty for espionage, desertion, theft, adultery and, in the case of a merchant, being declared bankrupt for the third time. It also forbade washing or urinating in running water, as streams and rivers were thought to be alive. The *Yasa* became the institutional foundation of the empire, evidence of Genghis's wisdom and his vision of how the future empire should be governed.

However, modern historians cast doubts upon whether there was such a vision of a future well-governed empire, and suggest that a large proportion of what we know as the *Yasa* is really a body of case histories – accounts of

36

judgements which became precedents for future cases. There is also an account from the great Persian historian, Rashid al-Din, of a large number of decrees uttered by Genghis. These maxims, or *biligs*, were recorded and have been mistakenly assumed to be fragments of the *Yasa*, but they were not a code of general laws. In addition to Genghis's decrees and the body of case law, there is an inheritance of Mongol customs and traditions. In other words, the *Yasa* is no longer seen as the great foundation stone of the empire, but rather as a mixture of enlightenment and superstition that is as much an account of Mongol lore as law.

REVITALIZING THE ARMY

There was, however, a far more influential institution which was structured and regulated by Genghis Khan and which strictly governed the way most Mongols lived their lives – the army. All men over the age of fourteen were expected to undertake military duty. Only physicians, undertakers and priests were exempt. Upon being summoned, the men were expected to leave their flocks, take with them four or five changes of horse, and travel to wherever their unit happened to be based. Wives and children were expected to follow, and if the army was abroad the family travelled with the herds. As new arrivals rode into the *ordu* (military camp) they would find it laid out along standard lines, so they knew exactly where to find the physician's tent, or the armoury to collect their allocation of weapons. They would then move out to join their unit, which might be an *arban* – a simple unit of ten; a *jagun* – ten *arbans* or 100 men; a *minghan* – a regiment of ten *jaguns* or 1000 men; or a *tumen*, a division of ten *minghans* or 10000 men. The *ordu* was run by quartermasters, or *jurtchis*, who secured supplies and organized the running of the place.

A soldier was responsible for making sure his equipment was kept up to standard and was regularly inspected by officers. Failing to look after one's equipment usually meant being sent home from the regiment. A soldier's equipment began with a silk undershirt, a novelty learnt from the Chinese. If he was unlucky enough to be hit by an arrow, although it might pierce the armour it was unlikely to penetrate the closely woven silk shirt. What tended to happen was that the silk was dragged into the wound with the arrow head.

Overleaf: The Mongol vanguard, known as a *mangudai*, were
usually lightly armed – two bows, a quiver of sixty arrows and a scimitar.
It was their task to engage the enemy and draw it towards
the rest of the Mongol army.

Removing an arrow embedded in flesh creates a much larger wound than when it entered, but with the silk wound tightly round the arrow head this became easier. By gently pulling the silk around the wound, the soldier or physician would turn the head of the arrow and remove it without ripping further flesh.

Over the silk he wore a tunic, and if he was part of the heavy cavalry he was given a coat of mail and a cuirass made of leather-covered iron scales. Each soldier carried a leather-covered wicker shield and a helmet of either leather or iron, depending on his rank. He was armed with two composite bows and a large quiver containing no fewer than sixty arrows. Light cavalry carried a small sword and two or three javelins, while the heavy brigade carried a scimitar, a battle axe or a mace and a 4 m (12 foot) lance. Soldiers were also equipped for travel. They were expected to carry on the horse clothing, cooking pots, dried meat, a water bottle, files for sharpening arrows, a needle and thread and other useful little items. The saddlebag itself was usually made from a cow's stomach which, being waterproof and inflatable, also provided a useful float when crossing rivers.

One important institution Genghis Khan developed was to transform the nomadic horsemen's favourite sport, the hunt, into a military drill. Whether the quarry was wolf, wild boar or deer, the hunt became a way of instilling into the minds of his soldiers the virtues of working and acting as part of a large single entity. These hunting exercises were conducted during the winter for about three months and every soldier participated. A variety of techniques were employed, depending on the size of the unit.

A small party would be ordered to deploy themselves at various points in an arc. The quarry would be herded or drawn towards the most advantageous ground by a series of carefully orchestrated strikes. Sometimes the quarry might even be goaded into attacking one or two horsemen, who would gallop away, drawing the quarry after them into a trap. The use of the feint became a standard tactic of the Mongols and was employed successfully again and again. Once the quarry was in the intended place, the waiting circle of horsemen would move in for the kill.

Another approach was to string an entire division of the army along what might be described as a starting line, sometimes 130 km (80 miles) long. On a signal the entire complement, fully armed as if for battle, would ride forward at a walk towards a finish line hundreds of kilometres away. This was usually situated at a point in the shadow of a hill, where the proceedings could be watched by the khan and his entourage. Over the following days the massed cavalry would march forward, sweeping or herding before them all the game they encountered along the way. Something approaching this sport is still

practised today in Mongolia during Naadam festivals – modern-day tourneys where traditional Mongol skills such as archery, a particularly moribund form of wrestling and horse-riding are celebrated. The horse race takes place over 30 km (20 miles) or more, often involving as many as 500 riders who begin the race at a leisurely walk, only gradually spurring their horses towards a gallop as they approach the finish.

During the hunt, as the riders approached the finish line the flanks would begin to ride ahead of the centre, and so slowly describe a massive arc. Still further on, the flanks would turn and ride towards each other, thus trapping all the game that had been herded over the hundreds of kilometres of countryside. During the march it was forbidden to kill anything, but it was even more of a disgrace if a rider let some beast escape the net. Throughout the exercise officers rode behind their men, shouting orders and directing their movements.

The Mongols also employed an extremely effective and reliable system of signals, through flags, torches and riders who carried messages over great distances. This eventually provided them with one of the greatest advantages they ever took into the field: reliable and effective communications. It enabled all the Mongol units to remain in constant contact with each other and, through their remarkable corps of couriers, under the control of a single commander.

At the end of this elaborate piece of hunting choreography, the men were given the chance to show off their individual fighting skills. Once the flanks had met and the circle tightened, the khan would ride down from his vantage point into the circle and take his pick of the game. This was doubtless a somewhat daunting exercise, as the khan's own skills would be on public show before the entire company. When he had finished and returned to the hill, it was the turn of the soldiers. Now it was the opportunity for each individual, in front of his officers, to show off his skill with sword, bow and arrows or lance. Many wrestled the beasts by hand and tried to kill them with nothing more than a dagger, and it was not uncommon for some soldiers to be torn to pieces by frenzied packs of wolves. Eventually, the elderly and the youngest in the party would beg the khan for the lives of the animals still left in the ring, and once that was granted the great hunt was formally finished.

With exercises like this the Mongols developed a regime that enabled them to train and maintain an extremely professional army – something of a novelty for the thirteenth century. Alongside the skills of riding, shooting and swordsmanship, each Mongol warrior learned the importance of discipline, co-ordination and obedience. Although their tactics in the field were no different from those of any other nomadic tribe, their strategies became

masterpieces of originality and daring. The pursuit of the quarry became the pursuit of the enemy; and soon commanders began developing strategies that were to leave their enemies nonplussed. What was being forged, under Genghis Khan's direction, was a modern cavalry that would have no equal anywhere in the world.

FOREIGN EXPANSION

It was not for some three years after the *quriltai* of 1206 that Genghis Khan began any campaigns abroad. The political situation on his borders presented no threats; the various sedentary empires were stable and largely uninterested in the internal politics of the Turkic Mongol tribes. China at that time was divided into three separate kingdoms. South of Mongolia, in what would be the most western extremities of modern China, was the Hsi-Hsia, easily the weakest of the three; its people were largely Tibetan Buddhists. To the east of Mongolia, northern China was under the domination of the Jurchen, the semi-nomadic people from Manchuria who, like the dynasty before them, had conquered and established their own dynasty, the Chin. South of the Chin was the real heart of China, governed by a pure Chinese dynasty, the Sung, that traced its heritage back hundreds of years. To the west of Mongolia lay the empire of the Qara Khitai and the Uighurs, and beyond them the vast lands of the Khwarazm Shah, the northern Persian empire.

In many traditional accounts it is assumed that, once all internal resistance had been thoroughly put down, Genghis turned his attention to building his empire. It is also assumed that the first and most likely conquest would be China, as this had always been the country into which nomadic horsemen had ventured when seeking to extend their influence. But this explanation only holds good for the semi-nomadic horsemen who had periodically ridden out of Manchuria. These people had always shown an interest in exploiting and governing an agricultural nation like China. Having established themselves as the legitimate rulers, they were particularly adept at handling the illiterate bands of horsemen that occasionally came thundering out of Mongolia to raid Chinese towns and settlements. The Chinese referred to the Mongols as the 'uncooked'. These raw horsemen had never shown any interest in conquest before; terror and extortion were their ambitions – not government. The conquest of China was the last thing the Mongols set out to do. China had always been, and particularly to the horsemen from the eastern steppe, simply a rich quarry to be plundered at will – and it was exactly so under Genghis Khan. China was a raid that turned into an occupation.

The first expansion of the Mongol's influence came when the Uighurs

abandoned their relationship with the Qara Khitai in 1209 and offered their submission to Genghis Khan. They were welcomed as a 'fifth son'. As such, the Uighur's state remained autonomous throughout Genghis's life; later it became the most valued client state in the empire. It became the preferred policy, wherever possible, to seek out alliances with local rulers who, in return for their acknowledgement of the Mongols' supremacy, would be granted a kind of vassal-like autonomy. A similar arrangement was extracted from the Tanguts, the rulers of Hsi-Hsia; however, the latter had to be encouraged to accept Mongol terms. Genghis had launched a raid into Hsi-Hsia in 1207, and then again in 1209. The first of these was a typical raid intended to gather booty with which to finance the new nation, but the second was a far more serious affair and found the Mongols placing the Tangut capital under siege. The experience was a salutary one for the Mongols, just as it had been for all previous nomadic empires when they encountered enemies that preferred to fight from behind large fortifications. The Mongols had no immediate answer to these tactics, but nevertheless were able to force the Tangut king to accept their terms. In addition Genghis also extracted a promise that the king would send troops to aid the Mongols, should they ever be requested. Finally the Tangut king gave his daughter in marriage to Genghis, thus cementing the relationship. In return he was not required to renounce his sovereignty.

THE INVASION OF CHINA

But the Tanguts and Uighurs were relatively small kingdoms, and Genghis really made no impression on the international stage until the campaigns against the Chin, which began in 1211. They started with the time-honoured practice of extorting money and other concessions out of the wealthy Chinese. What went wrong, however, was that the Chin decided to respond to the Mongol initiative with military force. To begin with the Chin had constructed a chain of intimidating fortified cities to protect the empire from invasions from the north; they also maintained a large and powerful body of cavalry plus an equally large army of foot soldiers, which they had every intention of using if provoked. Genghis marched into Chin territory with a sizeable force which divided into smaller units and rode in all directions, systematically laying waste small towns and villages which they found in their path. They tended to avoid the larger, fortified cities and were happy to continue in this fashion until they eventually encountered a vast Chin force at Huan-erh-tsui. Instead of beating a hasty retreat, Genghis decided to attack. In their first serious engagement with a large foreign army, the Mongol cavalry proved devastating. They completely outmanoeuvred the Chin, virtually destroying a force of some

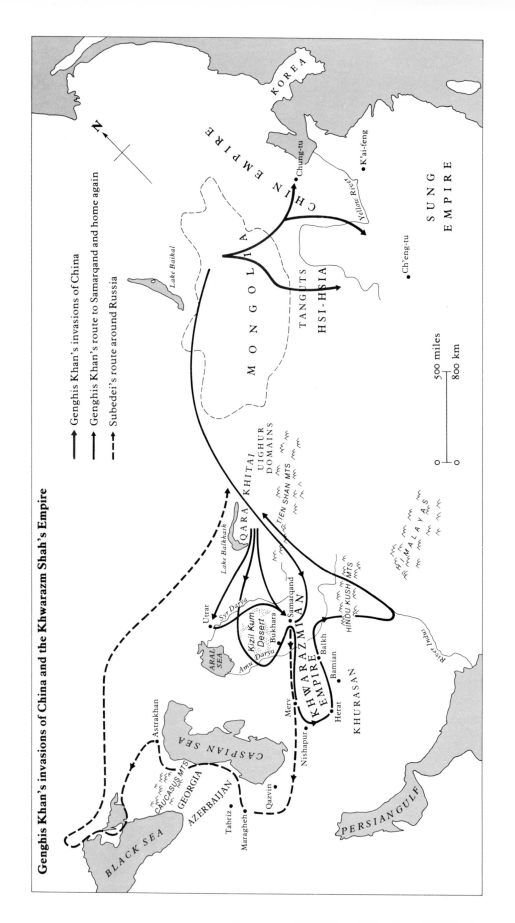

Genghis Khan's invasions of China and the Khwarazm Shah's Empire

Genghis Khan's invasions of China
Genghis Khan's route to Samarqand and home again
Subedei's route around Russia

N

500 miles
800 km

KOREA

CHIN EMPIRE

Chung-tu
K'ai-feng
Yellow River

SUNG EMPIRE

Ch'eng-tu

MONGOLIA

TANGUTS
HSI-HSIA

Lake Baikal

QARA KHITAI
UIGHUR DOMAINS

TIEN SHAN MTS

Lake Balkhash

HIMALAYAS

HINDU KUSH MTS

Utrar
Syr Darya
Kizil Kum Desert
Samarqand
Bukhara
ARAL SEA
Amu Darya

KHWARAZMIAN EMPIRE

Balkh
Bamian
Herat

KHURASAN

River Indus

Merv
Nishapur

Astrakhan

CASPIAN SEA

Qazvin

CAUCASUS MTS
GEORGIA
AZERBAIJAN
Tabriz
Maragheh

BLACK SEA

PERSIAN GULF

70 000 within a matter of hours. Nine years later, a Taoist monk on his way to visit Genghis travelled through this area and reported that the battlefield was still littered with human bones. Jochi, Genghis's eldest son, went on to the very gates of the Chin capital, Chung-tu, near the site of modern Peking, but since he had no knowledge or experience of siege warfare he withdrew. Although the Mongols had also gained control of the key passes into China and a number of small fortifications in the Chin defensive perimeter, they had no use for these; so in February of the following year the invaders rode back to southern Mongolia. They had failed to extort much out of the campaign, and the Chin quickly reoccupied those towns that had been destroyed by the Mongol raiders.

The Mongols returned to their homelands having learnt one important lesson: even though they had routed a huge Chin army, they would never extract a submission from the Chin emperor so long as he and his government remained safe inside their large fortified cities. It had never occurred to the Mongols to stay and occupy the lands they had conquered, so the campaign achieved almost nothing – either by their standards or by those of any other conqueror. However, once back in Mongolia Genghis sought to strengthen his hand before conducting any further raids. He effected an alliance with the Khitans, a small neighbouring kingdom who had been ousted from northern China by the Jurchen less than a century before. They were not particularly powerful, but because their territory lay north-east of the Chin the new alliance would make the Chin feel almost surrounded. Genghis then launched another campaign, with the Khitans, across the Chin's northern frontier. On this occasion the Mongols were more successful at capturing fortified towns, but the campaign was brought to an abrupt end when Genghis was wounded by a stray arrow. The Mongols decided to take as much booty as they could and depart.

In the autumn of 1213, the Mongols returned for the third time. They marched in three large columns, with Genghis in command of the largest while his sons Jochi, Chaghadai and the youngest, Tolui, shared command of the others. When they reached the outskirts of the Chin capital, Chung-tu, they again realized it was far too formidable, so they turned south and marched across the North China plain towards the Yellow River. In the process they crossed the fertile plain north of the Yellow River, seeing for the first time some of the vast area of land that lay under cultivation, and, of course, the huge numbers of peasants who worked it. Throughout 1213 they rode back and forth across Chin territory and in the process slaughtered countless thousands of the population. They also gathered the most prodigious amounts of booty: massive quantities of silk, gold and silver, plus hundreds of young boys and

girls who were marched back as slaves. However, as the campaign dragged on the Mongols became victims of an outbreak of the plague that periodically swept through these lands. When the three columns reunited to lay siege to Chung-tu, Genghis's force had come to resemble a much reduced host of rag-tag ruffians rather than a conquering army. He had neither the skill nor the men to take Chung-tu, nor was he inclined to stay and try to starve the city into submission. However, internal disputes within the Chin court brought things to a conclusion when the Chin emperor suddenly indicated that he wanted to make peace. Genghis responded by asking what the Chin might offer in return for the siege being called off. When the negotiations had been concluded, the Mongols departed with even more silk and gold, together with another 500 children to be added to those already headed for slavery. Once again the Mongols turned and rode back towards their homeland: 'Our soldiers laden [with] satin and goods as many as they could carry, tied their burdens with silk and went away.'

Genghis also accepted a marriage with a Chin princess, assuming, as his shabby army departed China, that the Chin now took him to be the pre-eminent sovereign in the region and that this situation would not be challenged. From a Mongol perspective the campaign was a great success, and Genghis's status was much enhanced by the enormous quantities of booty to be shared out. But from the Chin perspective the outcome could also be seen as a success, for once again they had survived simply by paying off the invaders. Once the Mongols were gone, the Chinese would return to their lands and continue where they had left off. As ever, the Mongols had shown not the slightest interest in permanently occupying or supplanting Chin control of northern China.

In the meantime the Chin emperor, thinking that Chung-tu was a little too close to the northern passes that led to Mongolia, decided to move his court to the city of K'ai-feng, south of the Yellow River. According to a Chinese account, having assumed that the Chin had accepted his supremacy, Genghis interpreted this as a breakdown in trust. 'The Chin emperor made a peace agreement with me, but now he has moved his capital to the south; evidently he mistrusts my word and has used the peace to deceive me!' It seems likely that, had the Chin still been prepared to appease the Mongols, they might have

Genghis pursuing the Chin through the mountains, from
a manuscript of Rashid al-Din. At the beginning of this campaign,
the Mongols captured many of the Chin fortifications
that guarded the mountain passes.

46

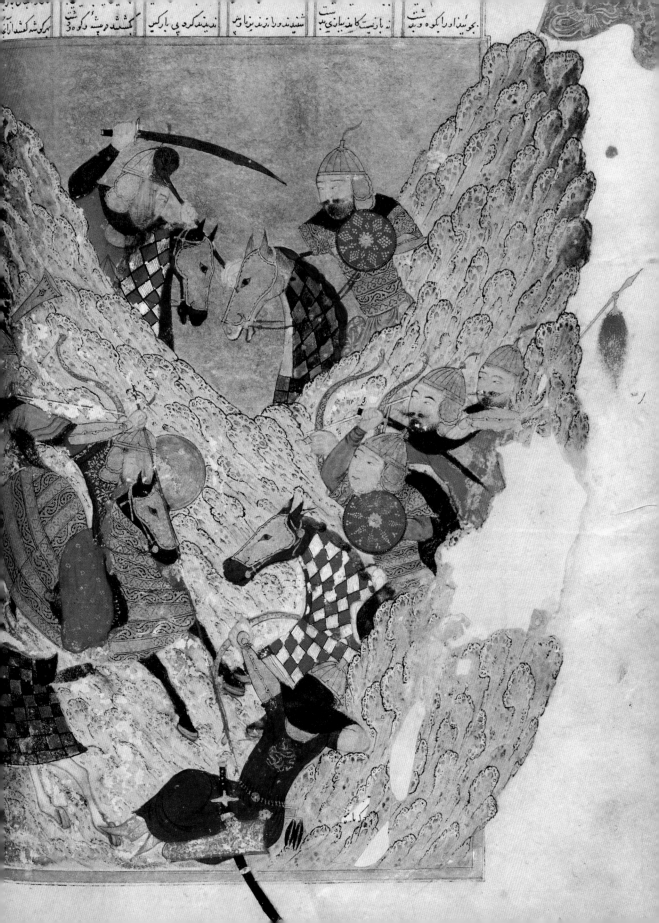

escaped destruction. In the autumn of 1214 the Mongols returned to the siege of Chung-tu, this time with a much larger army that included Chinese and Khitans as well as Mongols. This time the city was invested by a force prepared to stay for as long as it took. The inhabitants, distraught that their emperor had deserted them and terrified of the retribution they expected at the hands of the Mongols, remained behind their walls and suffered appalling deprivations. As the months passed they even turned to cannibalism, and the longer they held out the greater Mongol retribution would be. In the spring of 1215, as there seemed to be little progress, Genghis left the campaign to one of his generals and returned to the northern frontier. So he was not present when finally, in the early summer, the Chin commanders abandoned the city and the Mongols entered unopposed.

Once the Mongols were inside the city walls, the inhabitants' worst fears were realized. Chung-tu had been one of the largest cities in northern China, and it was utterly laid to waste. News of the destruction must have sent a shiver of dread through all the courts in the region. For the first time the Mongols were seen not merely as a significant military force, but as a force capable of appalling levels of destruction. Squadrons of Mongol horsemen rode the streets firing incendiary arrows into the wooden houses, while others put thousands of the civilian population to the sword. Entire districts were reduced to ash, and a visiting ambassador from the Khwarazm Shah, the leader of the great Islamic empire in western Asia, reported that, after all the slaughter and the fires, the streets were greasy with human fat and littered with carcasses.

There was, however, some method in this madness. Genghis preferred to secure submission from his neighbours without resort to warfare, the military successes were clearly meant to send a signal to others. In 1218 the Koreans, no doubt heavily influenced by reports of the fate of Chung-tu, made their submissions to the Mongol court along with substantial payments; and so they avoided destruction. The annihilation of the former Chin capital was both an act of appalling retribution and a warning to others, for the singular fact appreciated by all Mongol commanders was the enormous discrepancy between the size of the Mongol nation and that of other nations that lay on its borders. Slaughter on a grand scale, or the threat of it, was the only way to get their own way. Those that accepted Mongol terms, like the Uighurs, Tanguts, Khitans and Koreans, could expect clemency; those that did not or – worse – who reneged on their agreements could expect no mercy.

With the fall of Chung-tu large numbers of Chinese, Khitan and Chin troops surrendered, along with the administrators and officials responsible for the government of the northern part of the Chin empire. Under their influence, the Mongols took their first hesitant steps towards assuming

responsibility for the administration of a conquered land. It was a role for which they had little enthusiasm, but it was being forced upon them. Even so, the Chin were still not conquered and remained so for nearly twenty years.

THE PUNISHMENT OF GOD

But by now Genghis had already lost interest in the campaign in China, and had become absorbed in matters further west. Reports of the fall of Chung-tu had inspired the Khwarazm Shah to open a dialogue. Khwarazm Shah 'Ala' al-Din Muhammad II had inherited an empire founded by a Turkish merce-nary, Qutbeddin Muhammad, in what is today Uzbekistan. 'Ala' al-Din also took over a massive army largely made up of Turkish mercenaries from the tribes west of the Aral Sea, and with this force he had expanded his empire south into the Persian territory of Khurasan. In reality it had been little more than an easy annexation, given the size and reputation of his army, yet it was enough for him to declare afterwards that he was 'the chosen prince of Allah'. Indeed, so impressed were his own sycophantic courtiers that they proclaimed him the second Alexander. To the north-east of Khurasan lay the empire of Transoxania with its grand cities of Bukhara and Samarqand, and beyond that the powerful Buddhist empire of the Qara Khitai, which stood between the Muslim world and the expanding empire of the Mongols.

Following the neighbouring Uighurs' submission to Genghis Khan in 1209, the territory of Qara Khitai seemed far less powerful, especially as it was currently being ruled by a survivor of the war between the Mongols and the Naimans, the hated and despotic Kuchlug. 'Ala' al-Din chose this moment to march into Transoxania, which he finally conquered in 1210. These lands lie between the rivers Oxus and Jaxartes and are on the whole fairly barren. But it was across these lands that the caravans of both the East and the Middle East had crossed for centuries, and they had brought extraordinary wealth to the cities that produced or traded in carpets, silk, woven cotton and silver lamé. The greatest of these was Samarqand, which the Khwarazm Shah had made his capital. By some accounts it was a magnificent city of some 500000 inhabitants, a community of craftsmen, merchants, Chinese artisans, leather workers, goldsmiths and silversmiths. In the fields beyond the city walls aubergines and melons were grown, to be packed in snow inside lead-lined boxes for export. The streets were lined with shady trees, cooled by fountains and decorated with gardens, and under the Khwarazm Shah Samarqand became one of the most magnificent cities in Asia.

Since the Khwarazm Shah had found conquest a somewhat effortless exercise, he had given serious consideration to conquering China. However,

his plans had been halted by reports of the Mongol victories against the Chin – hence the presence of one of his envoys at the sacking of Chung-tu. He had been sent to report on the new power that had emerged from the steppe. Genghis would have long known of the Khwarazm Shah's reputation. Now they were both aware of each other.

In 1216, Genghis sent to Samarqand three envoys bearing magnificent gifts of gold, jade, ivory ornaments and cloaks spun from the wool of white camels. They were delivered with a letter:

> I send you these gifts. I know your power and the vast extent of your empire and I regard you as my most cherished son. For your part you must know that I have conquered China and all the Turkish nations north of it; my country is an anthill of soldiers and a mine of silver and I have no need of other lands. Therefore I believe that we have an equal interest in encouraging trade between our subjects.

The letter was sealed 'God in heaven, the Kah Khan, the power of God on earth. The Seal of the Emperor of Mankind'. Opinion varies about the real motives behind the letter, given the ambiguous language; but its ostensible purpose seems clear. It was an acknowledgement that he, Genghis Khan, was lord of the East while the Khwarazm Shah was lord of the West, and that perhaps it would be a good thing if there was a trade agreement between their respective empires. In due course an agreement was established allowing the free passage of merchants and traders through their respective territories.

Nevertheless, Genghis's intentions must be questioned in view of the barely veiled insult in his letter, describing the vastly more powerful Khwarazm Shah as his 'son'. Could he possibly have been trying to incite trouble with his great neighbour? Even though he had just won some important victories in northern China, the war there was a long way from being concluded. Indeed, it had only just begun. The Mongols had been absorbing new territories to the east and the west, and their meagre manpower was sorely stretched. To have undertaken another campaign at this juncture and against such an adversary would have been reckless in the extreme. Yet to judge from the Mongol chroniclers who recorded these events sometime afterwards, it was only a matter of time before Genghis Khan struck out in the west. In the event, however, it was 'Ala' al-Din Muhammad II himself who took the initiative.

In 1218 a caravan of some 450 Muslim merchants, travelling from Mongol territory, arrived at the frontier town of Utrar to inaugurate the trade agreement. The Khwarazm Shah's governor in Utrar, Inalchuq Khwadir Khan, suspecting that the merchants were spies – which they almost certainly were – had them all killed and their property confiscated. When Genghis sent

three envoys to the court of the Khwarazm Shah to demand reparations, he responded by killing one of the envoys and burning the beards of the other two. This was tantamount to an act of war, for the Mongols always accorded ambassadors the greatest respect and assumed that the persons of their own ambassadors were sacrosanct.

The Khwarazm Shah must have realized that such contempt would lead to war. Perhaps he had come to believe his own courtiers' claim that he was, indeed, the new Alexander, and calculated that a swift and effortless encounter with this pagan horseman would render him undisputed master of all Asia. After all, it is thought he had a massive army of some 400 000 men in Transoxania alone, with reserves scattered throughout the empire – there was no other army to match it anywhere. Whatever his motives, this vain, arrogant, self-deluding individual succeeded in bringing down one of the most appalling disasters ever to befall the eastern Islamic world.

But before Genghis embarked upon a war with the mighty Khwarazm Shah there were a number of irritating issues that had to be settled closer to home. First he had to deal with an old enemy named Kuchlug, a survivor of the Naimans, who had set himself up as ruler of the Qara Khitai. The second was the threat of insurrection from the survivors of the war against the Merkids, whom Genghis had defeated in 1208. To contend with these problems he despatched two of his leading generals. The first was Subedei Bat'atur of the Reindeer people, an obscure tribe that still exists today in north-western Mongolia. They still ride and herd reindeer and are regarded by the rest of the Mongolians as the most unsophisticated barbarians. The other was a man named Jebei Noyan. As soon as Kuchlug had been dealt with the kingdom of Qara Khitai fell into the Mongol dominion, which meant that Genghis's frontiers now abutted those of the Khwarazm Shah. First blood was drawn when Subedei's attachment, while in pursuit of the remaining Merkids, had a somewhat bruising encounter with a force led by the Khwarazm Shah's son, Jalal al-Din, in the Fergana valley, below the Tien Shan Mountains.

Unlike his father, Jalal al-Din had natural gifts as a military leader and would have been a match for any of the Mongol princes had he been given command of a force of significant size. Having assumed that war with the Mongols was now inevitable, Jalal al-Din had counselled his father that the best strategy was to deploy their massive force in a series of highly mobile corps that could be despatched to encounter any invading Mongol troops. Instead, his father had elected to spread the entire force in a thin line along the River Syr Darya. Jalal al-Din argued that the line was not strong enough to withstand a determined assault, and that the best thing would be to launch a pre-emptive strike before the Mongols could put together any kind of substantial force.

Again, he was ignored, although he was given permission to patrol the frontier in case of any incursions.

It was Subedei's ill-fortune to be leading some 30 000 exhausted Mongols, doggedly in pursuit of renegade Merkids, through the passes in the Tien Shan Mountains and straight into 50 000 of the Khwarazm Shah's soldiers led by Jalal al-Din. Although the battle was inconclusive and both sides suffered heavy losses, the Mongol column was forced to retreat with its wounded back across the passes. The encounter served as an object lesson. Jalal al-Din would be a serious obstacle to any invasion, and his whereabouts would have to be carefully monitored.

To help him plan this expedition, Genghis called a great *quriltai* of his most senior generals. It would not be like a raid against the Chin; this would be the largest military expedition the Mongols had ever conducted. As he became more involved in the planning, Genghis was urged by one of his wives to give some thought to the succession of the empire. He was already fifty-six, and the outcome of the adventure was by no means certain. In considering the problem, he examined the qualities of each of his sons. Despite his obvious qualities as a general the eldest son, Jochi, was ruled out because of doubts about his paternity. His mother, Borte, had given birth to him after being rescued from the Merkids, who had captured and raped her soon after her marriage to the young Genghis. His second son, Chaghadai, the so-called guardian of the *Yasa*, was a scrupulously fair administrator; but Genghis was not fond of him, regarding him as a somewhat narrow-minded and obstinate character. Ogedei was clearly the most intelligent and educated of the sons; an able if not distinguished commander, he was extremely generous, fond of good company and good alcohol, and, although far less athletic than his father, he seemed the most open to new ideas. The fourth son, Tolui, even more of a drunkard than Ogedei, was already regarded as a brilliant general but was also thought to be too quick tempered. Genghis struggled over the choice between his two youngest sons, and finally settled upon Ogedei. The other three were made to promise that they would not oppose Ogedei's succession, and with this matter resolved Genghis returned to planning the campaign.

In the meantime, from right across the eastern steppe tens of thousands of men were being summoned from their herds and ordered to report to Genghis's *ordus*. Gradually the army swelled to perhaps something between 150 000 and 200 000. It represented the largest concentration of Mongol power that had ever been mustered – yet it was still less than half the size of the opposition. Given these hard facts, it was decided to co-ordinate an attack against the Khwarazm Shah on a number of different positions at the same time. The Mongol force was divided into four corps: the first commanded by

Genghis and Subedei, the second by his sons Ogedei and Chaghadai, the third by Jebei and the fourth by Jochi. Still conscious of his meagre forces, Genghis decided to call in the agreement he had made with the Tanguts, that they would furnish him with soldiers whenever and wherever he requested them. The Tangut king's reply was disappointing: he said that if he [Genghis] didn't have enough men of his own, then he didn't deserve to be khan. Stung by this response, Genghis grimly set forth alone on the campaign in the west.

The first move was in the autumn of 1219 against the city of Utrar, where a force of some 50000 Mongols led by Chaghadai and Ogedei advanced on the city walls. The governor knew he could expect no mercy, so he poured scorn on the Mongol demand to surrender and, with his 80000-strong garrison, settled down to a long siege. Meanwhile, the forces under the command of Jebei and Jochi moved south. Jebei had command of 20000 men, with whom he was ordered to draw off any major enemy force guarding the southern approaches, and then advance into Transoxania. While all eyes were on him, Genghis and Subedei moved their contingent quietly out of Mongolia, crossed the Syr Darya River into Transoxania and then, instead of riding south, turned due west and promptly disappeared. It was as though they had ridden off the map. Meanwhile Jochi's force roamed up and down the Syr Darya with orders to attack the Khwarazm Shah's strongholds at Khojend, and to harry their defences before also crossing the river.

Genghis and Subedei were in fact leading their forces on a secret route through the Kizil Kum Desert to the north-east of the Khwarazm Shah's territory. This region was thought to be impenetrable, but the Mongols had a guide to show them the way. Genghis knew the Khwarazm Shah's spies could not follow his progress; as far as the enemy were concerned, the entire division did not exist. It emerged, however, in March 1220 some 650 km (400 miles) behind the enemy lines, when the people of Bukhara sighted the Mongol force on the outskirts of their city. Stunned by this remarkable apparition, the Turkish garrison burst from the city gates and attempted to fight their way free. They were slaughtered to a man. According to the Persian historian Juvaini, the plain 'seemed to be a tray filled with blood'. Totally demoralized, the inhabitants surrendered without a fight.

Once Genghis had entered the 'cupola of Islam', as Juvaini described Bukhara, he rode into the largest mosque thinking it was the Sultan's palace. When it was explained that it was a house of God, he ordered it to be converted into stables and the cases that held the Koran to be used for mangers. As copies of the Koran were thrown to the four winds, Genghis mounted the pulpit inside the mosque and lectured the citizens about the treachery of their Sultan. 'I am the punishment of God,' he told them. 'If you had not committed great

sins, he would not have sent a punishment like me.' Genghis, determined there would be no hindrance to the plundering of the city, ordered the entire civilian population to abandon everything and leave with nothing but the clothes they stood in. As the city was being sacked, a fire broke out and swept through the closely packed wooden houses. When the fires were out all that was left were the most prominent stone structures; the rest had become 'a level plain'. Juvaini estimated that upwards of 30 000 had been slain, while thousands more women and children were led off into slavery in Mongolia along with cartloads of booty.

However, the majority of the population had been allowed to escape, to roam the countryside and seek refuge where they could, and take with them terrible accounts of the fate of Bukhara. The object was to terrify and demoralize the inhabitants of Samarqand, the Khwarazm Shah's capital. When Genghis approached that city he forced prisoners from Bukhara to march ahead, which swelled the ranks of his army and, of course, provided shields against the enemy's arrows. Samarqand was expected to hold out for a year; it capitulated after five days. Neither Genghis Khan nor any of his army had ever seen anything quite like it. They roamed the streets and avenues, drinking at the fountains and gorging themselves on the exotic fruits and sherbets. The Turkish garrison, all 30 000, were put to the sword. The population was divided into sections: women were set apart to be raped and then sent off as slaves; the clerics were all spared; while the entire population of craftsmen and artisans were also transported to the Mongol homeland where they would be employed at Genghis's court.

While Genghis and Subedei had captured the jewels of the Khwarazm Shah's empire, Chaghadai and Ogedei had still been engaged in the siege of Utrar. It had taken five months before the walls were breached, and another month to take the citadel where the garrison and most of the inhabitants had taken refuge. When the citadel walls too had been breached almost the entire garrison and most of the citizenry were slaughtered, but Genghis had sent orders that he wanted the governor, Inalchuq, taken alive. He and his wife, knowing they were doomed, had taken to the roof of the armoury from where his wife ripped off tiles which he then hurled at his pursuers. The Mongols began demolishing the building stone by stone, until they had Inalchuq in their

Genghis berating the citizens of Bukhara.
'I am the punishment of God,' he told them. 'If you had not
committed great sins, he would not have
sent a punishment like me.'

وعظ نفس جگر خان
برمسجد بخارا

grasp. They took him to Samarqand, where he was executed by having molten silver poured into his eyes and ears. Utrar was than put to the torch, and later levelled to the ground.

FUGITIVES FROM MONGOL WRATH

Although Inalchuq had been dealt with, the Khwarazm Shah had escaped Genghis's troops. The Sultan had ignored his son's appeal to stay and carry the fight back to the invader, and instead took flight in the hope of finding refuge in Mesopotamia. Genghis sent Subedei and Jebei in pursuit. They followed him from town to town, from province to province – and the Khwarazm Shah found no refuge. Jalal al-Din had also departed Samarqand, but it was his intention to stay in the field and harass the Mongols in an attempt to halt their progress. In the event, however, he too became a fugitive, and for as long as he remained at liberty the Mongols were prepared to burn and slaughter everything in their path in their efforts to capture him. Genghis and his son Tolui took up this task themselves. They rode south across the Oxus River, pursuing Jalal al-Din down through south-eastern Persia into what is now Afghanistan, then into Pakistan and across the Indus River. The destruction that was wrought along the way was on a scale never before experienced in steppe warfare. When Merv fell in 1221, the Persian chroniclers claim that Tolui slaughtered 700000 sparing just eighty craftsmen. Nishapur suffered just as badly, as did Balkh; once one of the greatest cities of the age, filled with magnificent mosques, hospitals and palaces – a place where Alexander had visited and Zoroaster had once preached. Today it is an empty arena of walls guarding a windswept plain.

Jalal al-Din evaded capture throughout the campaign and in so doing became, in Persian chronicles, a figure of epic qualities. His exploits stirred the citizens of a number of cities to revolt, but this only brought down Mongol wrath on an even greater scale. For a week the Mongols devoted themselves to the slaughter of the inhabitants of Herat, after which most of the city, bar the citadel, was levelled to the ground. Jalal al-Din continued to trouble the Mongol forces for years to come, but was never able to concentrate his forces into any significant size and was never again a serious threat. His father, on the other hand, was hunted into ignominy.

Subedei and Jebei pursued the Khwarazm Shah through Tus and Rayy up to the western shores of the Caspian Sea. Subedei had been ordered to finish off the Khwarazm Shah, and in the process was given leave to carry out a reconnaissance in force of the lands between the Caspian and Black Seas. The Khwarazm Shah was eventually pursued to Astara on the shores of the

Caspian, where he discarded his fine clothes, took up the rags of a beggar and, with a small group of followers, attempted to slip out of the town unnoticed. Penniless and anonymous, he boarded a small fishing boat just as a Mongol troop raced to the shores, firing their arrows in vain after the little boat. The mighty Khwarazm Shah made it to the tiny island of Abeskum, where he finally died of pleurisy in January 1221. He had fallen from the greatest heights to utter poverty, and was buried in a torn shirt borrowed from one of his servants.

The rest of Subedei's campaign has entered the annals of military history as one of the greatest adventures in cavalry warfare. His contingent continued through Azerbaijan and into the Christian kingdom of Georgia, then around the western and northern shores of the Caspian Sea into Russia. Once he had made his way through the pass at Derbent, his column emerged on to the plain north of the Caucasus. Here they were confronted by an alliance of Turkic tribes from the western steppe: Alans, Cherkes and Kipchaks. Though both sides suffered serious losses, these Western tribesmen proved no match for the easterners and Subedei continued his 'Great Raid' across the Russian steppe. When the Russian princes heard news of the foreigners' progress through their territory they put together a united force to challenge what had by now become a much weakened detachment – it was no longer an army. But again the locals came off worse in a crushing defeat at the battle of Kalka in 1223. It was now five years since the Mongols had gone to war.

FINAL REVENGE

As far as the main army was concerned, military operations ceased once Genghis reached the waters of the Indus. Messengers had brought news of the Khwarazm Shah's death: his army had been decimated, and Jalal al-Din was no longer thought to be a threat. Almost as if he had suddenly had his fill of carnage, Genghis retired to pastures south of the Hindu Kush and from there summoned a famous Taoist sage, Ch'ang Ch'un, to leave his monastery and come to the Great Khan's side. In an uncharacteristically philosophical vein, Genghis had become preoccupied with questions of his own mortality and was anxious to know if the sage knew of any elixir that might postpone death

Overleaf: Once the fabled city of Balkh, in what is now
northern Afghanistan. A thousand years before Christ Zoroaster
preached here; seven hundred years later Alexander
passed this way. Then came Genghis Khan.

indefinitely. The learned one knew of no such potion; nevertheless Genghis was so impressed with Ch'ang Ch'un's wisdom that he granted the Taoist sect valuable privileges. In this somewhat reflective mood he travelled, during the autumn of 1222, back to Transoxania where he stayed for some time in Bukhara. Here he listened for some time to the clerics expounding upon the virtues of Islam. He remained attentive throughout their lectures, but admonished the imams over the annual pilgrimage to Mecca, insisting that God could not exist in a stone but was present throughout the entire world. In Samarqand he ordered the imams to pray for him in their mosques, but was not content to stay and, in the spring of 1223, began the long journey back to Mongolia. He was apparently in no hurry, having taken up with a young and attractive new consort along the way. But it was not her charms that caused him to dawdle. He had learnt that his first wife, Borte, was furious that he had taken up with a new wife; and so, as the conqueror of the world approached Mongolia, he sent forth emissaries to report on Borte's temperament.

It was 1225 before his great caravans, laden with booty and trailing long lines of slaves, finally returned home. Subedei and Jebei had by this time completed their march through the Russian principalities and had brought a great deal of intelligence about the lands that lay in the western steppe and beyond. Genghis was by now nearly sixty, and new campaigns into these lands were beyond even his remarkable faculties. However, his soldiering days were by no means finished; there were a number of problems that he would deal with now that he was back. During his absence from the Chin campaign, the general he had left in command had died and the small contingent that he had commanded had returned to Mongolia; the Chin had therefore been able to reoccupy much of the territory that Genghis had taken from them ten years before. But before an expedition could be mounted for China, there was even more pressing business closer to home.

Seven years earlier, the king of the Tanguts had refused to supply Genghis with soldiers for the campaign into Transoxania. According to the *Secret History*, before setting out to deal with this miscreant, Genghis had been troubled by a number of bad omens. The Mongols were a deeply superstitious people and even the most learned of them were easily ruled by the vagaries of a shaman's wisdom or the encoded messages in the charred shoulder-bone of a sheep. Yet, despite these omens, revenge had always been the most vital motivation, and so in 1226 he set out at the head of his army. From a military aspect everything proceeded according to plan, yet in other respects the years spent on this campaign were dogged with misfortune. After just a few months he was badly thrown from his horse during a hunt. When he returned to his camp, the surgeons discovered that he had suffered serious internal injuries

and pleaded with him to give up the war until he had recovered. Genghis refused, struggling to hide his pain from his soldiers. He was determined to stay with the army at least until the Tanguts were vanquished.

Chinese chroniclers echoed the accounts written by Persians about the war in Transoxania, describing dreadful scenes of slaughter, destruction and fields littered with bones. At times the Mongols employed ingenious tactics against the enemy cities; like damming up rivers and then letting loose the flood to engulf a city and the surrounding countryside. On one occasion a battle took place on the frozen Yellow River, when the Tangut commanders saw an opportunity for a full-scale charge across the ice. But the Mongols coped with frozen rivers all the time in their part of the world, and the Tanguts were hopelessly outclassed. Their horses slid and crashed into one another, losing their mounts which were then picked off by Mongol archers. The Mongols had taken the precaution of scattering grit over their section of the ice and tying felt around the unshod hooves of their horses. But it was a victory that gave Genghis little comfort. Some weeks before he had learnt that his son Jochi had died. On hearing the news he had retired into his tent and remained there for some days, unwilling to let his soldiers witness his grief.

By the summer of 1227 the war against the Tanguts was nearly over, but by then Genghis and his surgeons knew that the life of the Great Khan was ebbing. He summoned his sons before him, and when Ogedei and Tolui arrived they found their father wrapped in blankets and shivering before a small fire. He was delirious with pain, and ranting: 'My descendants will wear gold, they will eat the choicest meats, they will ride the finest horses, they will hold in their arms the most beautiful women and they will forget to whom they owe it all.' Gradually he rallied and found the strength to explain to his youngest son how the campaign ought to be completed. 'A deed is not glorious until it is finished.' He extracted a promise from them to continue the war against the Chin, and they discussed how that campaign ought to be waged.

Some time in August 1227 Genghis Khan finally died, but in accordance with his orders his death was kept a secret from his army. The Tangut capital had not yet surrendered, though its inhabitants had sent word of their wish to sue for peace. When the city gates were finally opened the Mongol soldiers were finally told of Genghis's death. They swept inside with their swords drawn and showed no mercy. Every living thing inside the city walls was put to death.

The procession carrying their commander back to the steppe took many weeks. Anyone who met the bier along the road was instantly dispatched 'to serve their master in the other world'. He had chosen to be buried on a mountain named Burkhan Kaldun, in a range that rises near the Onon, Tuula

61

and Kerulen rivers. According to tradition, it was near this mountain that the original forebears of the Mongol nation, the Blue Wolf and the Fallow Doe, had mated. It was, and for most Mongolians still is, the spiritual heartland of the nation. Genghis's body lay in state for three months while princes and ambassadors travelled to pay their respects. At his burial, forty jewelled slave girls and forty of the finest horses were sacrificed and buried alongside him. Then a thousand horsemen rode over the ground to disguise the site. Within less than a generation the mountainside was covered with fresh undergrowth and Genghis Khan's final resting place was devoured by the steppe.

Portrait of Genghis Khan, from the
National Palace Museum, Taipei.

3

THE PROMISE
FULFILLED

THE CAMPAIGNS OF GENGHIS KHAN were far and away the most far-reaching in world history; never had so much territory been conquered by a single man. At the time of his death the empire was four times the size of Alexander's and more than twice the size of the Roman empire; yet it had barely even begun to expand. Moreover, just like the Greek and Roman empires, it would have a tremendous impact upon world history even though it survived less than 200 hundred years. All of this was forged around the genius of a single figure, born within an insignificant nomadic tribe which for hundreds of years had anonymously tended its sheep and horses in the eastern Asian steppe.

By any standard Genghis Khan was a major figure in world history, and yet the true scale of his success has never been properly recognized in the West. Here his name has largely become synonymous with scenes of unbridled barbarism, the rape of civilization and the threat of pagan hordes. He has never enjoyed the status of great empire builders like Alexander, Tamerlane or Napoleon. Nevertheless, his accomplishments greatly outshine these more familiar names, and not simply in terms of scale. For one thing the Mongol empire was far more enduring. When Alexander died his empire was divided up amongst his generals, who then descended into a series of petty quarrels which quickly led to the collapse of the fragments that remained. The Mongol empire did not lose its sense of purpose once the charismatic figure at its heart was gone, as was the case with the empires built by Tamerlane and Alexander.

Genghis had ensured a secure succession and at the same time established the beginnings of an administration that would grow with the empire. Like Napoleon, he had been blessed with generals of great calibre – men who were promoted through the ranks of a modern army where talent and ability were rewarded. In most armies of those days, nobles and princes of the blood automatically assumed military command regardless of their competence. Another quality that Genghis shared with the little Corsican was his ability to provide his army with a seemingly endless string of victories, and with it incredible wealth, which was repaid with uncompromising loyalty. But unlike Napoleon, Genghis never abandoned his armies nor sacrificed them for his own vainglory. Nor did Genghis ever meet his Waterloo. His victories were won through brilliant strategy, organization, discipline and courage. There are simply no comparisons in military history with the breathtaking conquests undertaken during the last twenty-five years of his life. The whole of Asia resounded with the name Genghis Khan – though at an enormous cost.

A TERRIBLE PRICE

The unprecedented slaughter, particularly of civilians, that occurred through-out his campaigns has always given historians reason for pause. Yet it is too simple to dismiss the huge degree of carnage as unbridled barbarism. In his favour it has to be said that Genghis never employed murder as a political weapon, as Tamerlane and other more recent tyrants did, and indeed the death penalty was used for very few crimes. During Genghis's reign conquered subjects were immediately emancipated, and there was never any form of political or racial tyranny. The Mongols were extraordinarily tolerant of other religions and this was a tradition that they maintained for most of the history of the empire – a rare quality in a world where Christians and Muslims had been at war with each other for nearly 500 years. Yet, in the words of the historian Dr David Morgan, these highly enlightened attitudes must always be seen in context: 'Assuming you survived your first encounter with the Mongol armies,' he once mused, 'it was highly improbable you would be subsequently persecuted for your religious beliefs.' Before the how and why of Mongol war-making policies are examined, it is important to try and grasp the scale. No one suffered more than the people of Transoxania, Khwarazmia and Khurasan. There was nothing in living or recorded memory that compared with the catastrophe, and one Persian chronicler writing a hundred years after the event described the parlous state of the country in these words: '. . . as a result of the eruption of the Mongols and the general massacre of people which took place in those days . . . there can be no doubt that if for a thousand years to come

no evil befalls the country, yet it will not be possible to repair the damage, and bring the land back into the state it was formerly.'

All the chroniclers seemed to vie with one another in trying to capture the sheer scale of the disaster. They make grim reading. One writer claimed that when the town of Herat suffered Genghis's terrible retribution, having rebelled and challenged Mongol rule, the Mongol general Elchidei is supposed to have exterminated no fewer than 1 600 000 people. Another chronicler puts the figure at 2 400 000. At the destruction of Nishapur, the death toll was supposed to have reached 1 747 000. The heads of their victims were stacked in three pyramids: a pile each for men, women and children. When the bones had been picked clean the piles of skulls stood as macabre warnings to anyone who might challenge Mongol supremacy.

No modern historian takes these figures as a realistic account of the death toll. For a start, no one has any idea what the populations of these areas were in the mid-thirteenth century, though it seems unlikely that any city there could have matched the population of a Chinese city like K'ai-feng or Hang-chow, both of which numbered over a million inhabitants. Even making allowances for people from the countryside who sought refuge behind the city walls, these figures are certainly exaggerations. But even if they cannot be taken literally, they do begin to suggest the enormous psychological shock that had swept through the population. There is no precedent for these figures in Persian histories, which suggests there was no precedent for the amount of death and destruction that had been endured. Throughout Khurasan, the Mongols continued the same policy. At Bamian, Balkh and Merv the entire populations – even domestic animals – were slaughtered. The generals Jebei and Subedei brought similar disaster to Azerbaijan, destroying the towns of Rayy, Qum, Zanjan, Qazvin and Maragheh. Interestingly, nearly all the cities dealt with this way had been those whose inhabitants had rebelled against Mongol rule. It is also worth adding that not all the inhabitants were thought to be expendable; officers and nobles were invariably spared, as were artisans, craftsmen, scribes, clerics, merchants and occasionally administrators – all of whom the Mongols held in high regard. The opposite was the case, however, when it came to peasants, the majority of human life in the thirteenth century. Whether in China or western Asia, the peasants who worked the land were regarded without exception as having no greater status in life than a flock of sheep. When the order came to put the population to the sword, they were herded together like sheep – and dealt with as such. Being pasture-based horsemen, the Mongols viewed men and women who worked on their knees in the soil as the basest form of human life. Even a horse was far more valuable.

But as we know from more recent experiences of mass extermination,

The citadel of Herat in western Afghanistan, built on the remains
of a fort raised by Alexander the Great. It was claimed that just
twenty-five citizens survived the Mongol attack.

one cannot believe that the soldiers of a conquering army would go to all the effort required to slaughter many hundreds of thousands of people simply because they had a loathing for agricultural labourers. It is quite clear from the evidence that the Mongols preferred to gain submission without having to resort to mass-murder. Their strategy was to avoid Mongol casualties whenever possible, so any city that surrendered without resisting was spared – and the Mongols usually kept their word. However, any sign of resistance was met with merciless retribution; the resulting massacre was intended as a warning to others. Judging by the large numbers of cities that surrendered upon the Mongols' demand, the tactic seems to have worked.

But the slaughter that went on during the fighting was nothing compared

to the destruction wrought in its wake. The Persian plateau does not have many great rivers, and so agriculture had always been supported by a very sophisticated and widespread system of artificial irrigation known as *qanats*. This consisted of an elaborate system of underground channels constructed to carry water from the mountain sources across – or under the land – to the fields. From the surface this system appears as a long line of shallow wells from which are dug long trenches that carry the water at right-angles to the line of wells, irrigating the land on either side. All irrigation systems, and *qanats* in particular, need to be regularly maintained. Unless they are regularly dug out they silt up and the entire system collapses. With the population either dead, or frightened away, the *qanat* system gradually broke down and the land dried up. Agriculture ceased to be possible and the cities of the region that had depended upon it withered, or, like the city of Bukhara, were not rebuilt to anything like their previous size and opulence. The Mongol legacy lasted for centuries.

These devastating consequences lead one to wonder why an army bothers to conquer a place if in the process there is nothing left worth ruling. The answer is that, under Genghis Khan, the Mongols were not really engaged in a campaign of conquest. As soon as fighting came to an end, the armies withdrew from all the territories except Khwarazmia which was put under the control of Mongol-appointed administrators. There was no real interest in occupying and exploiting the lands through which they had swept like a juggernaut. Despite the vastness of his conquests, Genghis's vision of the world at the time of his death was still centred upon the steppe. While Mongol territory had expanded to include all the lands previously controlled by all the other Turko-Mongol tribes, it was almost coincidental that it also consumed some of the lands of sedentary peoples that surrounded its frontiers. Genghis Khan's invasions of northern China and Khwarazmia were designed to gain submission, not so that he could rule the world. He had set out originally to gain control of the steppe, and from his perspective the sedentary territories on his frontiers were of marginal importance

This was quite the opposite view to that of the new ranks of advisers and administrators that had joined the Mongol court; for them, of course, the steppes were of marginal importance, lying as they did between the frontiers of one civilization and another. It was this fundamental distinction between the nomadic and the sedentary view of the world which had led to the most devastating effects on the populations of farmlands and cities.

But there was another crucial factor that influenced Mongol attitudes towards the sedentary populations, and that was the Mongols' inferior numbers. They simply didn't have the manpower to station garrisons in the

territory they had conquered, so they relied upon a country's collective memory of the most terrifying and brutal assault upon one or two cities to ensure loyalty in the absence of the main army. Though it lasted for seven long years, the entire campaign through Khwarazmia, Khurasan and the Russian steppes was really one gigantic raid, intended to terrorize the massive populations in those regions into submission. Any sign of revolt was, from the Mongols' point of view, much better dealt with by wiping out the entire population.

Through all these considerations of Mongol attitudes, there was one singular principle that informed all their ideas – their almost total lack of contact with sedentary civilizations. Their proud nomadic traditions had led them to look contemptuously upon the great agricultural producers like China. They had traded for centuries with border posts and had received, indirectly, gifts and money from the Chinese courts, but China was seen as nothing more than a vast treasure house to be plundered. Perhaps the most chilling statistic that illustrates this stunning disregard for their sedentary neighbours comes from their own records. A census taken by the Chin empire in 1195 showed a population in northern China of fewer than 50 million people, yet when the Mongols took their first census of their newly won domain in 1235–6 they counted fewer than 9 million. Even assuming that enormous numbers of people may not have been counted because of the general state of chaos in northern China, this kind of discrepancy in the numbers suggests that Mongol policies of terrorism were akin to genocide. As was pointed out earlier, although the population of western Asia was far lower than that of China, the effects of the Great Raid were, if anything, proportionally much worse.

China's recovery from these disasters took longer than necessary because of the Mongols' unwillingness to assume responsibility for their conquests. They continued to be more than satisfied with the regular payment of tribute: silk, grain and precious metals, as well as sophisticated war machinery built by captured artisans. Though they had acquired rights over vast areas of land in China and Persia, both with long traditions of complex and sophisticated self-administration, the Mongols saw no immediate need to rely upon these traditions in the running of their new domains. Indeed, for some

Overleaf: *Qanats*, the Persian system of irrigation.
Underground channels drew water down from the mountains across
the plains to fill lines of shallow wells and trenches in the fields.
After the Mongol attacks the *qanats* were neglected, the system
silted up and Persia reverted to a desert.

time they saw no need for an official government structure at all; and when pressed to deal with a crisis they would respond in a somewhat *ad hoc* fashion, usually delegating responsibility to a foreign official who carried out his job under distant Mongol supervision.

So although at the end of Genghis Khan's life it cannot quite be claimed that he had forged an empire, nor is it accurate to suggest that, having withdrawn their armies, the Mongols took no further interest in the conquered lands. Quite the opposite; and it is in this particular respect that the legacy of Genghis Khan differs dramatically from, say, that of Alexander, Attila, Tamerlane and Napoleon. It is clear that Genghis believed he had established a dynasty that had won the submission of most of western and central Asia and northern China – and that he expected it to endure long after his death. But it was also clear that no steppe nation had ever conquered this much territory before and that the Mongols would have to employ new policies with regard to it. Quite what those policies would be was not yet certain, but the Mongols were above all things practical and were never too proud to learn from others.

THE GOLDEN CLAN

As the empire expanded, eventually to encompass all of the Middle East and China, the Mongols became much more sophisticated in their methods of government, though initially they were not seduced by the obvious sophistication of either the Chinese or Persian administrations. They preferred to employ the administrative experience of people who had an acceptable nomadic pedigree, like the Uighurs, who occupied the lands to the east of the Tien Shan Mountains, and the Khitans, who had been the rulers of northern China before the Jurchen Chin. From the Uighurs, of course, the Mongols had adopted an alphabet and their traditions of commercial law, while from the Khitans they borrowed such intangibles as concepts, vocabulary and institutions.

The most significant institution they took from the Khitans was the *darughachi*, a sort of all-purpose Mongol official who was stationed in conquered territory and became, in effect, a kind of provincial military governor. It was his responsibility to ensure that the local communities did not renege on the submissions they had made to the Mongols. These officials had a swift and reliable line of communication with the Great Khan, and any hint of revolt was dealt with immediately. However, the *darughachi*'s most vital responsibility was to ensure that the appropriate taxes were collected and forwarded to the central chancellery in Mongolia. *Darughachis* had been recruited from the ranks of the *keshig*, the imperial guard, whose allegiance was

to the life and wellbeing of the Great Khan. All lines of communication led to him – or the aristocracy that had been created around him. This aristocracy, or the Golden Clan as it was known, were the families that could trace their lineage to Genghis Khan himself. The most important of these were Genghis's four sons born of his first wife, Borte. It was only they and their descendants who had the right to rule.

These four – Jochi, Chaghadai, Ogedei and Tolui – formed the bedrock of the dynasty. To ensure the Golden Clan's endurance Genghis had devised a system of appanages, or *ulus*, that were distributed amongst the members of his clan and honoured commanders who had distinguished themselves in warfare. These tracts of territory extended only over lands where nomadic peoples tended to dwell and provided the holder with a source of wealth, for along with the land came a contingent of army units plus animals, artisans and artists. The holders of these *ulus* also shared in the tax revenues from other parts of the empire. The *ulus* varied in size, depending upon the age of the recipient and the esteem in which he was held, and his subsequent wealth reflected his status within the Clan. The majority of *ulus* were of the order of many hundreds of square kilometres; however, those distributed to Genghis's sons were much larger.

Before he set out on the campaign into western Asia, Genghis had already settled the question of succession, and before he died he had also set out the geographical shape of the future empire through the *ulus* he designated to his four sons. It was Mongol tradition to pass to the eldest son the lands furthest from home. Jochi, the eldest, had died some months before his father, and so all the lands 'to the west as far as the hoof of a Mongol horse trodden', were divided amongst his sons. The eldest, Orda, was given possession of the land from the north-east shores of the Aral Sea and the districts around the Sari Su River. This was later called the White Horde, and precious little is known about it. His younger brother, the able but youthful Batu, received land to the north-west, stretching from the northern shores of the Caspian as far west as the Volga and east as far as the Irgiz River. This became known as the Golden Horde, and would in time prove extraordinarily extensive. Chaghadai, a kind of Lord Chancellor, was given the lands in Central Asia that had previously been the land of the Qara Khitai, to which was later added Transoxania. Ogedei received the lands north-east of Chaghadai's – the Ala Kul, the Tarbagatai Mountains, the Kara Irtish River and the region extending from the Altai Mountains to Lake Baikal. Tolui, the youngest son, received the Mongol 'heartland', the traditional inheritance of the youngest-born.

Although Genghis had already decided upon Ogedei as his successor, it was two years before he actually assumed the title of Great Khan. Some

suggest it was because Ogedei himself was reluctant, feeling that Tolui might perhaps have been better suited, while other sources suggest it was Tolui who was unhappy about being passed over. At any rate, a *quriltai* was called in 1229 at which the issue was finally settled.

THE GREAT KHAN OGEDEI

Ogedei was, by all accounts, the most intelligent and certainly the most generous and tolerant of the four brothers. Judging from the number of stories that have survived about him, it would seem that he spent a great deal of his time devising expedients by which those who had fallen foul of Chaghadai's stern judgements might escape the death penalty. Ogedei was also a great *bon viveur*, having a well-developed taste for wine. After being admonished by his elder brother for his excessive drunkenness, Ogedei is supposed to have meekly foresworn his past behaviour and promised to restrict himself to a specific number of cups of wine a day – though not before taking the precaution of obtaining the most enormous wine goblet!

But these accounts of Ogedei do not paint his full character. Under his control the proto-empire established by his father expanded into a commonwealth of the most prodigious size. The first and most important action undertaken was the long-overdue conquest of the Chin. This campaign, begun by Genghis in 1211, had been continuing for more than twenty-five years. Ogedei was determined to bring matters to a swift conclusion, but first he had to make up lost ground. After the death of Muqali, the general whom Genghis had left in charge of the campaign, the Chin had reconquered a large tract of territory around the Wei valley and in Shensi. Genghis had always known that defeating the Chin would not be easy and he had advised his sons that they would probably need the aid of the Sung empire, to the south in the traditional heartland of China.

In 1230 a new Mongol offensive began, but it was soon repulsed. In 1231 they returned under the command of Subedei and, although they made some ground, they were again repulsed from the Wei valley. Ogedei finally decided to take his father's advice and make a supreme effort to court the Sung. The Mongols' aim was to try and approach K'ai-feng, the current Chin capital, through Sung territory. If they could also exploit a hundred-year-old hatred

The enthronement of Ogedei Khan, from a manuscript of Rashid al-Din.
Beside him is his wife Toregene and, on the right, his children. Future successions
would be a struggle between Ogedei's sons and those of his younger brother Tolui.

between the two dynasties and actually recruit the Sung armies to their cause, then that would be a bonus. Ogedei took command of the bulk of the Mongol army and marched it in an easterly direction along the banks of the Yellow River. Tolui took a contingent of 30 000 in a large sweeping movement down into Sung territory, taking the city of Hang-chung, then moved south towards Szechwan. There he turned and moved north-west again, crossing the Han River and suddenly appearing inside Chin territory. By early 1232, his forces depleted from disease and malnutrition, he had joined up with Ogedei Khan's army again. Almost immediately the Mongols were confronted by a Chin army led by one of their most able generals, Wan-yen Yi.

The battle was hard fought, with the outcome turning many times, but eventually the Chin were defeated. Wan-yen Yi was captured and the Mongols, impressed by his ability, tried to persuade him to join their side. He refused, preferring death to dishonour. The Chin, in the meantime, had withdrawn their forces to K'ai-feng, abandoning the rest of their territory. The subsequent siege of K'ai-feng was undertaken first by Ogedei; but, when the Chin emperor refused to submit to Mongol rule, the inevitable long drawn-out campaign against one of the largest and best-fortified cities in China was left to Subedei. It turned out to be a far more difficult exercise than any other that the Mongols had faced. According to a Chinese account, it seems that the Chin were employing a new weapon that was having a devastating effect on Subedei's forces: '. . . great mortars that roared like thunder in the heaven'. The Mongols were confronted by what is thought to have been their first experience of gunpowder and their forces were in danger of being destroyed at the very gates of the city.

While Subedei was left to get on with the investment of K'ai-feng, Ogedei and his brother Tolui returned to the mountain passes to spend the summer. While they were together, both Ogedei and his brother became seriously ill and news reached Subedei that the Great Khan was not expected to survive. There are many different stories about the events at the mysterious summer retreat. One legend has it that Ogedei's illness caused so much concern that the great Lord Tengri, the Mongol God, was called upon to come to his aid. The Lord God in heaven agreed to take the life of another in place of Ogedei's, and Tolui volunteered. This particular legend was developed amongst the later rulers of the empire, who were to be descendants of Tolui. It is far more likely that the story was invented to enhance the circumstances of Tolui's death, which was probably caused by nothing more mysterious than alcoholic poisoning. The two of them had perhaps partaken of a less than wholesome brew, and only Ogedei recovered.

In the meantime, Subedei's own situation was becoming desperate. As

he was losing men at an alarming rate he had to find a quick way of bringing the military stand-off to an end. He took the initiative and approached the Sung for help. The Sung emperor agreed, in return for a couple of Chin provinces – Honan and K'ai-feng. Soon 20 000 fresh Sung troops arrived at the gates of K'ai-feng, and the city collapsed shortly afterwards. The destruction and plundering of K'ai-feng in 1234 was followed by the execution of all the male members of the Chin Dynasty, while the women were deported to the Mongol court. These scenes were witnessed by the Sung generals and would haunt them in the years to come. Subedei was about to set upon the rest of the population when one of Ogedei's advisers, Yeh-lu Ch'u-ts'ai, intervened.

LIBERAL INFLUENCES: YEH-LU CH'U-TS'AI

Yeh-lu Ch'u-ts'ai already had a reputation at the Chin court at Chung-tu even before he entered Mongol employment, where he later shone as a great statesman. A Khitan by birth, he was related to the old Liao dynasty, though his father and grandfather had been functionaries in the Chin court. Educated as an astronomer/astrologer, he was brought up with Buddhist ideals though his future lay as a typical Confucian administrator. After the fall of Chung-tu, Yeh-lu Ch'u-ts'ai was amongst the prisoners brought before Genghis Khan. When Genghis asked if he was not glad that his forefathers had been avenged now that the Chin were defeated, Yeh-lu Ch'u-ts'ai reminded Genghis that both his father and grandfather had served in the Chin court. 'How can I, as a subject and a son, be so insincere at heart as to consider my sovereign and my father as enemies?' Genghis was impressed with the young man's strong sense of loyalty and immediately recruited him into his budding administration. Before long Yeh-lu Ch'u-ts'ai was recruiting others from the ranks of the Chin, Khitan and Chinese prisoners. He rescued libraries from the torch, gathering up documents and books wherever the Mongol armies travelled, and along with his growing staff fashioned a makeshift, mobile civil service. After Genghis's death he was inherited by Ogedei and became one of his closest advisers.

It is Yeh-lu Ch'u-ts'ai who is credited with having moderated the Mongols' worst excesses, and in particular with radically altering their

Overleaf: The festival of Qing Ming in the city of K'ai-feng, painted before the Mongol conquest. This great city of more than a million people was briefly the Chin capital until it fell to a combined Mongol and Sung force in 1260.

approach towards gathering revenue. But it was after the fall of K'ai-feng and the conquest of the Chin that he is said to have made his most important stand. It had been seriously proposed by Subedei and the other generals that, after the artisans, merchants and scholars had been rounded up and sent off to Mongolia, the rest of the population should be put to the sword – not the population of K'ai-feng, but the entire population of north China.

The millions of Chinese peasants had been a source of concern to the Mongols for some time, not just because their labour seemed incomprehensible, but because their sheer numbers were so disquieting. They made utterly useless soldiers; besides which, the vast amounts of good land they occupied might be better used as pasture for the Mongol herds. As mass extermination was being seriously debated, Yeh-lu Ch'u-ts'ai energetically argued against it. He pointed out that if the peasants were left alone and allowed to prosper, and he was granted permission to introduce a fair and progressive system of taxing the product of their labours, the Mongols' income from north China would be massively enhanced. Yeh-lu Ch'u-ts'ai's scheme was to try and introduce a proper budget for the running of the Mongol court and army. This meant raising a tax that would be uniform throughout the empire. A settled population would pay 10 per cent of its harvest, while nomadic people would provide one animal for every hundred owned. In particular he wanted to do away with the Mongols' unproductive methods of gathering tax. Yeh-lu Ch'u-ts'ai's reforms came slowly, though once the increased revenue and produce started flowing Ogedei became more sympathetic and talk of mass extermination ceased.

Although Genghis held Yeh-lu Ch'u-ts'ai in high esteem, his influence within the Mongol court as a scribe, astrologer and principal minister was not really felt until the reign of Ogedei. The second Great Khan was more open to foreign ideas and prepared to practise foreign methods, although by comparison with his principal minister he was still a determined nomad. It had been Genghis's great wish that the empire should remain largely steppe-based – that, however large it grew, the centre of power would not shift to any of the settled societies but remain firmly in the Mongol heartland. However, with the empire now expanding on all sides, a burgeoning administration struggling to keep pace, coupled with an ever-increasing traffic of supplicants and envoys arriving to pay tribute to the Great Khan, the traditional encampment of tents and *gers* was inadequate. The Mongols had to have a capital.

CAPITAL OF A NOMADIC PEOPLE

Rather in the manner in which cities like Washington DC, Brasilia and Canberra were constructed out of nowhere, Qaraqorum emerged from the

midst of a great grassy waste to be the notional focus for the greatest land-based empire in history. After the collapse of the empire it quickly fell into decay, and the majority of its permanent buildings were plundered for materials during the construction, in the sixteenth century, of a nearby Buddhist monastery. The location of Qaraqorum was subsequently lost to history until it was rediscovered in the nineteenth century, and excavated by the Russians during the first half of the present century. Evidence from these excavations suggests that the site had been used by a Buddhist community long before the Mongol empire, and that during the time of Genghis Khan it was a kind of tent city, being both a military camp and a trading centre for commerce and handicrafts.

In some respects it was a curious location for the seat of government. It was not in original Mongol territory but in the border regions, roughly midway between Ogedei's and Tolui's *ulus* in the Orkhon valley – territory that had once been occupied by the Naimans. However, for the steppe peoples the location had great significance. It was close to the crossroads of a series of traditional highways that had been used by migrating nomads and merchants' caravans for centuries. Forest-dwelling nomads passed through the area during their annual migrations to and from the south, while Islamic merchants journeying to and from China passed through the same valley in an east–west direction. These ancient highways were will being used, so it made great sense for the capital to be placed at this important point.

Work began on the city while Ogedei was still on campaign against the Chin, and the first walls went up in 1235. According to the archaeologists, it was constructed on an artificial hill composed of alternate layers of sand and clay. The city itself was surrounded by an earthen wall about 1 km (1100 yards) across the northern face, 1.5 km (1650 yards) down the western side and about 2 km (2200 yards) down the opposite wall. These were only about 1 m (3 feet) high but some 15–18 m (50–60 feet) thick. To the west of these, in the south-western corner of the site, was Ogedei's palace area, which was itself a walled compound. At the southern end of this compound there were two massive gates, set one in front of the other; an outer gate was some 30 m (100 feet) high. Inside the compound were two large halls used for audiences, banquets and the reception of guests. The largest was more than 80 m (250

Overleaf: The remains at Qaraqorum. There are a number of these large stone tortoises which are thought to have supported imperial stelae – official pronouncements from the court carved in stone.

feet) long and was described by Friar William of Rubruck, a French friar who went to the Mongol empire as an evangelist:

> And the palace is like a church, with a middle nave, and two sides beyond two rows of pillars, and with three doors to the south, and beyond the middle door on the inside stands the tree [a fountain that produced a selection of liquors], and the khan sits in a high place to the north, so that he can be seen by all; and he himself sits up there like a divinity. There are twelve idol temples of different nations, two muhummeries [mosques] in which is cried the law of Mahomet, and one church of Christians is in the extreme end of the city. At the eastern end is sold millet and other kinds of grain; at the western one, sheep and goats are sold; at the southern, oxen and carts are sold; at the northern, horses are sold.

Within the palace compound, behind the main halls was a low, circular mound where the Mongols erected large residential tents. Despite the existence of numerous large buildings, they preferred to sleep under canvas. The major buildings seem to have been built on a Chinese model, with high-pitched, tiled roofs. The halls were supported off the ground by regularly spaced pillars. In public places stone tortoises formed the bases of imperial stelae. By all accounts the Mongols lavished considerable sums on the decorations of the buildings, and yet the site itself was not that imposing. One European traveller compared it with a village on the outskirts of Paris.

> As for the city of Qaraqorum I can tell you that, not counting the Khan's palace, it is not as large as the village of Saint Denis, and the monastery of Saint Denis is worth ten times more than that palace. . . . There are two quarters in it; one of Saracens [Muslims] in which are the markets, and where a great many Tartar gather on account of the court, which is always near this [city], and on account of the great number of ambassadors; the other is the quarter of the Cathayans, all of whom are artisans. Besides these quarters there are great palaces, which are for the secretaries of the court.

Despite having created a permanent seat of power, Ogedei did not forego the traditional seasonal migrations. He would be at Qaraqorum from February through to the spring, when he travelled north of the capital to the lakes and marshes of the Orkhon River. He would stay there for a month or six weeks, return to Qaraqorum briefly and then, to escape the baking summers, move to the high ground in the mountains to the south-east. By the end of August he would move once more, this time south to the Ongin River, where he had his hunting grounds and winter residence, and there he would stay until returning to Qaraqorum to begin the cycle over again.

Nevertheless, Qaraqorum did provide a focus for the expanding empire, and a place to house the administration. Yeh-lu Ch'u-ts'ai was instrumental in strengthening the authority of this medieval Brasilia. The Treasury was located there, as were the taxation and revenue-gathering services; and Chaghadai, the Lord Chancellor, held court there. But most importantly, it was the place to which foreign envoys, wealthy merchants and prominent clerics travelled for an audience with the most important man in Asia. It became the hub of all political and commercial life in the continent.

In order for this to be so, the empire had to develop a system of communication that would bind all the spokes to the hub. The great *Yam* was forged by Ogedei from a simpler system that his father had employed for keeping in touch with his generals. Its essence was a network of riders whose purposes were varied: they could act as escorts for visiting envoys, ensuring their safe passage over the thousands of miles of open steppe; or the system might be used to transport materials, especially along the roads from China. They might also be used for the gathering of intelligence from the far reaches of the empire and beyond. However, the most important use of the *Yam* was the swift transmission of royal orders across the length and breadth of Asia.

Ogedei established the system first in his own *ulus*. At regular stages along the roads, roughly 40–50 km (25–30 miles) or a day's ride, post stations were constructed that provided messengers with food, shelter and fresh horses. These horses were provided by the local population, while the system itself was maintained by the army. The messengers carried with them a form of identification, known as a *paiza*, that established under whose authority they travelled. Each *paiza* was about 50 cm (18 ins) long and was usually made of wood, though *paizas* representing some-one of high authority might be of silver or even gold. They were also highly decorated, bearing engravings of tigers or falcons – which also testified as to the rank of the holder.

Two bronze *paizas*, a kind of identification worn by messengers of the *Yam* – the imperial communications system.

Riders on the *Yam* were sometimes expected
to ride without stopping for hundreds of miles,
changing horses while at full gallop.

There are reports of couriers covering some staggering distances through
the *Yam*; Marco Polo claimed 300–500 km (about 200–300 miles) a day.
These express couriers galloped day and night from one post station to
another, swathed in a garland of bells that signalled their approach. The

custodian at the station would hear the courier and have fresh horses saddled and ready. On one occasion, when a message was sent from the court at Qaraqorum to Russia, the couriers covered 1600 km (1000 miles) a month.

EXPANSION INTO WESTERN ASIA

As Ogedei set about constructing the fabric of the empire, there were still military objectives that had to be met. Genghis's campaign through Khwarazmia and Khurasan had left appalling ruin and destruction in the countryside and swept away all remnants of central government control. In the anarchy that reigned, Jalal al-Din, who had fled to Delhi in 1221, had gradually clawed his way back to power in an attempt to fill the vacuum. It was precisely the same situation that had occurred in northern China, after Genghis had lost interest in that campaign. As the Mongols had not left garrisons to hold the territory they had conquered, it was only a matter of time before someone else moved in.

Jalal al-Din had a great deal to avenge and found no difficulty gathering supporters. By 1224 he had won back a large slice of territory, which he extended into Azerbaijan by the following year, and soon he was also launching raids into Christian Georgia. By 1228 he had virtually restored the empire his father had occupied, and included with it the provinces of Fars, Kirman, Iraq-Ajemi, Azerbaijan and Mazandaran. In his obsession to reconquer his birthright, Jalal al-Din had no hesitation in conducting a murderous campaign no less terrible than that of the Mongols. Though he was clearly a commander of some distinction, he had no political skills; having reconquered most of Persia, he failed to unite the kingdom against any outside threat. This came in the form of a new Mongol invasion in 1230, when Ogedei sent an army to put an end to the unexpected restoration of the Khwarazm sultanate. The Mongols moved swiftly through Khurasan and up to Azerbaijan, where they completely surprised the defenders at Tabriz. Jalal al-Din fled from his old enemies and led them on another chase, though on this occasion he found no sanctuary. The Mongol commander, Chormaghun, kept up a relentless pursuit, and the longer he continued the harder it was for Jalal al-Din to hold on to his support. He fled north-west towards the plains of Mughan, west of the Caspian Sea. He was crossing territory that his father had crossed when he too was being pursued by the Mongols ten years before. Eventually, just like his father, Jalal al-Din found himself bereft of allies and he died around 1231, probably murdered by Kurds.

The Mongol general who had led the campaign, Chormaghun, remained as *darughachi*, or military governor, in the areas of Persia he had

conquered, and established his residence in the plains west of the Caspian Sea. Over the next ten years Chormaghun worked his way through the many small states of the Caucasus, subduing them all before turning towards the kingdom of Georgia in 1236. The reputation of the Mongols had already reached these lands, so that by the time Chormaghun and his army arrived the famous Queen Rasudan had already fled to the neighbouring province. Thus Georgia too became a vassal state. Another *darughachi* was despatched to govern the lands to the south-east, Khurasan and Mazandaran, and gradually the Mongols extended more effective control over western Asia. This policy of strengthening the Mongol presence in western Asia would soon pay dividends when decisions to expand the empire even further west were taken.

THE DECISION TO INVADE EUROPE

Following the destruction of the Chin empire in 1234, Ogedei had returned to Qaraqorum to supervise the construction of his city, which was now well advanced. With the capital still rising out of a grassy wilderness, in 1235 he called a *quriltai* at which the Golden Clan and its advisers took stock of the state of the empire. It was perhaps one of the most important *quriltais* in the history of the empire, setting down a number of institutions that survived for many generations, and also directing the empire on a new course that would dramatically transform the history of the rest of the world.

Yeh-lu Ch'u-ts'ai used the *quriltai* to impose his taxation reforms and establish a number of new institutions that would serve the expanding empire. Having instructed Ogedei that 'although the empire had been conquered on horseback, it would not be ruled on horseback', he established a set of rules and precedents for the running of the Mongol court and established libraries for the precious books and documents that he had rescued from the remnants of the Chin capital. He also built schools where Mongol children would be taught to become civil administrators.

It was also at the meeting in 1235 that the formal establishment of the *Yam* took place. The order was given for the construction and supply of staging posts throughout the empire, but especially along the route between the main residences of Ogedei, Chaghadai and Batu way out in the west. Wells were dug at regular intervals to supply water, while Yeh-lu Ch'u-ts'ai saw to the provision of grain, horses and cattle for every outpost.

When the discussion came round to military activity, the generals reported action on a number of different fronts. With the conquest of northern China complete, Ogedei could now contend with one or two irritating problems. Since 1211, when Genghis Khan had first extracted a submission

from the Korean rulers, the Mongols had been irritated by the Koreans' persistent streak of independence. In 1231 a Mongol army had crossed the Yalu River, not to conquer but to raid and terrorize the Koreans into submission and the payment of tribute. Having succeeded, the Mongols left seventy officials behind to gather the revenue they had exacted. However, it was reported at the *quriltai* that in the absence of Mongol forces most of these officials had been murdered.

Ogedei, determined to deal with the Koreans once and for all, despatched an army across the Yalu. After three years of war that took a heavy toll upon the local population, the Korean rulers finally agreed to negotiate with their conquerors and peace came in 1241. Ogedei also decided to entrust his two sons, Koten and Kochu, with an army which they were to lead in a separate campaign against the Sung empire. This was in retaliation for some territorial infringements that had occurred following the collapse of the Chin. In the meantime, there were reports of General Chormaghun forging his way towards the kingdom of Georgia. In a sense, this operation was the vanguard for what was to be the most critical decision taken at the *quriltai* of 1235.

Batu, the orphaned son of Jochi, had inherited the westernmost reaches of the empire, though in fact these lands had never been conquered. They had, of course, been reconnoitred by the great General Subedei during his extraordinary Great Raid around the Caspian Sea and through Russia. Subedei saw great opportunities in these lands, but he also saw that the western steppes were the weakest point in the empire's defences, occupied as it was with numerous volatile nomadic groups. He argued that the Mongols ought to extend their empire west to the edge of the steppes and to protect their flank. Once that had been accomplished, the Mongols could push forward into Europe – conquering the separate nations one by one, just as they had done in China. As Subedei pressed his case it was greeted by growing enthusiasm, especially from Ogedei who became so enamoured of the idea that he suggested leading the army into the west himself.

Fortunately Yeh-lu Ch'u-ts'ai tempered Ogedei's enthusiasm, arguing that, unlike the situation in his father's time, the Mongols now had an empire which required someone at its head; his place, therefore, was in Qaraqorum. It was agreed instead that, since the proposed expedition was meant to conquer lands bequeathed to Batu, it was only appropriate that he should lead the campaign. It was the decision to invade Europe that above all else distinguishes the *quriltai* of 1235 from all others, and it quickly became the only real issue of discussion for the rest of the session. It would require an immense amount of planning and time; the campaign, Subedei estimated, would take eighteen years.

4

THE INVASION
OF EUROPE

THE FIRST OBJECTIVE OF THE OPERATION that emerged from the meeting at Qaraqorum was to secure the lands up to the banks of the River Volga. This meant taking the city of Bulgar, which stood at the confluence of the Volga and Kama rivers and dominated all commercial life between these rivers and the Ural Mountains. The Bulgars themselves had once been nomads, but had long since given up camp life for the city, growing rich on the fur trade. They had also taken up the word of the Prophet and were, at that time, the most northerly converts to Islam. In the seventh century those Bulgars who had not converted emigrated across the Danube, where the nation they founded eventually bore their name. Apart from the Bulgars, the Mongols would also have to subjugate the nomadic tribes that inhabited the lands to the south, along the banks of the Volga. Then the Mongol armies could cross the Volga safely, knowing their flank and rear could not be threatened. But before any military operations could commence, there would be a great deal of preparation.

The great push west was going to require enormous resources, and these were not immediately to hand. Batu, who had been given nominal responsibility for the campaign, had a miserably small army of some 4000 men. A form of conscription would have to be introduced. Subedei had estimated that the armies should be ready to move by the winter of 1237, which would give them

two years to recruit men from subjugated tribes, train them and prepare their *matériel*. By the spring of 1236, a formidable army had already been gathered: it consisted of 50000 men from the main Mongol army, plus several corps of Chinese and Persian engineers and some 20000 conscripts. No fewer than ten princes of the blood had joined the growing ranks, including Batu's brothers Orda, Shiban, Berke and Sinkur; Chaghadai's sons Baidar and Buri; Ogedei's sons Guyuk and Kadan; and Tolui's sons Mongke and Budjek.

With things advancing so well, Batu and Subedei set out northwards with an expeditionary force to attack the Bulgars, while Mongke and Budjek moved south to tackle the tribes along the lower Volga. The pursuit of the southern tribal groups turned into a classic Mongol hunt, with Mongke and Budjek spreading their forces out into a great arc and then sweeping along either bank of the river. The middle ranks floated on 200 barges down the river itself. The hunt led them to an island in the centre of the river, where fugitive tribal warriors and their princes thought themselves safe, given the swift currents and choppy waters. But they had not noticed a sandbar that ran from the river bank to the island, shallow enough to allow horses to cross. Within an hour all were slaughtered and resistance in the south put to an end.

Meanwhile, in the north, Batu and Subedei were working their way through the Bulgar territories. By the spring they had smashed all Bulgar resistance and turned yet another nation into a vassal state. Little is recorded of that campaign, except that the city of Bulgar itself was so utterly destroyed that it was never rebuilt. Before returning to Mongolia, Batu and Subedei charged through the foothills of the Urals, gathering up further conscripts for the great new army. By the winter of 1237, just as Subedei had predicted, a Mongol army of 120000 stood ready to cross the frozen Volga into Russia.

TWO ARMIES, TWO CONCEPTS OF FIGHTING

The army that had been forged under Genghis Khan and then tempered during the campaigns in China and Persia was by now easily the most formidable military force in existence. Its command structure and tactics were more advanced than any other army at the time, and would not be unfamiliar to soldiers of today. By comparison, however, the armies of Russia and Europe had evolved tactics that would seem hopelessly unimaginative to a Mongol officer. Though they were just as dependent as the Mongols upon the cavalry, or knights, as the most potent element of the army, the Europeans had neglected the mobility of the horse in preference to a host of head-bashers, for that is what the knights had become.

This may seem an unlikely description of European knighthood during

the age of chivalry. But chivalry was rather more a state of mind than a period of great military accomplishment. Thought to have emerged around the turn of the thirteenth century, the era of heroic European knighthood takes its name from the French word *chevalier*, meaning horseman or knight. Chivalry originally referred to the process of recruitment and training of knights, but it soon came to refer also to the curriculum of training that a young man underwent when learning to fight, hunt, serve his lord and govern his vassals. Ultimately it evolved into that courtly ideal in which the true knight was not only courageous and skilful in war but also generous, pious and courteous. He was a defender of the weak, often a poet or musician, and dedicated to serve some lady of his choice.

The other important aspect of the great flowering of European knighthood was the number of military-religious orders, such as the Knights Templars and Hospitallers and the Teutonic Knights. Their lives were bound by religious ritual, celibacy, vows of poverty, devotion to the Church and the restoration of the Holy Land to Christianity. In short, they were monks who were also professional soldiers. So the ideals of European knighthood were aesthetically quite sophisticated. But as an army they employed terribly crude methods.

The most important difference between European and Mongol horsemen was the development of armour. By the first half of the thirteenth century the northern European knight wore heavy steel mail that covered virtually every part of his body. Over his bare back he wore two separate linen undershirts, plus one that was padded called an aketon. On top of this he wore a long mail tunic, called a hauberk, that hung down to about mid-thigh. Underneath the skirt he wore thick woollen hose and then mail leggings that laced up to his crutch. Over his head he put on a linen hood called a coif, then a heavy mail coif, and on top of that the distinctive bucket-shaped helm. On top of his mail haubert he wore a simple linen surplice or surcoat that bore the emblem of his order, or coat of arms. The entire outfit, including broadsword, lance and shield, weighed well over 45 kg (100 lb), and with the rider himself it was an enormous burden to place on the back of a horse. In consequence the European horseman was far less mobile than his Mongol counterpart. He could not manage delicate or intricate manoeuvres; the day was usually decided on the basis of a rather basic head-on clash. Once the charge had taken place, most knights dismounted (or were brought down) and combat continued with blade and shield in ferocious hand-to-hand combat. First lance, then sword and axe were wielded against shield and mail in very close fighting, for the essence of knightly combat was a vicious duel to the death with an opponent.

Behind the cavalry would be the infantry, usually a mob of untrained and badly equipped peasants who had been forced into the army to serve the knights and usually got cut down by the enemy's horsemen. The knights themselves were not trained officers, and their individual combat skills were of no use when leading men into battle. The size of their retinue was an indication of their wealth, not their ability, and there was no clear chain of command down from the commander-in-chief.

The only area in which the Europeans excelled was in the construction of fortifications (the ultimate defence against horsemen) and in siege warfare. But nothing in the European experience had taught them any other form of warfare. Even during the Crusades most European armies were engaged either in the defence of fortified towns or in laying siege to them. Yet, in the event, these skills proved of little consequence when the encounter with the Mongols finally took place.

By contrast the Mongols were a tightly disciplined fighting machine, in which each soldier knew his place and his responsibilities. He did not fight as an individual, but as part of a massive formation that was led in and out of well-drilled manoeuvres. When the Mongol army advanced they approached as a series of long single ranks, made up of a number of units. The first two consisted of heavy cavalry, followed by three ranks of light cavalry. Out on either flank and up front were further, smaller detachments of light cavalry.

An encounter with the enemy was rarely a surprise because there were scouts out in the field who were able to communicate with the main body through a system of flags and messengers. When the enemy had been engaged, either on the flank or in front, the outer detachments quickly became the vanguard and were soon reinforced from the rear. Once the enemy's position and disposition had been discovered, the three rear ranks of light cavalry would move up through the ranks of heavy cavalry and gallop up to the line. Rarely would any of these detachments engage the enemy in close combat. Instead they would detach small squadrons of some ten or twenty riders to gallop across the enemy's line, pouring in a deadly shower of arrows.

The Mongols also preferred to manoeuvre the enemy's ranks to exactly where they wanted them. They did this by deploying the *mangudai*, a corp of 'suicide troops' that charged straight at the enemy line. As they approached within range of the enemy, they would suddenly break ranks, turn and flee. The sight of the Mongols in flight was a temptation that most enemy commanders could not resist. With the enemy cavalry in hot pursuit, the *mangudai* galloped to a prearranged spot – where the rest of the army lay in wait. By the time the enemy had reached the killing ground, their ranks were already spread out and made easy targets. From 200 m (180 yards) away the

European knights had developed suits of mail as a defence
against the sword. However, the weight of this armour, plus all their weapons,
meant that they lost a great deal of mobility.

Mongol archers would let loose a hail of arrows until the enemy's ranks had
been shredded, and it was time for the heavy cavalry to be deployed. This was
summoned by the sound of the *naqara*, a huge drum carried into battle on a
camel. The heavy brigade would begin at a walk, gradually breaking into a trot
– and then, on a signal from their commander and the appropriate beat of the
drum, a terrifying shriek would rend the air, lances would be lowered and the
horses spurred into a gallop.

But there was more to the Mongol army than cavalry. Following their

A craftsman making the traditional Mongol composite bow,
the most formidable bow of the Middle Ages. Made from bamboo and the horn
of a yak, it fires arrows at tremendous velocity.

long campaigns in China and Persia, they had acquired a great deal of expertise in siege warfare and artillery. From China they had taken up the rather lightweight Chinese siege machines and adapted them to the battlefield. There was a light catapult which could launch a 1 kg (2 lb) missile over 100 m (100 yards), and a heavier machine that would fire an 11 kg (25 lb) projectile over 150 m (150 yards). The advantage of the lighter device was that it could be dismantled and carried with the main body of the army. Both of these machines could be used either to launch rocks at walls or gates, or to hurl

naphtha or burning tar into the enemy's lines. But their range was not very great, and it was not until the Mongols had adapted machines captured from the Khwarazm Shah's army that they really had a formidable artillery. The Islamic designs were adapted to the lighter Chinese models to create something similar to the European catapult or trebuchet, with a range of more than 350 m (350 yards). They also adopted the ballista, which looked like a giant crossbow and fired a heavy arrow over the same range as a catapult, but with far more accuracy. These were light enough to be carried on to the battlefield, and could be part of a rolling barrage, to push back the enemy's front line, that was often set up before the army's advance.

But perhaps the most important war-making invention that the Mongols adopted was the Chinese discovery of explosives, which they probably first encountered during the wars against the Chin. It was used either in the form of rockets, which, fired *en masse* into the enemy's ranks, caused little damage but much alarm; or as grenades – clay vessels packed with explosives and hurled either by catapult or by hand. It might also have been possible for the Mongols to use cannon, as the Chinese had used them since the eleventh century, but there are no accounts of them doing so.

Virtually every new military invention was taken up and used by the Mongols and with these machines they quickly developed the modern principles of artillery. A prolonged battering from rocks, burning tar, grenades and fire bombs into the enemy lines would be followed up by an attack from mounted archers. These carefully rehearsed manoeuvres depended on great mobility and discipline. Although the bombardment was not nearly as accurate as the mounted archers, it spread fear and confusion amongst the enemy and made the archers' job much easier.

The image of the Mongol army on the march must have been an awe-inspiring sight. Each *tumen* (roughly 10000 men, but it was rarely up to that strength) was equipped with additional supplies of weapons and equipment carried on packhorses behind their ranks. Way off in the rear amongst the artillery and reserves was the main baggage train, made up of vast numbers of camels and wagons. Some of the wagons would be carrying supplies and equipment, but many would also be supporting mobile *gers*. In the midst of huge clouds of dust it would have seemed like a convoy of tents floating through the countryside; and behind it trotted flocks of sheep and goats that would provide food and drink for the thousands. Twentieth-century military historians have described the Mongol army as the precursor to the modern military force made up of tanks and artillery, and it is hardly surprising that two of the greatest exponents of tank warfare, Field Marshal Rommel and General George S. Patton, were both students and admirers of the legendary Subedei.

The European armies of the thirteenth century were ill prepared for what was emerging out of the East.

INTO RUSSIA

In the winter of 1237, the great Mongol juggernaut crossed the frozen Volga and set out, according to Subedei's plan, to drive swiftly deep into the heart of Russia dividing the dozen principalities that ruled the region and reducing the risk of a united opposition. The prospect for that was at any rate slim. Over the previous thousand years the Russians had gallantly withstood invasions from Swedes, French and Germans; however, the Mongols now found a nation perilously unable to produce a joint concentration of military force – even under the most critical circumstances. Their internecine rivalry made Mongol victory that much more likely.

Nevertheless, the Mongols' objective was total conquest and with that in mind they were not prepared to take any risks. The most powerful of the Russian princes were Grand Duke Yuri of Suzdal and Prince Michael of Kiev. The plan was to drive between the two and isolate Suzdal and Novgorod from the lands of Chernigov and Kiev. Having crossed the Volga, the Mongols rode north through thick forests to disguise their arrival. A woman ambassador was despatched with two riders to confront the first obstacle, the principality of Riazan which lay on the eastern frontier of Russia.

The citizens were so surprised at the sight of a woman at their gates that they were certain she was a sorceress and refused to let her in. But she had probably been chosen because she spoke their language. At any rate, the two sides were forced to conduct their business by shouting at one another. The Mongol demand was for submission, a tax of 10 per cent and reinforcements for their army. The Riazan prince replied contemptuously that, if the Mongols were prepared to wait, once the inhabitants had all gone they could have everything.

Subedei had already decided to make an example of Riazan. The city was surrounded by thick forests from which the Mongols now cut timber to construct a stockade that encircled the city walls. From behind this, Subedei's artillery could fire upon the city with impunity. After five days of relentless

Overleaf: The Mongol army on the march took with it
herds of sheep and cattle for food, camels and bullocks to carry equipment,
and vast herds of reserve horses.

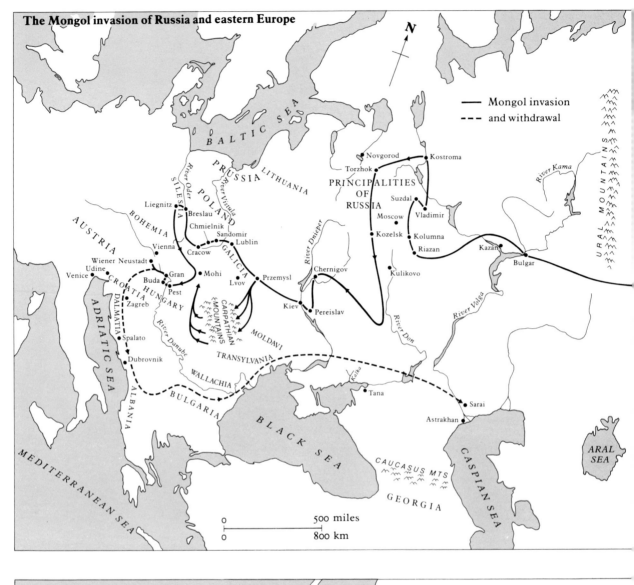

The Mongol invasion of Russia and eastern Europe

| Mongol invasion |
| and withdrawal |

BALTIC SEA

PRUSSIA

LITHUANIA

River Oder

River Vistula

SILESIA

POLAND

Liegnitz

Breslau

Chmielnik

Sandomir

Lublin

Cracow

Vienna

AUSTRIA

BOHEMIA

Wiener Neustadt

Udine

Venice

CROATIA

HUNGARY

Buda

Gran

Mohi

Pest

GALICIA

Lvov

Przemysl

River Dnieper

Chernigov

Kiev

Pereislav

MOLDAVI

CARPATHIAN MOUNTAINS

TRANSYLVANIA

DALMATIA

Zagreb

Spalato

River Danube

WALLACHIA

Dubrovnik

ALBANIA

BULGARIA

ADRIATIC SEA

MEDITERRANEAN SEA

BLACK SEA

PRINCIPALITIES OF RUSSIA

Novgorod

Kostroma

Torzhok

River Kama

Suzdal

Moscow

Vladimir

Kozelsk

Kolumna

Riazan

Kulikovo

Kazan

Bulgar

URAL MOUNTAINS

River Don

River Volga

River Kalka

Tana

Sarai

Astrakhan

CAUCASUS MTS

GEORGIA

CASPIAN SEA

ARAL SEA

0   500 miles
0   800 km

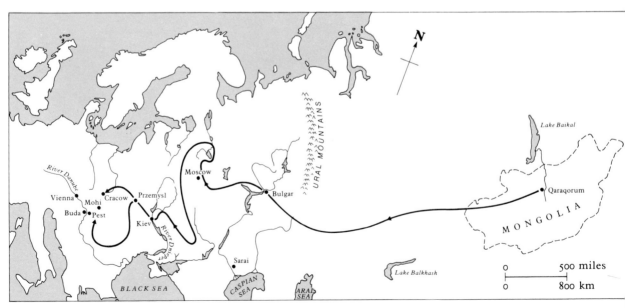

River Danube

Vienna

Mohi

Buda

Pest

Cracow

Przemysl

Kiev

River Dnieper

Sarai

BLACK SEA

CASPIAN SEA

ARAL SEA

Moscow

Bulgar

URAL MOUNTAINS

Lake Baikal

Qaraqorum

MONGOLIA

Lake Balkhash

0   500 miles
0   800 km

bombardment the city was taken, then systematically razed to the ground. The prince and his family were all slaughtered – some impaled, others flayed alive. The entire population of young women was raped including all the nuns, while others were forced to watch. As was intended, a few survivors were allowed to escape so that the warning spread elsewhere.

From Riazan the Mongols moved on to Kolomna and then into Suzdalia, where they took the town of Moscow. After Moscow they turned back again and rode east towards the city of Vladimir, where they also employed the stockade technique. After Vladimir they divided their forces and criss-crossed the countryside, bringing terror from one town to another, in an attempt to flush out the main army of Grand Duke of Suzdalia. By February they had located it and, without the hapless Grand Duke ever being aware, managed to surround the entire army before bringing down on it a deadly shower of arrows.

While Subedei was slaughtering Suzdalians, Batu had marched on to Novgorod. But his progress was delayed; he was caught out by the approaching thaw which turned the countryside into a maze of impassable marshes and the attack of Novgorod city was abandoned. Batu joined up with Subedei again and they rode south-west towards what is now the western Ukraine. Along the way they were held up at the city of Kozelsk. Here the defenders were prepared and had decided to ride out to meet the Mongols rather than find themselves besieged and bombarded as their neighbours had been. Their garrison managed to catch the Mongol vanguard unprepared and inflicted a great many losses. Unfortunately, this only meant that Batu and Subedei halted their march to the green pastures of the Ukraine and dealt with the upstart city of Kozelsk. The defenders' resistance was by all accounts heroic and lasted no less than seven weeks, but when it finally fell the population was put to the sword and there were no survivors. The slaughter was so great that the Mongols themselves renamed Kozelski the City of Woe.

By now the army was sorely depleted and in need of rest. They continued south and finally made their encampment in the great breadbasket that is the Don Basin. Reinforcements were summoned from across the various vassal states, fresh horses were driven from Mongolia and for a whole year the army

Overleaf: The Mongols were exceedingly practical people, and recruited Chinese and Persian siege engineers to construct sophisticated machinery – such as the huge catapult shown in this illustration from a manuscript of Rashid al-Din – for the campaigns against Russian and European walled cities.

جماعة من رجوم الفساد ونجوم العناد بعصيان السلطان وسلق أسيو
السقا، لما حصل لهم من بطن الرفاهية وشيطنه العصبية فلما عرف السل
أولئك المدبر مشى إلى بستان سبع عشرة الاف فارس وكان قد لجم
الطائي زعيم العرب نحاصروا أولئك المردة في قلعه أرك وشرعول

rested and rebuilt its strength. Small detachments were sent off on raiding expeditions to subdue the various nomadic tribes that inhabited southern Russia and north Caucasia – and in the process to gather in further recruits. This time it was the turn of the Circassians, Alans, Kipchaks and Cumans. Although most of the Cumans and Kipchaks were captured, their leader, Khan Kotian, managed to escape with a force of some 40000 through the Carpathian passes into Hungary.

Nevertheless the Mongol raids were so successful, especially those conducted by Batu's young brother Berke, that they actually gathered up more slave-soldiers than they could employ. Many were sold off for gold, in particular to the new Sultan of Egypt who was keen to establish himself as a power within the Middle East. It was an ironic transaction, since it had tremendous repercussions for the Mongols in the years to come. These Turkic nomadic slave-soldiers soon became the most powerful element of the Sultan's army. By 1250 one of their leaders, Aybak, had married into the Egyptian royal line, created the Bahri regime and become the first Mamluk Sultan of Egypt. The Mamluks and the Mongols were destined to meet again and again throughout the second half of the century.

MONGOL RIVALRIES

By the spring of 1240 the Mongol army had reassembled and was ready to continue the campaign. However, before it got under way a rift developed amongst the Mongol princes that was to have repercussions later. Although Batu had been given nominal command of a large and powerful army, it was made up of elements from every corner of the empire. With a vast array of resources and at the express will of the Great Khan, Batu's own personal realm was being expanded further and further west, adding very significantly to his own wealth and prestige. This situation apparently irritated a number of the princes in his entourage, but nothing was said until a trifling incident during a banquet to celebrate the recommencement of the campaign. It was the Mongol custom at a celebration for the most senior to have the privilege of drinking first. Batu, without thinking otherwise, lifted his glass and drank before any of the other princes. Although he was perfectly entitled to do so, he had shown not the slightest hint of offering to defer to any of his nephews or cousins, and some of the princes felt insulted by his presumption of superiority. They expected to be treated as equals.

Princes Guyuk and Buri, the son of Ogedei Khan and grandson of Chaghadai Khan respectively, were so incensed that they stormed out of the tent. Batu then complained to Ogedei Khan that he had been insulted in public

by his cousins, who had since both returned to Qaraqorum – to the great embarrassment of the court. Ogedei was now placed in a difficult position: his son Guyuk was already the focus of a campaign to become the next Great Khan and, unless Batu's charges were answered, Guyuk's chances might be jeopardized. Rather than be seen to chastise his son and nephew in public, Ogedei referred to the *Yasa* for a solution. There they discovered that Genghis Khan had once declared that any transgressions committed in the midst of a campaign had to be dealt with by the commander in the field. Batu himself would have to decide on the punishment. The two princes set out on the ignominious return to the western steppe, where it seems that Batu was only too glad to see them take up their commands again. There is no record of any punishment. However, the incident was not forgotten and beneath the surface animosity continued to brew.

With the campaign under way again, it was the turn of the principalities of Chernigov and Kiev to face the Mongol onslaught. For the past year most of the Russian princes had had time either to ponder the magnitude of the Mongol catastrophe or to dread the prospect of it. Once again Mongol progress seemed relentless and the cities of Chernigov and Pereislav fell in quick succession, causing Prince Michael of Kiev to decide that resistance was useless. He and his entourage fled to Hungary and from there to Silesia in what is now western Poland. The defence of Kiev, the political and religious capital of Russia, was left to the governor, Dmitri. Batu had entrusted the offensive to his cousin Mongke, the eldest son of Tolui; Mongke, conscious of the city's great importance to the Russians, attempted to take it undamaged. Unfortunately, Dmitri refused to surrender and sealed the city's fate by murdering Mongke's envoys. Russian chroniclers recorded how 'clouds of Tartars' approached the town, and claimed that the thundering sound of wagons, bellowing cattle, the hooves of thousands of horses, war cries and so on were so loud that people within the city walls could barely make themselves heard without shouting.

The bombardment began once Batu had arrived to oversee his cousin's efforts. The Mongols concentrated their attack upon the so-called Polish or Western Gate, where the battlements were made of wood. It fell quickly, and within a matter of days the outer wall had been breached. Since Kiev had no citadel the final battle had been fought at the church of the Virgin, which had been hurriedly fortified. But the work had been in vain as the entire structure collapsed under the weight of hundreds of terrified citizens who had climbed up on to the roof. Dmitri was captured but, because he had remained to defend his city while his lord had fled, the Mongols set him free. Again the destruction was appalling, and the only major structure to survive was the magnificent

Cathedral of St Sophia. Six years after the disaster a European traveller described the once-splendid city: 'Many valuable artistic relics and architectural monuments were reduced to rubble.' Kiev, 'the mother of Russian cities', lost its place as the principal city of all Russia; henceforth the focus of political power would lie in the north-east.

From Kiev the Mongols marched west to the Russian border into the foothills of the Carpathian Mountains. Along the way they over-ran the country of Galicia, taking the cities of Volhynia, Cherven, Lvov and Przemysl. It was near Przemysl, on what is now the Polish border, that Batu established his winter encampment – his springboard into Europe. The question was, where to attack and when? The logical approach would have been to wait until the spring and ensure the expedition had the best of the weather. Poland was the obvious target, because there was nothing but open country between it and the Mongols. But Batu and Subedei had a far more sophisticated campaign in mind, and in any case an issue had developed between Batu and the Hungarian king that required attention.

THE SWEEP INTO POLAND AND HUNGARY

A great many refugees had fled west into Poland and Hungary to escape the Mongol storm. Among the numerous princes and bishops that had taken flight were a large number of Cumans and Kipchaks, nomadic peoples that had escaped from southern Russia. The rest of their countrymen had made submission to the Mongols, but the Cuman leader Khan Kotian had fled with 40 000 soldiers and found safety in Hungary. The Hungarian King, Bela IV, had shown great promise as a leader since his accession in 1235, though in the months to come his reign came to resemble an exercise in survival. He already had one of the most powerful armies in Europe, made so by a first-rate cavalry that had no equal west of the Urals – provided, of course, he had the co-operation of all his nobles who commanded each detachment. In the past, during times of national threat, the Hungarian horsemen had successfully repelled nomadic raiders – in fact many of the Hungarian ranks comprised steppe horsemen who had drifted, or were pushed west, and settled in Hungary. So in 1240, when a large army of Cumans and Kipchaks suddenly

In contrast to European knights, the Mongol warrior's
only protection was a silk undershirt, a long felt tunic and
a leather cuirass. Consequently the Mongol soldiers could
fully exploit their mounts' speed and agility.

appeared looking for asylum, Bela was only too glad to grant it – provided the heathen converted to Christianity, which they were only too glad to do. Forty thousand horsemen would make a significant difference to the King's army – a thought that had not escaped the Hungarian nobility, who strongly advised against it. They claimed, somewhat disingenuously, that by harbouring refugees fleeing from the Mongols the Hungarians might incur the wrath of the great Eastern invader. They were right, but their actions did nothing to improve the situation.

When the Mongols learned of the Cumans' exodus to Hungary, Batu wrote to Bela: 'I have heard that you have taken the Cumans, who are my subjects, under your protection, I command you to send them away, for by taking them away from me you have become my enemy. It is easier for them to flee than it is for your people. They live in tents, while you live in houses and cities. . . .' Along with his letter Batu had sent no fewer than thirty envoys to Hungary, not all of whom arrived; but those who did were murdered. In allowing this to happen Bela had sealed his country's fate. But in any case the Mongols had already decided upon an invasion, because the terrain was the best in which to pasture their herds before the push into central Europe.

As the Mongols settled down for the winter near Przemysl, Subedei unveiled his extraordinary plan for the conquest of eastern Europe. Having established that Hungary was the primary objective, Subedei proposed that the expedition be put into operation as soon as possible, in the very depth of winter. The ground would be frozen and hard under hoof; but, more to the point, a winter expedition would provide the element of surprise. The Mongol army stood at around 130 000, since 30 000 troops had been left in Russia to maintain control. It was by no means a massive force, and yet Subedei's plan called for it to be divided into separate detachments. Before the conquest of Hungary could be certain, Subedei wanted to deal with any threat of a counter-attack from any of Hungary's neighbours; so he planned an invasion at several points along a front of no less than 1000 km (600 miles). By modern standards it was an extraordinary idea, but for those times it was positively majestic.

Twenty thousand men were to be sent into Poland under the command of the princes Baidar and Kadan. Their function was to sweep through Poland and Lithuania and draw off any substantial force from the north that might threaten the campaign in Hungary. Meanwhile, the bulk of the army under Batu would cross the Carpathian Mountains into Hungary, seek out Bela's army and draw it into battle. While this happened, the 20 000 in Poland, having crushed any opposition there, were to sweep down into Hungary to support the rest of the army. The two forces would be at times 650–1000 km (400–600 miles) apart, and to ensure success they had to remain in constant communi-

cation. Chains of horsemen would have to be assigned across the front, and the entire manoeuvre would have to be choreographed down to the day.

Poland had been a divided nation since the death of King Boleslaw III a hundred years before. The King had split his kingdom among his four sons and their lands were broken up again by later generations until the country had fallen into civil war among no fewer than nine separate principalities. By 1240 the struggle was between four dukes: Conrad of Mazovia, Miecislaw of Oppeln, Henry the Pious of Silesia and Boleslaw the Chaste of Sandomir. The latter also ruled Cracow, was married to the daughter of King Bela of Hungary and saw himself as the rightful king of Poland. The Polish dukes were curiously unmoved by the events that had been taking place in Russia. Though they had received countless warnings from Russia and from Bela of Hungary, they seemed little concerned that the Mongols would ever cross the Vistula. Even Conrad, who had sheltered one of the Russian princes, Michael of Chernigov, seemed barely conscious of the terror encamped on his doorstep.

In Hungary, things were markedly different. King Bela was making desperate preparations for the expected onslaught. Since his accession Bela had been obsessed with redeeming the authority of the Crown and the character of the Hungarian court, left in a parlous state by his father. However, a series of quite ruthless reforms had led to his being isolated by the majority of barons, who saw Bela's policies as an attack upon their freedoms. Without their support, Bela had no hope of putting into the field an army at full strength; hence his enthusiasm for the presence of Cumans. But the sight of this uncivilized soldiery trampling the crops wherever they camped inflamed the barons even further. They demanded that the newcomers should be expelled; but Bela was determined to defend his realm and, if he had to employ nomads to help him do it, it was a price he was prepared to pay. He refused to submit to the barons' demands and urgently set about constructing defences at the various passes through the Carpathian Mountains.

By January 1241 the Mongols had begun to deploy their armies according to Subedei's plan. Princes Baidar and Kadan were marching with their 20000 men towards Lublin and the Vistula. Meanwhile Batu and Subedei had broken up the remainder of the army into no fewer than three separate detachments. Batu led 40000 men himself; Prince Shiban, his brother, led another 10000 through a pass on the northern flank; while Subedei and Guyuk took 30000 through passes on the southern flank.

Reports began arriving at Pest, the Hungarian capital, that the Mongols were on the move. Having inspected the defences Bela called a council of war, to which the Cumans and all the barons were summoned. By now the barons were prepared to gather their separate armies, but they were still not prepared

to lead them into battle alongside the Cumans. In an attempt to placate the barons, Bela offered to hold the Cuman leaders hostage for their followers' loyalty. Still the barons were not satisfied, making even further demands for financial reward in return for the support of their armies.

The situation was becoming desperate by 10 March when Bela received reports that the Mongols had begun to attack the defences in the Carpathian passes. Four days later the commander in charge of the Carpathian defences arrived bloodied and exhausted, to report that the passes had fallen and that the Mongols were advancing steadily towards Hungarian territory.

Six hundred and fifty kilometres (400 miles) to the north, a separate drama was playing out. In Poland the inhabitants were taken completely by surprise. Baidar and Kadan had attacked the city of Lublin in early February and soon afterwards had crossed the frozen Vistula. Having done so, they laid waste Sandomir, destroying the Cistercian monastery. After Sandomir the two princes split their already meagre force and set off to spread alarm and destruction over as wide an area as possible. The purpose, according to Subedei's plan, was to draw off any of the northern armies that the Mongols expected would come to the aid of the Hungarians. In particular, the Mongols were concerned about the large number of Christian knights that had built garrisons along the Baltic coast.

The Order of the Teutonic Knights of St Mary's Hospital in Jerusalem had been formed in 1198. Though the order was originally established in the Middle East like the two older orders, the Knights Templars and Hospitallers, the Teutonic Knights soon moved to northern Europe where they established fortifications in Prussia and Lithuania, along the Baltic. Their strength grew as more and more German nobles flocked to the order, gradually turning their outposts into large independent estates loyal to the Pope. These Knights had developed relations with the Polish dukes, especially Conrad and Henry the Pious. The former, somewhat over-awed by the Teutonic Knights' growing power, had handed over one of his provinces; while the latter had allowed German immigrants to settle on his own territory in the hope that he might earn support for his own ambitions. The gradual intertwining of interests between the Teutonic Knights and the Polish dukes created the potential for a formidable alliance of northern European powers. Once the Mongol presence in Poland was confirmed, this alliance began to pull itself together. Duke Henry of Silesia was gathering together an army, enlisting support from the Teutonic Knights. They had in turn enlisted support from a small number of Knights Templars and Hospitallers from France. Altogether they would number almost 30000. In addition, King Wenceslas of Bohemia was riding to join them with an army nearly twice that size.

The Mongol force in Poland, now divided into two, had set about burning and pillaging wherever they went. Baidar's force, not having encountered any serious resistance, proceeded towards the Polish capital, Cracow. Duke Boleslaw the Chaste had established his garrison there and might have presented a formidable barrier to the Mongols had he not thrown caution to the wind. A vanguard of Baidar's force had ridden to within a few kilometres of the city walls. When they were sighted, Boleslaw's commander responded by putting together a large force and chasing after them. The Mongols turned and fled. When the invader failed to return in strength, Boleslaw commanded that they should be hunted down and forced into battle. The forces of Cracow and Sandomir marched forth in dogged pursuit – but it was a trap. Having lured virtually the entire army out into the countryside, Baidar ambushed them at a place called Chmielnik, about 18 km (11 miles) from Cracow. There they were cut to pieces under a shower of arrows.

When stragglers from the battle reached the city walls they raised the alarm. Boleslaw and his family packed all the treasures they could carry and set off for Hungary. Most of the citizenry followed their example and began leaving in droves. While the streets were filling with horses and carts loaded with belongings, a trumpeter had been at the balcony of St Mary's church, sounding the alarm. A small Mongol reconnaissance force arrived at the city gates even before the battle at Chmielnik was concluded. One of their number, realizing the alarm had already been raised, took an arrow from his quiver, laid the hilt against the string of the bow, drew back and took careful aim. Again and again the trumpeter blew his refrain, while beneath him the streets teemed with thousands of people doing their best to get out of each other's way. Suddenly the trumpeter's call was silenced, and when the crowds turned to look up at the steeple the horn was already somersaulting towards the ground. The trumpeter was staggering backwards, an arrow through his throat. When the main Mongol force reached the city walls, Baidar found the streets virtually empty. The city was burnt to the ground on 24 March.

In Hungary, Transylvania had already been ravaged, as had Moldavia and Wallachia. The princes from these regions never had the opportunity to shift their armies to Buda, so swiftly were they overwhelmed. While Guyuk continued the destruction throughout south-eastern Hungary, Subedei swept north around and behind them towards Tiza, where he rejoined the main force under Batu. They were reported to be covering no less than 100 km (60 miles) a day, heading south between Uzhgorod and Mukachevo. There they encountered a Hungarian army, sent forth to turn the Mongols back, and swept it aside on 12 March.

Three days later, the Mongols had reached the Danube and were in sight

of Pest. Batu brought his column to a halt in sight of Bela's army, which was camped on the other side. Batu was in no mind to advance until he was joined by Shiban's contingent; and Subedei too was still some distance away. Communications between the various commanders were critical over the following weeks as they manoeuvred towards the big encounter that would decide the fate of the Hungarian invasion. Shiban was advancing at a terrific pace along the upper Vistula on his way to the rendezvous. On 17 March he took the town of Vac, further up the Danube. While Batu awaited Shiban's arrival he watched the Hungarians' camp fires a few miles off, but he saw no sign of Bela being tempted to take advantage of the Mongols' relative weakness.

There were growing problems within the Hungarian camp that prevented Bela from making a move. The barons were still intent upon ridding Hungary of the Cumans and were trying to ferment an uprising against them. The Hungarians had captured a small Mongol reconnaissance column which had contained a number of Cuman horsemen – a perfectly likely occurrence, given that thousands of Cumans had been pressed into the Mongols' service. The Hungarian barons declared that the presence of Cumans within the Mongol ranks was proof that the refugees were actually fifth columnists. In the midst of the uproar the Cuman leaders were assassinated and the rest took flight, burning and killing everything in their path out of Hungary. Bela was now in dire straits, with the barons steadfastly refusing to unite with him unless it was on their terms.

It would seem that the Mongols knew little of the chaos within the enemy camp – otherwise they might have tried to take advantage of it. Batu knew that the Hungarians would be the hardest challenge of the entire campaign and he was not about to proceed until he was certain of victory. The weeks passed and eventually Shiban's columns arrived, but instead of proceeding to advance upon the Hungarian camp they packed away their *gers* and began to withdraw.

When news arrived at Pest that the Mongols were retreating, the barons, sensing that victory was now possible, threw their support behind the King. On 7 April, the Hungarians marched out from their positions. Batu moved his army eastward, drawing the Hungarians after them. Subedei, although some distance away, shadowed Batu's manoeuvre so as to confirm the impression that the Mongols were withdrawing. A day later they drew to a halt at a spot they had already chosen near where the Hernad River flows into the Sajo. Nearby, on the Mohi plains, Bela drew up his army of nearly 100000 and made camp. Even without the Cumans he still outnumbered the invaders by 20000. Mongol scouts reported that Bela was camped in an area far too small for the size of his army. He had also encircled them with a ring of wagons and tents, making it impossible for them to escape in the event of an attack. Although the

Hungarians were formidable horsemen, their commander was somewhat inept.

In the meantime, the Mongols under Kadan and Baidar rode deeper into Poland, crossing the Oder River before the end of March. Their scouts had located Duke Henry's army some days' march to the west. On their way, Kadan and Baidar took the town of Breslau and burned it to the ground. The inhabitants had taken to the citadel, but the Mongols were in too much of a hurry and left the citizens unmolested. Duke Henry's army outnumbered the Mongols by 10 000; and a few days' march away was another army of some 50 000, belonging to Henry's brother-in-law King Wenceslas of Bohemia. Among Duke Henry's 30 000 was a large contingent of Teutonic Knights, plus small numbers of Knights Templars and Hospitallers from France, some of the most formidable contingents in northern Europe. Though the knights made a dramatic sight, with pennants flying and helms glinting in the sunlight, most of the army was made up of infantry, dragooned from the local peasantry and armed with little more than pitchforks and scythes. It was to delay forces such as these that Kadan and Baidar had been sent into Poland.

DESTRUCTION OF THE EUROPEAN KNIGHTS

On 9 April, the two armies met at a place called Liegnitz (now Legnica), in western Poland. Having given each other a good sight of their respective ranks, the following day the Mongols began their well-rehearsed manoeuvre. A thinly armed vanguard rode up to the Europeans, then turned and began to gallop away from the Polish archers. Duke Henry fell into the trap and sent his cavalry, the flower of European chivalry, into a suicidal charge at the Mongol lines. Under the weight of their armour, lances and helms, the Europeans galloped after the fleeing vanguard.

Once the cavalry was separated from the infantry, the Mongols let loose a smokescreen that cut the two units off from each other. Then the cavalry suddenly found themselves surrounded by Mongol archers who had been lying in wait. The Knights Templars, Hospitallers and Teutonic Knights swirled round and round in search of the enemy so that they could engage them. If they saw anything of the Mongols through the smoke they would probably have been more than 100 m (100 yards) away, pouring a lethal shower of arrows from the brow of a hill. Meanwhile, another detachment of Mongols had moved round in an arc and come upon the infantry standing unprotected in the middle of nowhere. Neither of the two forces could see what was happening to the other, but the results were identical. The Mongols, able to stand back from their victims, fired volley upon volley into the hapless

The famous confrontation between Batu's forces and those of
King Bela of Hungary, on the bridge across the Sajo River, on
10 April 1241. The Mongols employed artillery in a 'rolling barrage'
to force the Hungarians back.

knightly ranks. Mail provided an effective defence against sword cuts, but was
utterly useless against arrows and spear thrusts.

The slaughter continued until it was time to send in the heavy cavalry.
When Mongol heavy cavalry met European knights in hand-to-hand combat
it was a ferocious and bloody affair, and the Mongols took heavy casualties.
But by then the outcome had already been decided and Liegnitz was a
complete disaster for the Europeans. Duke Henry was killed trying to escape:
his body was decapitated and mutilated almost beyond recognition. To taunt
the inhabitants, the Mongols carried his head round the city walls on the end
of a Mongol spear. Again the invaders were in no mood to lay siege and were
content with the slaughter they had inflicted on the battlefield. To prove the
scale of their success, Kadan and Baidar ordered that an ear be cut off every
victim. They sent nine sacks of ears as a tribute to Batu.

After Liegnitz, the Mongols were expected to push further west; instead
they turned south. When King Wenceslas heard the news of Liegnitz he

The Hungarian cavalry led by King Bela, from the
Hungarian Picture Chronicle, at the National Szechenyi Library, Budapest.
Easily the most formidable cavalry in the whole of Europe,
it was the only serious challenge to the Mongol invasion.

headed back towards Bohemia for reinforcements. The Mongols, despite having been badly mauled, chased his army most of the way. But rather than risk another encounter with a large army, the Mongols broke up their force into small raiding parties and set about terrorizing the countryside. As they dashed from village to town, causing mayhem and destruction, the Poles could only conclude that they had been completely over-run by a massive host. The Mongols seemed to be everywhere and nowhere with no clear objective. But that was not the case at all; their objective was Hungary.

GATEWAY TO THE ATLANTIC

On 10 April, on the banks of the River Sajo, Batu's army had received word of the battle at Liegnitz. That night, it began its attack. Batu and his brother Shiban moved forward, thinking to cross the river and engage Bela from the front, while Subedei took his contingent north in search of a ford so that they

could outflank the Hungarians and attack from behind. Unfortunately they found no crossing and were delayed while his engineers built a bridge between the villages of Girines and Nady Czeks. Before light, Batu's force approached a stone bridge that led across the Sajo and straight to Bela's army on the far side. The bridge was too narrow to let more than a few horsemen across at a time, making it impossible to advance in any strength. It looked as though the Hungarians could hold the bridge indefinitely. Then Batu brought up a battery of seven catapults and began to hurl curious-looking missiles across at the Hungarians, 'to the accompaniment of thunderous noises and flashes of fire'. The Hungarians drew back from the explosives, allowing the Mongols to cross the bridge in sufficient numbers. Every so often the catapults were brought up closer, sending the Hungarians back further and allowing more Mongols across. It is known in modern artillery tactics as a 'rolling barrage'.

Eventually, Batu and his army got themselves on to the opposite side of the river, but they were no longer fighting a typical Mongol encounter. Batu's force stood at no more than 40 000, while the Hungarians numbered 100 000, and it was beginning to look as though the sheer weight of numbers would eventually take its toll. The Hungarians mounted one mass charge after another against the Mongol lines, but each time they were beaten back by fire bombs and hails of arrows. Nevertheless, for the finest cavalry in Europe it was beginning to look as though victory would be only a matter of time. Subedei's force was long overdue and Batu's situation was becoming desperate. The only manoeuvre Batu could employ was to try and turn the Hungarians' flank; so like a rugby scrum the Mongols wheeled round, forcing the Hungarians to turn with them. In doing so Batu succeeded in turning the Hungarians' back to Subedei's approach – when and if it arrived. After two hours of debilitating attacks, Batu suddenly ordered his men to fall back against the river and spread out into a single rank. As the puzzled Hungarians watched, awaiting the next opportunity to charge, the Mongol ranks fanned out into a massive semi-circle that appeared to embrace the entire Hungarian army. Behind the Hungarians, Subedei and his army had just arrived on the scene and were doing precisely the same thing. Only when it was too late did the Hungarians realize they were about to be surrounded; but, more to the point, they had suddenly lost the advantage. They were minutes from being encircled by a deadly ring of mounted archers who were about to loose their arrows. It was like the conclusion of a hunt.

Doggedly, the Hungarians closed ranks, spurred their horses and charged out of the circle, making their way straight for their fortified camp. Worried that his soldiers might not be up to a chase, Batu signalled to call off the attack. But Subedei was made of sterner stuff. He quickly roused the army,

led them in hot pursuit and soon had the camp surrounded. When he eventually had his artillery in place he sent a concentrated barrage of exploding missiles into their tents and wagons until the camp was in ruins. Those left standing were finally cut to pieces by the heavy cavalry.

A small group of Hungarians succeeded in escaping the attack, and fled in a thin column through a gorge back towards Pest. But they had fallen into another trap. Mongol light cavalry pursued them on either side, cutting them down with lethally accurate archery. The road to Pest was described as having been littered with bodies, 'like stones in a quarry'. The Hungarian dead were estimated at 60 000. Bela managed to outride his hunters, swim the Sajo and scramble into one of the forests on the other side where he found somewhere to hide. Meanwhile the Mongols reached Pest and put it to the torch. Then they rode along the Danube, making threatening lunges at Buda on the other bank. It had been a long day, and at times an uncertain one; but at the end of 10 April 1241 an army that had travelled nearly 10 000 km (6000 miles) from the eastern steppes of Asia was now in complete command of the Hungarian plain, and no power between it and the Atlantic Ocean seemed able to stand in their way.

5

FROM
PRESTER JOHN
TO ARMAGEDDON

M ORE THAN 700 YEARS AFTER THE EVENT it is still difficult fully to appreciate the massive geographical scale upon which the Mongols had fought their campaign; how, with such extraordinary precision, they co-ordinated so many separate army corps, developed and maintained long and complicated supply lines, operated communications systems over hundreds of kilometres, and then fought with courage and imagination against an enemy defending its own territory. The Asian armies – Mongol, Chinese and Persian – were unquestionably the masters of the art of war during the medieval period. Europe could barely comprehend what had happened, and was left in thrall as to what would follow.

Europe's first military encounter with the Mongols had been no more one-sided than that of the armies of China and Persia during the first half of the thirteenth century. However, the psychological impact was in every sense far more traumatic and long-lasting. Civilizations in both China and Persia had a long history of encounters with nomadic armies, whereas Europe had lived in blissful ignorance of the rest of Asia and nothing had prepared them for the Mongols. Europe in the thirteenth century was completely ignorant of the lands to the east of the Urals. Although there had been trade with the East dating back to the pre-Christian era, this had always been conducted through

Medieval European scholars invented
a highly sophisticated pantheon of monsters and
other creatures that were said to inhabit
the unexplored lands to the East.

merchants who plied between the Latin world and China without ever enlightening the one about the other.

The best-known product from the East was of course silk, which the Romans were convinced had been combed from the leaves of trees. India was a country that was only vaguely known, and even this chiefly because of Alexander's legendary march into the great subcontinent and the many weird and wonderful tales that had been spun about his exploits there. These tales, probably invented by merchants to enhance the exotic quality of their wares, were taken up by historians and had been perpetuated right up until the time of Marco Polo (1256–1323). India, which was then synonymous with most of what we call Asia, became a land occupied by men with the head of a dog (Cynocephali), or a single foot (Monopodes), or whose feet pointed backwards with their heels facing the front (Antipodes). There were creatures with neither neck nor head, but with a face set into the middle of their chest. There

were wild hunters who lived on the mere smell of flesh. And there were curious pygmies who were supposed to live a thousand years, Satyrs, Amazons, Brahmans and Gymnosophists, enchanted mountains, unicorns, griffins and ants that dug for gold. It was also the land of rare jewels, pearls, aromatic woods and spices.

All these fantastic creatures became a feature in medieval art and literature, and their likenesses were carved in perpetuity on the exteriors of Gothic churches. We know them today as gargoyles, but 700 years ago they were imaginative stone likenesses of the inhabitants of the East.

Europeans were not unique in depicting such fantastic creations; the Chinese had a remarkably similar pantheon of creatures which they believed inhabited the unknown West. These included the creatures with the head of a dog, the single-footed beings and the headless beasts with their faces in their chests. The Chinese also had fanciful notions about the origins of cotton, a commodity they imported from western Asia, and which was supposedly clipped from the fleece of 'water sheep'.

The reasons why these curious fantasies survived for so long was the complete lack of cultural exchange between the two hemispheres. The Roman empire had never extended further than the River Euphrates, beyond which were fierce nomadic horsemen, rugged mountains and deserts – a realm the Romans failed to penetrate. It is claimed that the Chinese made a number of attempts to contact the civilizations in the West, though there is a record of only one: Kan Ying, an envoy despatched in AD 97. He reached the Persian Gulf but was warned by his Arab hosts, keen to maintain their privileged position as international go-betweens, that the rest of his voyage would take two years and that most who ventured into those uncharted lands perished. Kan Ying turned back. By the seventh and eighth centuries, with the rise of Islamic power in the Middle East, both land and sea routes had fallen under the control of the Muslims. Islam's inevitable confrontation with the Christian West led to Europe becoming even more isolated; though trade in silks and spices continued at higher and higher prices through Arab middlemen.

It was not just ignorance that sustained ideas of a land populated with monsters and fantastic beings; they were also given credence by the writings of early Christian scholars. St Augustine had written about the existence of monsters, declaring their creation to have been an important part of God's great plan, so that man would not be perplexed by the birth of the malformed or insane. Under the authority of Christian teaching the regions to the east also became associated with certain biblical localities, like Terrestrial Paradise and the land inhabited by Gog and Magog – the latter being the land beyond Alexander's Gate (the Derbent Pass in the Caucasus Mountains) where

Alexander is said to have imprisoned the two foul giants, Gog and Magog. According to the Book of Revelations, they would be released by Satan to destroy Jerusalem and bring destruction upon the world. It is hardly surprising, therefore, that contemporary chroniclers, reporting the Mongol attacks, laced their accounts with flesh-devouring monsters, and that congregations were told to expect the imminent apocalypse. The tall tales of travelling merchants became part of the Christian view of the real world.

But there was another Christian fantasy, a far more recent one, that both disarmed and confused European monarchs about the origins and purpose of the invader. This had its origin in the story of the Magi – the three wise men from the East invested with the dignity of kings, as described by St Matthew. This was supported by stories which claimed that St Thomas had journeyed to India, where he had preached the gospel, met the Magi and baptized them. Out of these stories developed the conviction that, somewhere in the vast uncharted Orient, ruled a number of Christian kings. Add to this rich brew the great literary tradition that developed around the heroic exploits in India of Alexander, who had become an important figure in the world of chivalry and courtly love, and you soon have a medieval picture of Asia as a land inhabited by grotesques, and in some part of which there reigned heroic Christian kings who performed romantic deeds.

THE LEGEND OF PRESTER JOHN

By the eleventh century, with Europe locked in a war with the Islamic world over the possession of the Holy Land, these centuries-old tales were given some contemporary relevance with the creation of the extraordinary character of Prester John, or John the Presbyter, the legendary Christian king of the Orient who was bound to come to the aid of Christendom in its hour of need. With the Crusades going badly, that hour was at hand. The legend has its origins in a visit to Rome in 1122 by a prelate named John. He claimed to have come from India and was possibly from a Christian community on the Malabar coast, part of a flourishing community of eastern Christians whom the Roman church referred to as Nestorians. Since Rome had severed relations with the Nestorians, and with virtually all the Christian communities east of the Constantinople, Europe lost a golden opportunity to develop contacts with Asian civilizations and expand its knowledge of the world. Rome simply had no idea just how much Christianity had flourished in the East.

In the early sixth century the Nestorians moved from a strong base in Persia into west Turkistan, and from there progressively east to China. At the

L es erapout les veines e li lunaton
S i de luy enuertte ne prenge vengeison
E si ne faiet del regne eissil e destruction
D el tostrelles auet ne sai donc la acheison
D e gog e magog ke manguent la gent.

D e coe ke les illes di naiet alisandre nul ieruur
A lir ilbs de dratonte e des y sles ertur
D e gog e de magog sauuret la veruur
H e quid ke aiet homme alquer nen aur poiur
U el seublant ke faitet illes en aueret hidur
A iuem e dono ills di ma nenr aror uisur

Above: Prester John, the fictitious Christian king of the East,
depicted in a thirteenth-century Portuguese atlas. According to legend,
concocted during the time of the Crusades, Prester John would come to
the aid of Christendom during times of trouble.

———————————

Left: The Mongols were thought to have been
the offspring of Gog and Magog, two terrible giants seen here
feasting on their victims; from the *Romance of Alexander*
at Trinity College, Cambridge.

———————————

beginning of the eleventh century there were Christians even amongst the Mongol tribes, and by the height of the Mongol empire Christianity was expanding throughout Asia.

Given that contacts between Rome and the eastern Christians had been extremely rare, a visit of a prelate from the East was guaranteed a fascinated audience. Accounts claim that he lectured the Roman cardinals about life in India and the extraordinary miracles that regularly occurred in that kingdom during the great Christian festivals. Historians today believe that the prelate was probably an imposter, yet at the time of his visit the stories he told seemed plausible to medieval scholars because they appeared to confirm St Matthew's account of the Magi; that is, that there existed an Eastern kingdom ruled by the descendants of the three wise kings who had visited the holy family in Bethlehem.

Twenty years later, when the memory of the prelate's visit was still relatively fresh, a bishop in Syria reported the existence of a powerful Eastern king named Prester John who had inflicted a heavy defeat upon the Muslims. He also reported that this monarch, who was descended from the Magi, had decided to come to the aid of the crusaders in Jerusalem, in emulation of his illustrious ancestors, but had been prevented from doing so because of the untimely flooding of the River Tigris. It is now thought that the report was a garbled account of the wars fought against the Muslim rulers of Persia by the Qara Khitai empire in the twelfth century. So here we have a suffusion of the best medieval legends – a wise king with impeccable antecedents who was also heroic and therefore in the best traditions of Alexander. Whatever the claims for Prester John's ancestry, the mere fact that he was reportedly killing Muslims virtually guaranteed his Christian credentials.

Then, in 1165, a letter purporting to be from Prester John began circulating in Europe. From here on this character is clearly exploited for political reasons. The letter came in many forms, addressed to many different European notables: the Byzantine Emperor Manuel I Comnenus, the Pope, the Holy Roman Emperor and other monarchs. In his letter Prester John claimed to rule over a vast kingdom that extended from the tower of Babel to where the sun rises. He declared his intention to rescue Jerusalem from the Muslims, defeat the enemies of Christ and visit the Holy Sepulchre. He then went on to catalogue his treasures and the marvels of his kingdom. The letter was, of course, a complete fabrication, though it proved an enormous fillip for the crusading movement – which was probably the author's intention.

The figure of Prester John gained further verisimilitude when in 1177 the Pope despatched an envoy to seek him out in the lands east of the tower of Babel. Although the envoy disappeared, the crusading movement had re-

ceived the necessary boost. However, for thirty years the next three Crusades met with one disaster after another until enthusiasm began to waver again. In 1217, with remarkably good timing, during the preparations for yet another Crusade, fresh news began to circulate about the legendary Prester John and other 'Christian kings living in the Orient'. The Bishop of Acre, conducting a vigorous propaganda campaign for what would be the Fifth Crusade, had decided to employ the legend in many of his letters to the Latin settlers in the Levant. The Bishop claimed that Prester John and his Oriental colleagues had heard that a new Crusade was imminent and were about to set forth to help sweep the Saracens from the Holy Land.

Three years later, these claims were given further credence when a somewhat apocryphal document appeared called the 'Report on King David'; a description of the victorious advance into Persia of 'King David, Christian King of India, sent by the Lord to crush the heathen and destroy Mahomet's teaching'. There are many accounts of this letter; some of them equate King David with Prester John himself, while others claim he was his son or grandson. Again the letter affirmed prophecies that Prester John's arrival was imminent. It is at this point that Christian propaganda becomes entwined with historical fact, for what undoubtedly provided the basis for this report was Genghis Khan's breathtaking campaign against the Khwarazm Shah. The Church had taken a harbinger of disaster and transformed it into a prophecy of salvation.

The irony couldn't have been more bitter. During the following months, as further reports arrived, the Pope announced repeatedly the victorious progress of 'King David' through Persia and predicted the forthcoming liberation of the Holy Land. Even when this failed to occur, it did not diminish faith in the existence of Prester John. In 1223, when Subedei's army was engaged in the great raid through Georgia and the Russian states, the King of Hungary sent a letter to the Pope claiming that 'a certain King David or, as he is more usually called, Prester John' had recently entered Russia with a vast army and slaughtered 200 000 people. This terrible work was explained at first as the great Christian King setting upon the heretical Georgians, followers of the Greek Orthodox Church, with the same vigour as he had attacked the Islamic Persians. So firm was the belief in this character that, even when Queen

Overleaf: Legends about Genghis Khan became entwined
with those of Prester John. In this illustration, from an English manuscript
c.1400, the two are engaged in a fight to the death. The story is probably
based upon Genghis's war with the Christian king
of the Kereyids, Wang Khan.

Rusudan of Georgia sent an accurate account of the Mongol armies, it was dismissed in preference to the semi-fictitious reports of 'King David'.

Nevertheless, given the growing contradictions from various sources, there is no doubt that the Christian West was becoming a little alarmed and confused, especially by accounts of the most incredible amount of slaughter. Clearly Prester John was no longer quite the pious Christian so beloved of those early prophets, despite his hatred of the Muslims. As Europe pondered these contradictory reports, the great Novgorod Chronicler recorded a more accurate account of the 'Great Raid' through the Russian principalities: 'They turned back from the River Dnieper and we know not whence they came, nor where they hid themselves again; God knows whence he fetched them against us.' Their sudden disappearance left a great many questions unanswered, but these preoccupations disappeared as Europe soon became more deeply concerned with its own internal problems.

CONFLICT BETWEEN CHURCH AND STATE

The single most important issue that exercised most of the courts during the 1230s was the growing enmity between the Pope and the Holy Roman Emperor. It was a conflict that had its origins in the Investiture Conference of the eleventh century, when Pope Gregory VII formulated the doctrine that the Church exerted universal rule over the whole of Christendom and over all Christian kings and emperors. It was a split between the successors of St Peter and Charlemagne that turned from a political issue into open warfare under the Emperor Frederick II. He was an extraordinary figure, sometimes described as the *enfant terrible* of medieval Europe. He had been educated at the Norman court at Palermo in Sicily, where he had absorbed the *mores* of an exotic society that combined the sternness of the Norman court with heavy influences from the Middle East. Frederick combined brilliant intelligence with a taste for the cruel, the sensual and the strange. He had a deep love of Arab culture and great sympathy for Islam. His failure to take part in the Fifth Crusade almost certainly caused its failure, for which he was excommunicated by the new Pope in 1227. In spite of that he sailed to Palestine the following year, in the wake of the Sixth Crusade, and through some stunning diplomatic moves secured control of Jerusalem, Nazareth, Bethlehem and the territory between Jerusalem and Acre without spilling a single drop of blood.

Frederick's intimate knowledge of Middle Eastern politics enabled him to conduct negotiations with the Sultan of Egypt at the best possible time. Following the destruction of his father's empire, Jalal al-Din had escaped to India from where he emerged in 1223 to reconquer those lands. His campaign

had been short-lived, following the Mongols' return to reaffirm their control. Nevertheless, during a brief period in 1225 Jalal al-Din was proving a serious threat to the current rulers of the Muslim world, having won control of western Persia and Azerbaijan, invaded Georgia and launched an attack on Baghdad. In other words, Frederick had caught the Sultan at a bad moment and was able to extract a heavy price for peace with the Europeans. But although the Sixth Crusade had been a success, and as a result Frederick was absolved of his sins and taken back into the Church, the rift between Church and Empire had been too deep to be easily resolved. Hostilities had broken out again by the late 1230s, dividing Europe into two separate camps just at the time when Ogedei Khan had set in motion the conquest of Europe.

INTELLIGENCE IGNORED

When Batu's army first rode into Russia, Europe showed very little interest. Russia's remoteness, the tenuous relationships between the various principalities and her adherence to the Eastern Church meant that she had remained somewhat estranged from the rest of Europe. The flight of the various Russian princes alerted few to the true nature of the approaching threat, but amongst those taking note was the Hungarian King, Bela IV. It had been Bela's practice to send out Christian missionaries to try to convert the various nomadic tribes in the western steppe and perhaps even entreat them to accept him as their king. In 1237 he sent forth the most famous of these missionaries, the Dominican Friar Julian, to eastern Russia with instructions to gather information on the invader from the East. The monk's journey was interrupted by the Mongol advance; nevertheless he returned with a great deal of intelligence, much of it extremely accurate.

Julian produced a detailed account of how the Mongol armies relied upon great mobility, and of their strategy for conquering fortified towns. He claimed that the Mongol invasion had its origins in a conflict between two of their chieftains, one of whom is supposedly the young Genghis Khan and the other an older and more powerful figure who had refused the younger man permission to marry his daughter. This story had been in circulation for some time and in fact survived long after the European invasion, to be picked up again and again by Western travellers in the years to come. In more detailed versions the 'powerful chieftain' is identified as Prester John of India, or his son King David, and is apparently killed by Genghis Khan in the ensuing conflict over the issue of the daughter. At a Papal Council held in Lyons in 1245, a version of this story was presented in a report containing a general account of the Mongols. In this version, 'the King of the Tartars' (Genghis) is supposed

to have killed Prester John and then married his daughter, and their son was presumed to have been the present 'king'. The story is probably based upon accounts of the civil wars amongst the steppe tribes during Genghis's rise to power; the Prester John figure is Wang Khan, chief of the Kereyids and an eastern Christian or Nestorian, who was defeated by Genghis in 1203 and whose niece the Great Khan later married.

Julian's report managed to keep dimly alive the spirit of Prester John. On the one hand, according to the account, Genghis Khan was supposed to have killed Prester John, and so then destroyed Christendom's great saviour; yet on the other hand the Khan, Genghis's son, had maintained the Prester John bloodline. European chroniclers were still clutching at stories of saviours, even when the bulk of Julian's intelligence formed alarming news for King Bela. The Mongols' declared ambition, Julian reported, was nothing less than world domination, with Rome as their ultimate goal. It is thought that Julian was the first European writer to use the term 'Tartari' to identify the Mongols, a name he had probably picked up from the Cumans and which was eventually taken up by Westerners because of its similarity to the Latin word Tartarus, meaning hell. In the accounts that appeared a little after the Mongol invasion, they are depicted as devils released from hell.

Julian also brought back with him the message from Batu demanding that Bela hand over the Cumans to whom he had granted asylum, which was, in reality, a demand for the Hungarian King's unconditional surrender. Although Julian's report was quite widely disseminated, it is remarkable how little notice seems to have been paid to its contents by other monarchs. It seems that Frederick, the Holy Roman Emperor, even received a specific order of submission from Batu, which was accompanied by an offer that if he agreed, then he, Frederick, would be rewarded with some high office under Batu's rule. Frederick is reported to have replied, somewhat contemptuously, that as falconry was one of his favourite sports, perhaps he might be suited to the role of the Khan's chief falconer. The distinct impression is that Frederick would not have been too distressed about an invasion from the East, and that it was certainly not something he would have been interested in trying to prevent. The Pope too had received accounts of Julian's report, but he was too involved in his dispute with Frederick and paid very little attention to the threat, or to requests for help from Queen Rusudan of Georgia, or later on from Catholic Poland and Hungary. The image of Europe at this stage is of a land cocooned within the limits of its own imagination, and heedless of reliable evidence that disaster approached. Even when the reports clearly identified the approaching armies as having caused unimaginable death and destruction, there still persists a vestige of hope in some tenuous link with Prester John.

In 1238 Europe again received word of the Mongols, this time from a most unlikely source. The chronicler Matthew Paris gives us this account:

> About this time, special ambassadors were sent by the Saracens, chiefly on behalf of the Old Man of the Mountain, to the French King, telling him that a monstrous and inhuman race of men had burst forth from the northern mountains, and had taken possession of the extensive, rich lands of the east; that they had depopulated Hungary Major [the region between the Volga and the Urals], and had sent threatening letters, with dreadful emissaries; the chief of which declared that he was the messenger of God on high, sent to subdue the nations who rebelled against him. . . . This powerful and noble Saracen messenger, who had come to the French King, was sent on behalf of the whole of the people of the East, to tell them these things; and he asked assistance from the Western nations, the better to be able to repress the fury of the Tartars: and he also sent a Saracen messenger to the King of England [Henry III], to tell these events and to say that if they themselves could not withstand the attacks of such people, nothing remained to prevent their devastating the countries of the West.

The 'Old Man of the Mountain' was Hasan-i Sabbah, the chief of the Ismailis or Assassins, an Islamic Shia sect which had its headquarters in northern Persia and a branch in Syria. They had been at war with the Sunni Muslim leaders for some time, but had also fought against the crusaders. The reason behind their unexpected appeal to the West was the Mongol campaign under Chormaghun, which had been sent to pursue Jalal al-Din and reconquer Persia and the Caucasus. The Assassins, having been cast out as heretics, could expect no help from other Muslims. However, in view of the fact that another Mongol army was attacking Christian countries to the north, the Assassins naïvely assumed that Westerners might join with them in common cause against the Eastern threat.

Once again it was an opportunity for Europe to gain hard information about the new emergent Eastern power; however, the approach of the 'Saracens' was greeted with utter contempt. The Bishop of Winchester, Peter des Roches, able to see the world divided into just two camps, replied: 'Let us leave these dogs to devour one another, that they might be consumed, and perish; and we, when we proceed against the enemies of Christ who remain, will slay them, and cleanse the earth, so that all the world will be subject to the one Catholic Church, and there will be one shepherd and one fold.'

But not all of Europe was unmoved by the accounts of slaughter that were filtering through. One of the most fascinating stories connected with the Mongol invasion, also recorded by Matthew Paris, was of the fate of the

Yarmouth herring industry. As the Mongols were making their approach on Novgorod, during the winter of 1237–8, word of the destruction they were causing penetrated a number of fishing communities in northern Europe.

> The inhabitants of Gothland and Friesland [the Baltic Islands and the Netherlands], dreading their attacks, did not, as was their custom, come to Yarmouth, in England, at the time of the herring fisheries, at which place their ships usually loaded; and owing to this, herrings in that year were considered of no value, on account of their abundance, and about forty or fifty, although very good, were sold for one piece of silver, even in places at a great distance from the sea.

It would seem that ordinary folk in northern Europe had received abundant warning from the communities in Russia, and although their response was typically superstitious, it would also seem that their lords and masters were still untroubled by the same intelligence.

Having devastated the northern Russian principalities, Batu rested his forces in the lower Don throughout 1239 and the following year moved on Kiev. As has been seen, during the winter of 1240–1 Batu's army gathered near Przemysl, ready to launch out upon Europe. Within three months the political map of Europe had been torn in half. The disasters at Liegnitz in Poland and Mohi in Hungary, fought within two days of each other, had transformed the European perception of the Mongol threat. The last remnants of hope that these invaders might somehow be the armies of Prester John, or of his descendants, were finally and utterly extinguished. With the sudden and absolute destruction of two great Christian kingdoms, Europe was propelled from a state of naïve hope into an abyss of utter incomprehension.

PANIC AND CHAOS IN EUROPE

Within a week of the battle at Liegnitz, the Mongol army in Poland had rejoined the main force in Hungary which then moved on to secure the eastern half of the country, thus making it impossible for King Bela to muster a new army and renew the struggle. The invaders moved swiftly to gather up the reins of power and encourage the local people to return to their farms and trades. Though there was a great deal of looting and Pest itself was almost stripped to the bone, Batu's army did not engage in the wholesale slaughter and rape of the countryside that had been the hallmark of his grandfather's campaign in Khwarazmia. Nevertheless, Hungary was in a parlous state. Bela and his family had taken flight through the Carpathian Mountains on their way to Austria. While staying overnight at the monastery at Thurocz the Hungar-

ian King encountered another fugitive, Boleslaw the Chaste, who was heading south from Poland. With Hungary abandoned and still reeling, Boleslaw's domain was at the mercy of the fates.

The population was no less bewildered by the storm that seemed to have swept across their country, and for a long time the Poles simply could not comprehend what had happened nor why. This state of confusion was made worse by the crude and fanciful reports that were being spread in the aftermath. The Mongols' mobility was something that Polish chroniclers never understood; the only way they could explain the speed and vast distances the enemy covered was to over-estimate the size of the Mongol army by some five times. The staggering defeat at Liegnitz was explained by the heathens' vile use of some foul-smelling gas that incapacitated their soldiers. The Mongols' sudden departure from Poland was explained not by the events in Hungary, but by the notion that Polish armies had finally beaten them off. Polish chroniclers perpetuated these fallacies long afterwards, and Polish histories still include fictitious accounts of gallant victories fought and won against the invader. Even the battle of Liegnitz itself is regarded in some central European histories as a pyrrhic victory for the Europeans.

During the second half of 1241 Europe was on the verge of chaos. The chronicler Vincent of Beauvais vividly described the atmosphere when he claimed that the Mongols had let loose a series of evil spirits to destroy their enemies: 'the spirit of fear, the spirit of mistrust and the spirit of discord'. Having at first been stunned into complete inactivity, an aging and nervous Pope Gregory finally gathered sufficient presence of mind to declare a Crusade against the Mongols. In an uncharacteristic show of solidarity the Holy Roman Emperor, Frederick II, announced he would lead it. He despatched letters to all the courts of Europe, calling for their support: '. . . to Germany ardent in war, to France who nurses in her bosom an undaunted soldiery, to warlike Spain, to savage Ireland and to frozen Norway'. The response was varied. In numerous northern European castles, great caches of arms were stockpiled in preparation for the great united counter-attack. However, at the other extreme the Duke of Austria, whose borders ran with Hungary's, seemed supremely indifferent to the Mongol menace. He was more preoccupied with taking advantage of Hungary's plight, having demanded an enormous indemnity from Bela in return for granting him and his family protection. The Duke also took the opportunity to annex three Hungarian departments that lay against his borders. During their march into Hungary, the Austrians came face to face with Mongol reconnaissance patrols that were probing unexplored territory. One of these was repulsed by the Austrians; from this evidence the Duke was convinced that the Mongol threat

133

had been greatly exaggerated, and he boasted to those who would listen how his soldiers had killed hundreds of Mongols in hand-to-hand combat. The Duke's accounts did little to pacify the alarmists.

Elsewhere in Europe there was little evidence of any united crusade, and there were other ambitious monarchs who, like the Duke of Austria, tried to take advantage of the chaos wrought by the invaders. In Russia the Swedes, allied with contingents of the Teutonic Knights, landed at Neva in an attempt to take Novgorod. They were beaten off by the legendary Alexander Nevsky, who, though subsequently acclaimed as a Russian national hero, was nevertheless one of Batu's vassal princes. Frederick II, having agreed to lead the crusade, proved utterly ineffectual – he claimed that his ongoing conflict with the Pope prevented him from taking any significant action. Such were the internecine intrigues throughout the European courts that even the Pope himself was rumoured to be in league with the Mongols against his rivals.

By the winter of 1241–2 it had dawned upon the rest of Europe that neither the Church nor any individual Christian nation was powerful enough to withstand the next inevitable onslaught. Messages laced with portents of doom and bitter recrimination flew from one court to another. This letter from Count Henry of Lorraine to his father-in-law is typical: 'The dangers foretold long ago in Holy Scripture are now, owing to our sins, springing up and erupting. A cruel tribe of people beyond number, lawless and savage, is now invading and occupying our borders, and has now reached the land of the Poles, after roaming through many other lands and exterminating the people.' It seemed that the servants of Satan had finally been let loose, that the apocalypse was at hand, retribution for the sins of mankind would soon follow, the collapse of Western civilization and the extinction of Christendom itself were expected – if not the end of time itself.

Within this apocalyptic atmosphere, chroniclers drew freely upon their imaginations to provide the most gory accounts of Mongol practices. The arrival of the Mongols in medieval Europe was akin to an invasion of extra-terrestrials. The narrow, intolerant Christian world could only interpret the unknown in terms of salvation or damnation. Having been deprived of their hoped-for Prester John, chroniclers explained the harsh reality of the Mongol attacks by fantastic references to Armageddon. To the Hungarians they were

A scene from a Persian manuscript, the *Shah Namah* or
Book of Kings, c.1300, showing the execution of a prisoner,
while others have been buried alive upside-down in
typically brutal Mongol fashion.

چنین گفت داننده دهقان پیر
که هر کس که دارد خرد یادگیر

باز شاهی کسری چهل سال بود

creatures with the heads of dogs who, not satisfied with merely defeating their enemies, were intent upon devouring the corpses as well. Here are Matthew Paris's sadistic imaginings of Mongol destruction.

> For touching upon the cruelty and cunning of these people, there can be no infamy [great enough]; and, in briefly informing you of their wicked habits, I will recount nothing of which I hold either a doubt or mere opinion, but what I have with certainty proved and what I know. . . . The Tartar chief, with his dinner guests and other lotus-eaters [cannibals], fed upon their carcasses as if they were bread and left nothing but the bones for the vultures. . . . The old and ugly women were given to the cannibals . . . as their daily allowance of food; those who were beautiful were not eaten, but were suffocated by mobs of ravishers in spite of all their cries and lamentations. Virgins were raped until they died of exhaustion; then their breasts were cut off to be kept as dainties for their chiefs, and their bodies furnished an entertaining banquet for the savages. . . .

Matthew Paris had never seen a Mongol nor, from all accounts, ever met someone who had. Even the more informed reports were not without some embellishment. Friar Jordan of Giano, a Franciscan vicar in Bohemia, described in some detail the Mongols' fighting practices yet also claimed that the army contained large contingents of women. 'She who fights best is regarded as the most desirable, just as in our society she who weaves and sews best is more desired than the one who is beautiful.' No account could be too gruesome: 'They eat frogs, dogs, serpents, and all things alike. The men are inhuman and of the nature of beasts, rather to be called monsters than men, thirsting after and drinking blood, and tearing and devouring the flesh of dogs and human beings. . . .'

The Mongol invasion had transformed vague Christian ideas about retribution into an almost obsessive conviction that the end of the world was nigh. In northern Europe, the churches were filled every day of the week with terrified congregations whom the clergy led in hysterical prayers for deliverance. Flagellants trailed across the country spreading predictions of the approaching apocalypse, while in Germany those ubiquitous scapegoats, the Jews, were slaughtered in large numbers because it was believed they were somehow smuggling arms across the border to the Mongols. To Matthew Paris the end of the world was so certain that he confidently prophesied the year 1250 would be the advent of the Antichrist and the end of the sixth and last age. Even powerful monarchs like Louis IX of France were already resigned to martyrdom. 'We have this consolation from heaven,' he told his mother. 'If these people whom we call Tartars come against us, either we shall

send them back to hell where they came from, or else they will send us to heaven, where we shall enjoy the bliss that waits for the chosen.'

FURTHER POWER STRUGGLES OVER THE MONGOL SUCCESSION

As Europe awaited the sound of the last trumpet, the Mongols settled down during the summer months to rest and recuperate, allowing their herds to fatten and enabling reinforcements to arrive, receive training and be absorbed into the ranks. During those months another dispute broke out amongst the Mongol princes – or more likely it was a continuation of the same dispute that had alienated Batu from Guyuk and his followers. There is no account of what precipitated the incident, but suddenly the princes Guyuk and Buri returned to Qaraqorum. In the absence of anything concrete, some historians have speculated that Guyuk's sudden departure was part of some obscure manoeuvre to secure his succession. Ogedei Khan had in recent years become an alcoholic, his days spent in blind stupors, oblivious to the world around him. His fierce and somewhat rapacious wife Toregene had become the effective authority at Qaraqorum and was utterly dedicated to the promotion of her eldest son, Guyuk. Ogedei had nominated his grandson, Shiremun, but his declining faculties meant that there was little support for the young man.

Far away in Hungary, Batu's fabulous victories brought him immense power and influence. Six years earlier he had left Qaraqorum as the weakest and least significant of Genghis's princes; now his realm surpassed in area the empire in both China and western Asia. It is probable that, as news of Ogedei's decline filtered down to the imperial army in the West, Guyuk felt it wise to take advantage of the lull in fighting to return to court and lobby for his cause. But he was not the only Mongol prince concerned with the succession: Mongke, son of Tolui and one of Batu's staunchest supporters, also departed for Qaraqorum. He had gone not to present the case on behalf of Batu – who had no ambitions to be Great Khan – but to effect an alliance between Batu and the opposition at Qaraqorum who were determined to prevent a dynasty forming out of Ogedei's descendants.

RECONNAISSANCE FOR THE CAMPAIGN IN THE WEST

Meanwhile, in the capitals of Europe, the absence of any further Mongol advances meant that the impetus behind the Crusade against them dissipated and the great counter-attack itself was postponed. In August Pope Gregory died; his successor, the eighty-year-old Celestine IV, lasted only seventeen

[Column 1]

ñ existens. Clemonecø p̄ tduii g̃moratus: accepta
licentia a g̃phicib;. S; maledōne a q̄da ipoy episco
po cū suspec' eram: p̄modū ut audiui p̄ qda for
nicatōne ab eisde dcīto. nōie p̄gallo. inde cū qda
sine laico: canales ag̃legie sū ingressus peregrinans.
z sic mig̃ndo ulti': topido qd̄ frisac d̄r iacuimꝰ apud
fr̄es. S; ab eode sr̄e posito mane felice̅ carintha pe
rui soliuag'. de dein z q̄da opido auste qd̄ theutoni
ce Heustat d̄r id; nona ciuitas int̄ ead novos reli
giosos q̄ beguini vocant: hospitabar. et z p̄ima
ciuitate Vienna. locoseø etiā citeib; aliq̄t annis
dehtui. opa g̃fundē heube bona z mala. Viuēt enī
dīa istigante satis ītine̅t. Aie mee ng̃i aduisetar.
a nlos uer̄tū ab eirore revocat memorato. Hoc g̃
z multis aliis peñs int̄ nos ̄anos emigentib; ñas
dūs: fc̄s est uelut uastator hostilis z ultor formida
bilis. Hoc ideo dixim ex qda gens ingens. hōies ī
humani. e̅ fer exlex. ira furor. Uga furoris dira
tras infinitas pag̃ndo ferali deuastat. oīa obs
tancia cede z incendio horribil' exterminando. Iñ
hc̄ demū estate ipa gñs memorata q̄ tattari nū
cupaēt: pannoniā q̄ per ̄dicōne cepat: per mē
dein opidū in q̄ tc̄ forte morabar cū infinitis milī
b; obsedit. Zeulent. Hec erant ibide tū g̃ uecssi
uri bellici pt̄ milites L. ēs cū xi. balistariis dur
ī munucie reliq̄at. Hui oīs ex q̄bdam eminēciꝰ
ecclusiu' sr̄udentes exercitū: imane abhorrebant
seuiciam satellitū amit. z ascendūt ad dm ̄anoy
planctꝰ misabiles audiebant. q̄ subito z canua cen
te p̄icia p̄occupati. sine delectu g̃dicois. fortune.
serus z etatis. oīs indifferent diuisi supplicus
mitibant. Quoy cadaub; p̄icipes cū suis cenosa
riis. aliuseø locofagis q̄si pane uescentes: ñl pter
ossa uulturib; relinq̄bant. S; quod miru z famȩ
licȩ z edaces uultures: q̄ forte superant reliquiis
uesci minime dignabat. A mulieres aū uetulas
z deformes antropofagis q̄ p̄ uulgo reputat: in
esca q̄si p̄ diarrio dabant. ñ formosis uescebat.
set eas clamantes z eiulantes inī titudie cohitū
suffocabant. Vgies eø usque ad exanina cõm oppri
mebant. z clāde abscisis eay papis q̄si magistra
tib; p̄ delicus resuabant: ipsis uirgineis corpori
b; lautiꝰ epulabantur. Viderib; intim ipsoy
speculatorib;ex edam promontoy sūmitate: duce

[Column 2]

p̄incepi dalmacie cepit octo. Quoy dux austrie
noue unū Angliē nascōne. S; ipe q̄dam malefi
cia de regno Anglie perpetua baunaēōe p̄septū.
Hic ex pte regis necīssim̄ tattaroy: bis uenerat
ad regem hungarie: nuncei z int̄pres. Et mala q̄
fnmodū ôrigerunt: satis manifeste p̄muniendo
g̃minatus est: nisi se z regnū suū tattaree dede
siuiti. Hic a p̄incipib; ñis inductus ad dicen
dicendū ueritate de tattaris: ullin uisus: p̄mittee
uramentū. s; tanta g̃testas est: ut ut ipi credi po
set diablo. In p̄nus igit̄ de se ipo narrauit. q̄ istas
p̄ tempꝰ p̄sepcōus sue. id; añ xxx annos etatis sue
ī ciuitate Achon amissis in ludo oīb; q̄ habebat
ī ipsa hyeme nisi p̄ camisia de sacco. calceos de boue
capa de cilicio secū asportans: ignominiosa g̃pellēe
tedia cū infinitate consoratiis oīo ut fatuis z irreuisi
se clamans ut muis: mltas p̄ouincias libe p̄nus
sec. z holpites busicos iuenisi: z leuēiq̄lem uitāi
p̄txit: q̄mus cotidie ilboy leuutate z cordis istā
cia diablo se comendasset. Tande ex nimietate
laboy z assidua aeris mutatōe z aboy apud eas̄or
q̄n lang̃ore detent z ñ in tediū uite denisus est. Hō na
lens igit̄ p̄cede ut reuti paulatū respirando ibi
g̃morans: cepit ut erat alic̄nculū lit̄as ea q̄b; ipi
ferebant: tabul' cōmendare. z cito sca tā recte p̄
ferre: ut idigena putaretur. z eadem facilitate
didicit plures linguas. Ipm g̃ tattari per exp̄lora
tores suos eligentes sibi attr̄unt. z postq̄m de uen
dicando sibi toci mūdi dm̄o accep̄unt responsū:
multis sibi donariis ad fidelitatem suā z siuiciū
astr̄unt. p̄ eo qd̄ int̄p̄tib; indigebant. De
morib; aū eoy z sr̄ictōne. de disposicōne corpuꝫ
eoy z statura. de p̄a z modo pugnandi: iurauit
qd̄ sunt sr̄ oīis hōies auari. iracundi. dolosi. et
imisicordes. S; rigore puticōnis. z insanitate pe
nay per suos sr̄iores infligendaꝝ. a uirgis
z muutiis decepcōib; z seuicus: iuiēt cōh̄cent.
p̄incipia suas ē buu: deos uocant. z ceis colut
tēporib; solēpnitates eoy. a mltas qd̄ p̄iclares
ç; cū iiii. gñales. Et ipi se solos: oīta credut cō
creata. In exc̄endo seuiciam q̄ rebelles: ullin esse
credunt pctm. Habit aū pectora dura z robsta.
facies macras z pallidas. Scapulas rigidas z erectas
nasos distortos z breues. Mentu p̄minentia z a

Nephandi tartari ul' tattari humanis carnibus uescentes

Equi tartaroy qui sunt ua pascimini cum desint uberiora pabula frondibus z foliis iuuom z corticib; arbor' suis grentes.

days. The Vatican, hampered by Frederick's interference, soon descended into a protracted struggle to elect a new Pope.

As winter approached, the Mongols prepared the next stage in their campaign. The number of reconnaissance patrols was increased, gathering valuable intelligence on the strength and disposition of nearby armies and looking for the safest point at which Batu could get his army across the Danube. But before he had decided, he was granted a stroke of good fortune when the Danube froze hard. On Christmas Day Batu led his army into western Hungary and immediately attacked Gran (Esztergom), the ecclesiastical capital. This beautiful city, complete with royal castle and cathedrals, was stormed after the gates had been battered down by catapults. Vast quantities of Hungary's state treasures were captured and removed to Qaraqorum. A separate force led by Kadan entered Buda, sacked it and moved on to the next city, Gyor.

Throughout these encounters the Mongols were again little interested in prolonged sieges; if they met any serious resistance they preferred to ride on to the next objective. As western Hungary was being dealt with, Batu despatched a *tumen* ahead of the main force across the border into Austria. This force tore through the south-eastern territories, laying waste the countryside as far as Wiener Neustadt. The Duke of Austria, suddenly shaken out of his complacency, pleaded for support from his allies abroad – but none was forthcoming. The Austrians grew frantic when during the spring of 1242 a Mongol force attacked Klosterneuburg and scouts were sighted on the outskirts of Vienna.

It was during this reconnaissance in force into Austria that one of the most fascinating episodes of the European story took place. One of the Mongol reconnaissance patrols was attacked and eight of its number were taken prisoner. Amongst the prisoners was an Englishman, a knight who had been exiled for some unknown crime. Very little is known of this man, except that, having left Britain, he had journeyed to the Middle East where he had gambled away his wealth and soon afterwards joined the services of the Mongols. He is said to have spoken several languages and claimed to his captors that he had been in the Mongols' diplomatic service. If he had tried to

A wildly exaggerated illustration by Matthew Paris from his
Chronica Majora purporting to show Mongols cooking and
devouring their victims, while a woman prisoner awaits
a fate worse than death.

secure diplomatic immunity by this claim, it failed; the Austrians executed him, as they did the other seven.

Mongol forces also swept south-west, towards the Adriatic. About the same time that they were in Austria, Kadan was in command of a *tumen* engaged in pursuit of Bela who had fled from Austria into Croatia and Dalmatia. Patrols attached to this force were sighted as far away as Udine, just 100 km (60 miles) from Venice. Kadan moved on to Zagreb, sacked the city and then headed towards Spalato (Split) and Trogir, where Bela was in hiding. But Kadan's force had been badly mauled during this tour of the Dalmatian coast and, having reconnoitred the defences, passed Spalato by and moved on to Dubrovnik. By May, the *tumen* that had entered Austria had returned, having compiled a good account of the Austrian armies.

Batu was now prepared to begin the next stage in his campaign, the thrust into central Europe. The only thing that might stop him reaching the Atlantic would be a united European army of overwhelming numbers. No such army existed. Batu knew this and was impatient to get on with the task.

THE KHAN IS DEAD

Then, one morning in May 1242, quietly and with little warning, the Mongol encampment gathered itself together and prepared for action. But instead of heading west the armies turned east, recrossed the Danube and moved back into the territory they had just recently conquered. In the process they set about the most appalling campaign of slaughter and destruction that had yet been witnessed in Europe. This was not part of some elaborate manoeuvre designed to confuse and disable the enemy; this was a complete and total withdrawal. In the process, Batu was determined that the Hungarians and anyone else in his path would not soon forget the Mongols. Prisoners were released and then hunted down and slaughtered like rabbits, while whole villages and towns were erased from the map. Leaving in his wake a land turned to ashes, Batu rode back into southern Russia, towards Sarai, a base camp that stood near Astrakhan. He decided to make this the capital of his new empire, while Subedei took the imperial *tumens* back to Qaraqorum. Europe was abandoned. What had precipitated this dramatic change in strategy was news from Qaraqorum that the Great Khan Ogedei had finally died.

There was also news of great political confusion at the capital. Ogedei's widow was at the heart of a series of conspiracies to ensure Guyuk's succession. Against her the opposition was working away in support of their candidate, Mongke, son of Tolui. Although Batu had already thrown his support behind the opposition, Toregene, who was ruling as regent, had tilted

the odds in her favour by dismissing all her late husband's advisers and replacing them with her own sycophants. There was even a rumour that Toregene and her fellow conspirators had grown impatient with Ogedei's slow decline and had despatched him with poisoned wine.

Batu realized immediately that under Toregene's regency there was no question of his continuing the campaign in Europe. The imperial *tumens* would have been recalled, had they not already been sent back to Mongolia. Should Mongke succeed as Great Khan, it was certain that the conquest of Europe would be continued. In the meantime Batu's best strategy was to consolidate the lands he had already conquered east of the Carpathians and west of the Urals – a vast expanse by any standards. The future of the house of Batu was already assured. The future of Europe would be decided in Qaraqorum.

MISSIONS

TO

TARTARY

THE SUDDEN WITHDRAWAL FROM EASTERN Europe was initially regarded as something approaching a miracle, though it was also
assumed that it was merely a respite and that the Tartars would
inevitably return to complete their work. This view was encouraged by the Church, which was now more convinced than ever
that the Tartars were the tools of a vengeful God bent upon
retribution and so had renamed them the 'Hammer of God'. The
Mongols were clearly the descendants of Gog and Magog, released from their prison behind the Caucasus Mountains, and thus heralded
the coming of the Antichrist and of Armageddon. Indeed, there was a great
deal of theological debate about the Tartars, their origins, purposes and the
very meaning of their attack upon Europe.

But the Church was in no state to formulate a policy to cope with the end
of the world so long as it remained without a head. Pope Celestine IV had died
in September 1241 and Christendom was left to drift without a spiritual leader
for another two years. In addition to the constant threat of a renewed attack

The famous Thirteenth Ecumenical Council convened at
Lyons Cathedral in June 1245 by Pope Innocent IV at which the great threat
from the Mongols was discussed.

142

lesperance de tous ceulx qui se
trauoilloient cuidans quil feust
es angoisses de la mort. Il
ouurit la bouche et ses pre
mieres paroles quil dist fu
rent quil demanda la croix
et la print deuotement pour
aler oultremer. Et de puis
lors en auant il deuint de plus
en plus grant aulmosnier
et deuoit accomplir le saint
voiage et secourir la sainte
terre de promission. Laquelle
fut celle propre annee que le
Roy saint loys se avisa pres
que toute gastee et destruite
par une maniere de gens
Sarrazins appelles tiessame
Lesquelz entre aultres villes
prindrent par force la sainte

from the 'Hammer of God', there also came news that Jerusalem had fallen to the Muslim armies and Christian authority in the Holy Land seemed shattered. A new Pope, Innocent IV, was eventually elected in 1243 and almost immediately Frederick II renewed his attacks upon the Pope's territory in Italy. With internal quarrels in Rome and even the threat of rebellion, Innocent, fearful for his safety, left for Lyons and the protection offered him by the devout young King of France, Louis IX. From Lyons, Innocent immediately called what was to be the Thirteenth Ecumenical Council, which would be convened in June 1245. The new pontiff declared that the most important issue to be dealt with was the future security of Christendom, which most people understood to mean how it would cope with the 'Hammer of God'.

Innocent IV, a Genoese jurist before he had been elected Pope, took a far less superstitious approach to the problem than most people. A year before the Council was due to be convened he summoned to Lyons all informed persons or reports that could be gathered from Russia, Poland and Hungary. From these he learned a little about Mongol religious practices, a good deal about their methods of fighting and, perhaps most significantly, the fact that they accorded great respect and reliable protection to official envoys. Armed with this information, Innocent decided a few months before the Council to send forth a number of exploratory missions. They had instructions to travel to the Mongol court bearing greetings from Christendom, coupled with a somewhat audacious invitation to accept Christianity and be baptized. However, more importantly, the missions were charged with gleaning information about the Tartars and their intentions. A further objective was to extend invitations to the Eastern Russian and Greek Orthodox Churches and the eastern Christians to unite in common cause against the Mongol threat, and at the same time return to the bosom of Rome. Innocent chose to send monks from the newly founded Dominican and Franciscan orders for his mission 'Ad Tartaros'. These were both new and highly enthusiastic orders; the Dominicans in particular were friar-preachers, full of religious fever.

There were a number of legates despatched with letters from the Pope – Lawrence of Portugal, Ascelinus of Lombardy, Andrew of Longjumeau and Dominic of Aragon – all of whom took the route through the Levant. Their instructions were to deliver the letters to the first Mongol chieftain they encountered, and request that the letters be handed on to the Mongol king. One of the first missions to depart was that undertaken by the Franciscan John of Plano Carpini. His was by far the most difficult mission. He was instructed to take the overland route into eastern Russia first travelled by the Hungarian Julian in 1237, then continue all the way to the Mongol court – wherever that was – and deliver letters to the Mongol king in person.

This was a terribly arduous journey for a man already in his sixties and somewhat overweight. No doubt he had imagined he might see out his final years in quiet contemplation amongst other monks of his order. But he had been carefully chosen because of his experience in diplomatic circles, and because he knew personally a number of monarchs in eastern Europe who would be important contacts along the way. John had been born some time around the end of the twelfth century at Plano Carpini, a small town near Perugia in northern Italy. He was an early disciple of St Francis and had been sent by him in 1221 to Saxony where he established a number of monasteries, converted a great many friars to the new order and then sent them forth into northern Europe to spread the movement.

On Easter Day, 16 April 1245, Carpini left Lyons with a small party of companions that included Friar Stephen of Bohemia, and journeyed into Bohemia, Silesia and Poland where he was due to have consultations with the monarchs there. While in Breslau the party was joined by a Pole, Friar Benedict, who was fluent in Slavonic languages. From there they travelled to what was left of Cracow where they sought out Conrad, the Duke of Mazovia and Lanciscia, who was known to favour a union of nations and churches against the Mongols. It was also thought that Conrad's family links with the Russian princes, especially with the current leader Prince Daniel Romanovich, might exert some influence around the idea of an anti-Mongol bloc. Unfortunately, Daniel and the other Russian princes were already vassals of Batu and, so far as they were concerned, a rebellion against their Mongol overlords would have been suicidal.

At least the Franciscans did not depart for Kiev entirely empty-handed. They had learnt that it was the Mongol tradition to expect envoys to come bearing gifts, and so Carpini and his party purchased with what money they had a large collection of furs. In the depth of the Russian winter they travelled through a land firmly in the grip of the Mongol army towards Kiev, where they encountered a *tumen* commander. According to Carpini's own account, it was as they approached Kiev that they saw, in the most appalling detail, the worst evidence of the Mongol invasion three years before. The ground was still littered with the bleached bones of countless victims, and there were ruins all about them. Carpini's party, which by now had grown to about ten, was escorted south through Cuman country to where they first encountered Mongol camps. At the sight of Europeans 'some armed Tartars rushed upon us in a horrible manner, wanting to know what kind of men we were'. Struggling through a number of translators, Carpini explained the purpose of their mission and was eventually allowed to proceed. They would be escorted to Batu's camp, and it would be up to him to decide their future. Before

proceeding further they were required, as was the custom, to leave a hostage, and so Stephen and some of the servants remained behind.

While the Franciscans made their way towards their first encounter with a Mongol prince, in the Middle East the Dominicans were making their way slowly through the Levant towards Mongol settlements in northern Mesopotamia. The Frenchman Andrew of Longjumeau, accompanied by another monk of his order, journeyed through Syria trying to get to a Mongol outpost. They had little assistance from the various Sultans, who suspected the monks' real mission was to help form an alliance between the Mongols and Rome against Islam. To the papal envoys it must have seemed a most unlikely suspicion, yet it would prove remarkably prophetic in the years to come. So Andrew continued unassisted into northern Mesopotamia and then into Armenia, which was under the control of a Mongol military governor named Baiju. Toregene had sent Baiju to replace Chormaghun in 1242, as part of her policy of sweeping away her late husband's officials.

As the Dominicans made their way through Baiju's territory they encountered a number of Christian communities and eventually the prelate of the area, Simeon Rabban-ata, who had been appointed by none other than Ogedei Khan. Andrew discovered that the eastern Christians enjoyed a great many privileges under the Mongols and consequently were flourishing. Simeon had built many new churches, and the faith was spreading beyond northern Persia into Mongol-controlled western Asia.

The eastern Christians trace their history back to Thaddeus, one of the seventy evangelists sent forth by Thomas at Jesus's bidding shortly before his crucifixion. Thaddeus journeyed to the city of Edessa, now called Urfa in modern Turkey, and from there the gospel spread to the East. From the outset the eastern Christians had an independent nature; their language was neither Greek nor Latin but Aramaic, said to be the language spoken by Jesus, and their script Syriac – or biblical Aramaic. The Church spread into Persia where it flourished for the next four centuries, growing stronger and ever more independent. Following a series of wars between the Byzantine Roman empire and Persia, the eastern Christians sought to distance themselves from the Western Churches. The separation became permanent in 431, after most eastern Christians supported a Greek prelate named Nestorius who had been condemned as a heretic for teaching theology divergent from that of Rome; ever since then the eastern Christians had been regarded as followers of Nestorius – hence Nestorians. Eastern Christianity continued to develop in its own way, such as rejecting the doctrine of celibacy of the clergy. Over the centuries they became renowned as physicians, having gathered a great deal of knowledge from the Arabs, and churches were built in Merv, Nishapur,

Samarqand, Bukhara and Herat. Eventually their faith spread to the nomadic horsemen of the steppe and the Onghuts, Kereyids and Uighurs were converted.

AUDIENCE WITH BATU KHAN

During the spring of 1246, as Carpini was still making his way through the Ukraine towards Batu's camp, in faraway Qaraqorum the question of the succession was finally resolved. The regent, Toregene, with the support of the Chaghadai clan, had finally succeeded in winning sufficient support to ensure the election of her son Guyuk. This was apparently an unpopular decision; Guyuk had few devotees amongst the other Mongol princes, being even more devoted to drink and debauchery than his late father. Although the Mongke candidacy had been defeated, the opposition were far from satisfied and Qaraqorum continued to seethe with discontent.

Into this political maelstrom rode the portly John of Plano Carpini. He arrived at Batu's capital, Sarai, on the banks of the Volga, on 4 April 1246. As was the custom, John and his party were required to pass through various purification rites, such as walking between two fires to purge themselves of any evil intentions, and then bowing before a stuffed felt image of Genghis Khan. Batu made a deep impression on Carpini and his party, as did his magnificent tent city. They had numerous audiences in a particularly beautiful white linen tent that had once belonged to the Hungarian King, Bela IV. Inside the tent, lined in gold brocade, Batu Khan sat with his wives and officials offering his guests the best of their food and wine, to be eaten and drunk from gold vessels. Unfortunately, as it was the middle of Lent the good monks were obliged to refuse everything but gruel and water.

Batu had established himself as the supreme power throughout Russia and had received the submission of most of the Russian princes, starting with Yaroslav of Novgorod and followed by the princes of Chernigov and Galicia. Batu became adept at working the Russian princes' mutual animosities to his own advantage and succeeded in extending his rule from Bulgaria to Novgorod, even though his armies were rarely deployed further west than Kiev. Within a few years his power and prestige were unmatched anywhere outside of Qaraqorum. Seated on silk carpets, surrounded by beautifully adorned women, the simple Franciscans awaited Batu Khan's wishes. Having had the papal letters translated and read out to him, Batu decided the monks should carry them personally all the way to Qaraqorum, where they could be delivered to the Great Khan himself. Batu saw no reason for interfering in the relations between Europe and the empire, even though he had opposed the rise of the

new Khan. Guyuk was due to be enthroned within a few months, and Batu was keen that the Europeans should have the opportunity to witness the full splendour of Mongol wealth and ceremony.

So the envoys set off, under escort, towards the most important capital in the world. Qaraqorum was no longer the oasis of civilization that Ogedei and his Chinese architects had envisaged; the court had changed during the reign of the regent. For a start the great and wise chief minister, Yeh-lu Ch'u-ts'ai, had been replaced by a Muslim merchant by the name of Abd al-Rahman, who had immediately doubled the taxes in northern China. The royal house itself had become a den of intrigue. Toregene had become infatuated with a Persian slave named Fatima, whose influence upon the regent had caused great resentment – especially as a great many old favourites were purged from government. Virtually all the Chinese or Uighur officials were hounded out of the administration and some of them actually executed. Yeh-lu Ch'u-ts'ai himself left Qaraqorum a broken man and died in 1243, while even the military governor of Transoxania found himself being pursued by a unit of imperial guards and had to seek refuge in Batu's domain.

Although the significance of these developments was probably not appreciated by Carpini and his party, he was nevertheless aware of some form of division within the empire. To get to Qaraqorum they were led along the pathways of the now well-established Yam system; changing horses at each station, they sometimes arrived so late that they had no time to eat before collapsing into bed with exhaustion. The envoys followed a route that took them north of the Aral Sea through Khwarazmia, passing a number of towns including Utrar, the scene of the beginning of Genghis Khan's great westward expansion. They reached the Altai Mountains in July, entered former Naiman country, then proceeded eastward across the Khanagi range and arrived at Guyuk's *ordu* on 22 July. They had covered 5000 km (3000 miles) at a blistering 50 km (30 miles) a day, having arrived at their destination a little more than three months after leaving Batu's capital. The man from Plano Carpini had ventured further eastward than any European before him, and in the process had seen lands and people no European had ever dreamt of. His account of his travels includes a great deal of detail, filling countless blank pages in European knowledge. Yet there were still vast areas of Asia that the party did not explore, and in trying to fill in the blank areas on their maps Carpini fell back on traditional European geographical folklore. Hence there were still creatures 'who are said to have faces like dogs and live in the wilderness along the shores of the oceans'. His colleague Benedict also produced an account of their journey in which he claimed that northern Asia was populated by 'the dog-headed Cynocephali' and creatures called the

Parossies, whom he claimed ate no solid food on account of their having such narrow mouths – they survived on the mere smell of food.

A NEW GREAT KHAN IN QARAQORUM

On 24 August Carpini and his party were very much part of the real world, standing amongst a vast host gathered at a tent city at Sira-ordu, a few miles from Qaraqorum near Lake Koku-nor, for the enthronement of Guyuk Khan. Envoys, princes and other vassal lords had gathered from the four corners of the empire to be present at the enthronement. Grand Duke Yaroslav had travelled from Christian Russia; Sultan Kilij-Arslan IV from Seljuk Rum (Asia Minor); Constable Sempad from Armenia, the Egyptian Sultan's brother; an envoy from the Caliph of Baghdad; royal princes from Korea; and Prince David IV, son of Queen Rusudan of Georgia. There were representatives from northern China, from the Sung empire in the south, holy men from Tibet, shamans from the mountains and armies of retainers. All the Mongol aristocracy was present – except, that is, for Batu Khan, who preferred to remain in Sarai. This was a tremendous insult to the ruling family, and only served to widen the rift amongst the Mongol princes.

The ceremonies continued for four days, and on each successive day the colours worn by the court were changed. Carpini made particular note of the harnesses and breastplates that adorned the Mongol officers' horses, which he claimed had been made of 'about twenty marks' worth of gold'. He and his party were also greatly impressed by the vast quantities of silk, brocade, furs and jewels that had been brought as tribute for the new Great Khan. At the actual enthronement Guyuk was carried on a litter by four princes, so that he could be seen above the heads of the gathered host, to a large solid gold and ivory throne, encrusted with pearls and other gems, that had been made by the Russian goldsmith Cosmas.

Following the ceremonies the Mongol court remained at Sira-ordu, as did Carpini and his party, waiting patiently for their audience with the new Khan. In fact, Carpini never managed to get to Qaraqorum, though that doesn't seem to have deprived him of things to see and write about. He presents a curiously flattering picture of Guyuk the man, describing him as a

Overleaf: John of Plano Carpini, the first European known to have ventured to the Far East, vividly described the splendour and spectacle of Guyuk Khan's coronation ceremony which lasted for four days. According to Carpini, Guyuk declared 'From now on my own word shall serve as a sword.'

somewhat formidable man in his mid-forties. In fact he was considerably younger, of a sickly complexion, certainly an alcoholic and well on his way to an early grave. Nevertheless, Guyuk had sufficient presence of mind during the first months of his rule to make some dramatic changes to the court.

One of the first to go was Abd al-Rahman, the Muslim merchant whom his mother had made Prime Minister, and in due course it would be the turn of Baiju, the military governor in northern Persia whom his mother had promoted. Guyuk also dealt with his mother's confidante, Fatima, whom he had convicted of witchcraft and sentenced to be executed by suffocation – a peculiarly Mongolian practice. According to shamanistic tradition, blood contains an individual's spiritual essence; if the blood of a noble is spilt, it has an evil effect upon the ground on which it falls. Consequently, it was a form of respect towards enemy leaders or members of the aristocracy who had fallen from grace to be executed either by being wrapped in carpets until they were asphyxiated, or crushed under planks of wood. In Fatima's case, to make doubly sure her blood was not spilt, all her orifices were sewn up before she was rolled in a sheet of felt and then thrown into a river. Though the coming of a new reign seems to have brought with it the usual violent purge, Guyuk was also responsible for returning to power many of the former ministers who had previously been persecuted by his mother.

A FRANCISCAN VIEW OF MONGOL SOCIETY

Carpini described in some detail the comings and goings within Guyuk's administration, and in particular the return of an extremely able Uighur Christian named Chinqai, who had been Yeh-lu Ch'u-ts'ai's deputy. Carpini describes him as 'protonotary' or chief secretary, though he was more of a Chancellor or Prime Minister. It was Chinqai who acted as an intermediary in their efforts to arrange an audience with Guyuk. But the Great Khan was in no hurry to see the Europeans, partly because he already knew the content of the papal letters, which had been passed on by Batu, and partly because these so-called envoys from the Pope had arrived without any tribute or offering to make to the new Khan – a dreadful lapse in etiquette. Carpini had disposed of all the furs they had purchased in Russia as tribute to Batu. Indeed, not only was Guyuk prepared to let the monks wait, he was also prepared to let them suffer. He was so disappointed with them that he ordered them to be given hardly any food during their stay at his camp, and the wretched monks probably would have starved had not Cosmas, the Russian goldsmith, come to their rescue.

In reality, Carpini's request for an audience with Guyuk was little more

than a formality. He already had private information concerning the Great Khan's intentions towards Christendom, and it was not encouraging. In the meantime he made careful observations of the Mongols and their way of life, knowing that his report to the Pope was now even more vital. Yet, given the gloomy prospect that would underline his report, Carpini's account remained remarkably even-handed and in many cases extremely flattering. He devotes considerable space to describing Mongol religious practices: the making and worshipping of felt idols, particularly of Genghis Khan, horse sacrifices and so on. He briefly describes certain shamanistic rituals and the worship of Tengri, the Eternal Heaven or sky god.

As for his mission to convert the Mongols to Christianity, he seems to have swiftly concluded that any efforts in that area would be somewhat premature. Nevertheless, he does note the large number of 'Nestorian clerics' at the Mongol court and the fact that most of the royal family were either already Christian or heavily influenced by them. He also claimed that there was some hope for future evangelizing in China, of all places. Although he and his party got nowhere near China, there were a great many Chinese at Guyuk's court and, perhaps because most of these were Christians, they seem to have given him a distorted impression. Although the Church of the East had sent missions to T'ang China since the seventh century, Christianity had been in decline in China for more than a hundred years. Nevertheless, from his enquiries Carpini concluded that the Chinese have 'an Old and New Testament, and lives of Fathers and hermits, and buildings made like churches, in which they pray at stated times; and they say they have some saints. They worship one God, they honour Our Lord Jesus Christ, and they believe in eternal life, but are not baptized.' Although none of this was even remotely accurate, in what was the very earliest European account of the Chinese he goes on to give a very good description of their physical appearance and their marvellous craftsmanship.

When he comes to piece together a history of the Mongol tribes he is forced, again, to rely upon a mixture of fact and legend. Carpini is armed with his own thorough knowledge of the histories of the East, the Alexander romances and other European texts. With these in hand he is forced to make sense of the accounts gathered from Uighur scribes, travellers and any others that might shed light on the Mongols' origins. He provides Europe with an authoritative account of the importance of 'Chingiscan' and couples it, almost inevitably, with a further reference to that ubiquitous figure Prester John. In his account Carpini makes it clear that Genghis Khan was not Prester John, nor King David, but the founder of a great pagan empire. Prester John, on the other hand, is identified as the Christian king of Greater India, who is

supposed to have defeated Genghis Khan by using Greek fire (burning sulphur that was catapulted at the enemy) and manikins tied to horses.

This is a mixture of certain elements from the accounts of Genghis's campaign against the Khwarazm Shah, combined with legends surrounding Alexander's defeat of the Indian King Porus. Carpini heard these stories at a time when the Mongols were developing their own Genghis romances, having already elevated him to something approaching a deity. The Mongols were already familiar with the Oriental version of the Alexander romances and had blended themes from this with facts from Genghis's exploits. As for the account of Genghis's defeat, Carpini received this from Russian captives at the court, who had probably concocted the story as a way of ridiculing their masters.

By far the most important section in Carpini's account is that describing the Mongol army, its decimal structure, discipline and manner of fighting. It is an accurate and in parts detailed picture of a modern fighting machine. He ends this part by emphasizing that Europe's only hope of countering this formidable threat is to unite in common cause: 'Therefore, if Christians wish to save themselves, their country and Christendom, then kings, princes, barons and rulers of countries ought to assemble together and by common consent send men to fight against Tartars before they begin to spread over the land.'

It was November before Chinqai managed to secure Carpini a series of audiences with Guyuk Khan. At those occasions the contents of the papal letters were read out, chiding the Mongol Khan for the great destruction his armies had created in Christian Europe, entreating him to make assurances that these attacks would cease and offering him and his people the gift of baptism. Guyuk Khan's response was unequivocal. Chinqai was at great pains to record it accurately for the envoys to take back to Europe; a copy was made in Latin and another in Persian.

To the Pope's complaint about the destruction carried out in Europe, Guyuk replies: 'I do not understand these words of yours. Tengri [Eternal Heaven] has slain and annihilated these peoples, because they had adhered neither to Genghis Khan nor to Khagan [Ogedei], both of whom have been sent to make known God's command.' Mongol notions of political diplomacy had probably been borrowed from the Chinese, and Guyuk's response was

One of three copies of Guyuk Khan's letter to the Pope,
now in the Vatican Archives. The Khan's seal contains the legend,
'By the strength of Eternal Heaven, Order of the Universal Ruler
of the Empire of the Great Mongols.'

completely in character with Chinese principles. The fundamental concept was that the founder of a new dynasty clearly held the mandate of heaven; that is to say, the unquestionable proof that a leader held this holy mandate was his very success in seizing power. The spectacular achievements enjoyed by the Mongol armies had led them to see their holy mandate not simply in terms of a dynasty, but in relation to the entire world. The Mongol empire was not just another state, it was *the* supreme universal monarchy, and all the lands not within its borders were automatically regarded as subordinate and therefore potential vassals.

As to the Pope's request that the Mongols accept baptism, Guyuk replied: 'Thou, who art the Great Pope, together with all the princes, come in person to serve us. . . . If you do not observe God's command, and if you ignore my command, I shall know you as my enemy. Likewise I shall make you understand. If you do otherwise, God knows what I know.' The Great Khans saw themselves as God's representatives on earth, charged by God with the task of world conquest. Every nation would either have to submit or be destroyed. Cosmas, who had made the Great Seal used to stamp Guyuk's letter, explained the legend he had been asked to work into the design: 'By the strength of Eternal Heaven, Order of the Universal Ruler of the Empire of the Great Mongols. When it reaches the subject and rebel people, let them respect it, let them fear it.'

Before his departure, Carpini was approached by one of the soldiers detailed to escort him. He was told that Guyuk was keen to send his own ambassadors to the Pope and wanted another audience with the clerics to arrange this. It was the convention that the invitation to send Mongol ambassadors should come from the visiting envoys, but Carpini decided against it. He felt it would have been a mistake for Mongol ambassadors to travel on official business through Europe as 'they would see dissensions and wars among us and that it would encourage them to march against us'. On 13 November 1246, Carpini and his party finally departed Guyuk's tent city to begin the long journey home. They travelled through the depth of winter, arriving at Batu's camp in early May the following year. Batu granted them safe passage to Kiev, where they were greeted 'as if we had come back from the dead', sixteen months after they had departed.

While Carpini and his party had been struggling through another Russian winter, a Dominican named Ascelinus of Lombardy was making his way through the Levant, retracing the journey taken by Andrew of Longjumeau in search of Baiju's camp. Unlike Andrew, Friar Ascelinus managed to obtain good directions and arrived at the military governor's camp at Sisian in the Karabagh Highlands in May 1247.

Whatever qualified Ascelinus for this mission it was not any gift for diplomacy. Requested to make the obligatory genuflection, descending three times on the left knee, Ascelinus obstinately refused; nor did he bring with him the customary tributes so that he might be recognized as a serious envoy. Then Ascelinus made things even worse by referring to the Pope as 'the greatest of all men', and went on by demanding that Baiju and his followers should all become Christians.

Having first delivered Ascelinus a stinging rebuke – 'You ask us to become Christians and so [become] dogs like you?' – Baiju sentenced the monks to death, planning to flay them alive and then deliver their straw-stuffed hides to Rome. The monks escaped only through the intervention of Baiju's wife, who insisted that her husband show the customary Mongol respect for clerics – no matter how insolent. Despite his reprieve, the Dominican's obstinate nature was barely tempered and he might yet have come to grief had not an official from Qaraqorum arrived with orders to relieve Baiju of his command. The new governor, Eljigidei, an extremely wily tactician, was another of Guyuk's sweeping changes to his administration. Ascelinus departed soon afterwards, bearing letters that reiterated Guyuk's message to the Pope and with very little good to say of the Mongols.

OPTIMISM IN EUROPE

One year after leaving Sira-ordu, Carpini's epic journey was finally over; he arrived at Lyons on 18 November 1247, nearly two and a half years after having left that city. Innocent IV greeted him warmly and was delighted by the encouraging reports that the eastern Christians or Nestorians were prepared to recognize him as their 'particular lord and father and the Holy roman Church as lady and mistress'. However, the report from the Mongol court, coupled with Guyuk's letter, made him feel less optimistic. Europe had little option, in Carpini's opinion, but to prepare for the worst. The only chance of a reprieve, he suggested, was the growing rift he had observed between Batu and Guyuk, which he thought might possibly delay or distract the Mongols from renewing their advance in the West.

The papal court accepted this news grimly, and then listened hopefully for information on Prester John. The Franciscan confessed he could find no actual evidence of the man, nor of any large and powerful Christian king in the neighbourhood. However, the best piece of news, the one seized upon and broadcast throughout Christendom, was Carpini's description of the powerful influence that the eastern Christians enjoyed at the Mongol court. Clutching at this straw, Carpini even went so far as to predict that Guyuk would some

The illuminated first initial
of a copy of Carpini's
account of his journey
to the Mongol court.

day convert to Christianity. In what was, on the whole, a somewhat depressing – though fascinating – account, this singular fact was enough to generate widespread optimism, especially as it seemed to corroborate the report of Andrew of Longjumeau who had returned from Persia just a few months before.

The heady confidence that soon filled the papal court could not disguise some harsh realities: the Europe to which Carpini had returned was in no position to form a united front against a renewed Mongol attack – the 'dissensions and wars' had got worse during his absence. Three years before, at the Thirteenth Ecumenical Conference, Innocent had resolved to deal with the Mongols, not as the 'Hammer of God' but as a foreign invading power. It had also been decided to conduct yet another Crusade for the Holy Land, which the young and devout King Louis IX of France would lead. Innocent's strategy towards the Mongols was to try to draw the eastern Churches into a pan-Christian alliance – and first reports were encouraging.

However, these plans were put aside when the long-running conflict with Frederick II flared up again, spreading the fighting from Italy up into Germany and threatening to ignite central Europe. Within months of his return Carpini was despatched once again, this time to the court of Louis IX, to plead for assistance in the war against Frederick. But Louis would not abandon the Crusade, and by August he and his wife, Queen Margaret, had set sail for Cyprus. He had spent three years preparing, and had the foresight to take with him many followers with experience of the Middle East, including Andrew of Longjumeau.

MONGOL DECEIT, EUROPEAN NAIVETY

The French King left behind a Europe even more torn by internal strife, and praying for continued respite from the Tartars. He was unaware, however, that the hemisphere to which he sailed now contained a new and powerful

military presence. Louis made his first base at Limassol, but before he had even begun to deploy his army he received two envoys from General Eljigidei, the new Mongol military governor of northern Persia. Eljigidei's ambassadors were two wily Nestorians named David and Mark, one of whom was recognized by Andrew from his earlier travels through Georgia. They bore a letter from Eljigidei which claimed he had been charged by the Great Khan to protect all Christians in western Asia, rebuild their churches and pray for the success of Louis's Crusade. The letters went on to claim that the Great Khan had recently been baptized and that Eljigidei had followed his Khan's example. The ambassadors also delivered a secret message to Louis which they claimed Eljigidei had dared not commit to paper. It was a proposal for a military alliance.

According to David and Mark, Eljigidei was preparing his armies for a winter assault on Baghdad. If the King of France would co-ordinate his plans for an attack upon Egypt at the same time, then the two great Islamic powers, the Sultanate of Egypt and the Caliphate of Baghdad, would be unable to come to each other's assistance – and so the separate ambitions of the Great Khan and the great Pope would doubtless succeed. Eljigidei went further, and in a wonderfully bold stroke suggested that their respective armies should then converge and between them liberate the Holy Land.

To the young French King this was marvellous news. Eljigidei's message had confirmed Carpini's optimistic prediction, as well as more recent reports claiming that the entire Mongol court might soon be converted to Christianity. Soon Louis's court was wild with enthusiasm. He swiftly sent word to the Pope and then set about composing a suitable reply to the Mongol commander. He sent separate letters to both Guyuk Khan and Eljigidei, commending their decision to turn to Christianity and their offer of assistance in the war against Islam. Then, as a tribute to the Great Khan, he had a marvellous portable chapel constructed complete with decorations – all the paraphernalia necessary to celebrate Mass plus a few fragments from the True Cross. When it was finished, Louis sent Andrew of Longjumeau to Eljigidei's camp with the letters, gifts and secret messages regarding the forthcoming campaign.

The naïvety with which Louis responded to David and Mark's message only demonstrates how desperately Europe had come to believe in the Mongols' conversion – in the ancient legend of the powerful Christian kingdom of the East made manifest. While Christian influence at the court was well known, and Guyuk's baptism even possible, it is absolutely certain that neither he nor his court ever seriously embraced Christianity. Eljigidei's ambassadors were a most cunning ruse, executed with great aplomb.

There was one aspect of Mongol military endeavours that remained

essential to all their successes, and that was the gathering and exploitation of first-rate intelligence. It might be recalled that, while Ascelinus and his party were held captive in Baiju's camp, Eljigidei had arrived to take command. According to an account of one of the monks in that party, before they were released Ascelinus had been closely questioned about rumours that the Europeans were preparing to launch a fresh campaign to reconquer Jerusalem. It would have been obvious to a man of Eljigidei's calibre what advantages might be gained from a Mongol–European alliance. The scheme was simple, but ingenious. The Caliphate of Baghdad was the last significant power that stood in the way of Mongol ambitions in Persia, but to launch an attack would probably have invited a united Islamic response. If he could be certain that the Egyptian Sultan's armies would be pinned down at the same time, then he stood a better chance of success. The Mongols had no plans to march on the Holy Land, as yet.

Andrew and six other friars set sail with the portable chapel in late January 1249. By the time they arrived at Eljigidei's camp in the spring, Louis and his army were landing in Egypt as agreed. Eljigidei had not attacked Baghdad, nor had he even mobilized, for in the past six months the balance of power had shifted again in Qaraqorum.

A NEW POWER STRUGGLE IN THE MONGOL CAPITAL

In 1248 there had been an attempt to resolve the differences between Guyuk and Batu through a meeting between the two cousins in the Ili valley, about midway between their respective domains. But before Batu reached the rendezvous he received word that the planned reconciliation was in fact a trap; Guyuk intended to arrest him and have him executed. However, all Guyuk's plans came to nothing. His addiction to alcohol coupled with the rigours of the journey were finally too much for him, and he died somewhere along the road to the Ili valley. He was forty-two. His widow, Oghul-Ghaimish, assumed the regency until the next *quriltai* and, as was the custom, had begun conspiring to have her son Shiremun elected as the next Great Khan. This time, however, the house of Ogedei did not have the numbers. Tolui's widow Sorghaghtani Beki, with the support of Batu and most of the other princes, was gathering support for her son Mongke, whom Guyuk had defeated two years before.

Under the present circumstances Eljigidei, who owed his promotion to Guyuk, decided it would be unwise to launch a new campaign until the result of the election was known. So, in order to waste time, he sent Andrew and the portable chapel to Oghul-Ghaimish's camp in Tarbagatai. Nearly nine months later they arrived at the regent's camp, where the gifts intended for her

late husband were taken as tribute from the Christian West and proof of their submission to the Mongol court. Poor Andrew was then entrusted with a letter for King Louis which simply enjoined him to return each year with further tribute of gold and silver; if he did not, he would be destroyed. Andrew and his companions had naïvely expected to be welcomed into a Christian realm and treated as allies. Instead, Louis's envoys were hastened away as though they were messengers of a vassal lord.

In all respects the venture had proved a catastrophe. While the Dominicans had been fruitlessly trekking across Asia to the seat of the Mongol court, Louis had been in prison. Having landed in Egypt in June 1249, Louis's army quickly took Damietta unopposed and then marched on towards Cairo, firmly believing that at that moment Eljigidei's armies were laying siege to Baghdad. But Louis's progress was halted long before he reached Cairo by a unit of the Sultan's army led by a young Mamluk commander named Baybars. The Mamluks were Turkic slave soldiers who had entered the Sultan's service back in 1238. In fact they had originally been captured by Batu's son Berke during the raids that preceded the Mongol invasion of eastern Europe, and then sold to the Egyptian Sultan to help finance Batu's war. In the twenty years since, the Mamluks had become not only an indispensable element of the Egyptian army but also a significant force at court.

The confrontation between the armour-clad French knights and these once nomadic horsemen was as one-sided as the battles between the Poles and the Mongols. Louis's vanguard was utterly destroyed, forcing the army to fall back. It fought an effective rearguard action, but eventually was cut off from its supply lines and brought close to starvation. Louis had no option but to surrender and he was carried away in chains, stricken with dysentery and near death. He languished in prison until May 1250, when finally a massive ransom of one million gold bezants was paid and he and the remnants of his army were released. Out of 60000 men only 12000 sailed with him to Acre, where he made his base for the next four years.

The irony of Louis's situation couldn't have been more poignant. As he and his meagre army sailed from Egypt the Mamluks were in revolt, having murdered the Sultan's heir. The Sultan himself had died the year before, and following the revolt his widow, Shajar al-Durr, had married the Mamluks' commander-in-chief, Aybak. This created a new Islamic regime, but more importantly splintered the rest of the Islamic world and led to years of intrigue and civil war. There could have been no better time in which to launch a decisive campaign against Islam – but Louis did not have the means. He must have writhed with frustration.

In April 1251, Andrew of Longjumeau returned from Mongolia to be

received by his King at Caesarea near Acre. According to Louis's biographer, Joinville, the King was appalled at Oghul-Ghaimish's letter and at the Mongols' mendacity. Nevertheless, Andrew's mission was not entirely fruit-less; it did plant the seed of the possibility of Christian–Mongol *entente* – even if that response had probably been motivated by a lingering faith in an Eastern saviour. However, as things were, Europe would doubtless think twice before responding to any such suggestion again. In the meantime, as Andrew had been making his way back to Palestine, the question of the succession to the Great Khan was resolved. Oghul-Ghaimish's efforts on behalf of her son had become desperate and at one point she had even attempted to assassinate the other candidate, Mongke; however, the plot was discovered, Oghul-Ghaimish was discredited and on 1 July 1251 Mongke was duly elected. There followed the usual purge of opposition supporters, along with seventy advisers who were executed for their complicity; Oghul-Ghaimish suffered the same fate as Fatima; Chaghadai's grandson Buri had been part of the plot and was therefore doomed; and Shiremun was sent away to the wars in China and murdered there on Mongke's orders. Even Eljigidei and his sons were swept away in the purge.

Mongke Khan then immediately distinguished his reign by declaring his wish to renew the Genghis mandate of world conquest. There would be two massive imperial expeditions: the first was to take up properly the campaign against the Sung Dynasty in southern China and extend the empire's borders in the east. Mongke decided he would lead this campaign himself with the aid of his younger brother Khubilai. The other great expedition he gave to another of his younger brothers, Hulegu. This was the expansion of the empire in the west – not into Europe, but through Persia, down into Mesopotamia and Syria and eventually invading Egypt. This strike into the Middle East became the most ferocious and devastating attack that Islam ever encountered.

King Louis IX of France at Damietta in Egypt,
on his way towards Cairo. Tricked into thinking the Mongols
would support his Crusade, he met with disaster
just a few months later.

Comment le Roy print port a dunnete. ... chipre

la marsin pur   autres desllus nonimes le
le moyen dels   uindrent des contires del
ambaudeurs   susditcs atout grande
C estassauoir le patriar   quantite de nef et galees
che de sheiusalem et les   en chipre. Smdrct aussi

7

MONGOL

CRUSADERS

ITH THE ENTHRONEMENT OF MONGKE, the empire was once again in the hands of an expansionist. The motivating force behind the empire had lain dormant since Ogedei's reign and during that time it had shown distinct signs of decadence and internal decay. Mongke Khan was set to change all that. As this new sense of purpose moved through the Mongol capital, the Pope and his advisers struggled to decipher the confusing signals their envoys had delivered on the intentions of the 'Tartar hordes'. Louis's experience had been a bitter lesson.

However, though Europe waited to see what the fates delivered, this did not mean the end of European contact with the Mongol court. Among King Louis's entourage was a young Flemish monk by the name of William, who was soon to find himself at the very heart of the great empire just as it was about to make another stride on the world stage. Very little is known of young William, except that he was born in the French town of Rubruck around 1217, that he lived for some time at a friary in Paris, that he was passionately devout and that he had been in Louis's service at least since his departure for Egypt in 1248.

SPY AND EVANGELIST IN THE LAND OF THE MONGOLS

William of Rubruck enters the story because of his remarkable account of life and customs at the Mongol court. Far more detailed than previous accounts,

it describes the workings of the empire's capital at a critical time for both the empire and the rest of the world.

Friar William turned up at the Mongol court because of his own personal mission to preach the gospel among the pagans. He had been inspired by the stories of Andrew of Longjumeau and the writings of Carpini, amongst others, which described Mongol tolerance towards foreign religions. Rubruck had become concerned in particular about what he presumed was the pernicious influence of the 'Nestorians'. He had also been greatly moved by accounts of German slaves who were apparently labouring for one of the Mongol princes. This passionate friar saw it as his calling to travel the breadth of Asia, bring succour to the European slaves and, during this time of great evangelical fervour, convert the Mongols to the true Christian path.

Naturally Louis was reluctant to offer much encouragement to Rubruck's plan. He insisted that the friar should make quite clear to all Mongol officials the unofficial nature of his mission, in case they mistook his presence as an indication of Louis's submission to the Great Khan. However, in return for an account of Rubruck's observations from within the empire, Louis was prepared to give the monk a letter of introduction to Prince Sartaq, one of Batu Khan's sons and a recent convert, requesting safe conduct for the monk to fulfil his mission.

Rubruck set off from Acre at the beginning of 1253 with a party that included the Italian Franciscan Bartholomew of Cremona, a royal secretary named Gosset who brought with him gifts for the Khan, and a Syrian named Omodeo who was to act as guide and interpreter. They travelled by way of Constantinople, across the Black Sea and into Mongol territory, which Rubruck described as like 'stepping into some other world'. They arrived in July at Sartaq's camp, where the locals immediately presumed they were emissaries from King Louis; they were then sent on to Batu Khan's camp, three days' journey away. Batu also found Rubruck's explanations of a religious mission less than convincing, and he too sent them on – to the seat of the great Mongke Khan himself, at Qaraqorum.

During the three and a half months it took to get there, Rubruck made careful notes on the landscape and people he observed along the way. His extremely detailed account became one of the most important descriptions of Central Asia ever recorded by a European. Fascinated by the customs and beliefs of all the peoples he encountered, he was forever making enquiries of the whereabouts of the monsters and other strange creatures that were supposed to inhabit these lands. The friar was constantly astonished to find no evidence of such beings anywhere.

By October Rubruck and his party were south of Lake Balkhash where

he recorded that large numbers of villages had been destroyed 'so that the Tartars could feed their flocks there, for it is very fine pasturage'. Clearly old habits died hard. As with all journeys across the Asian steppe, the going was hard and gruelling. At times they were close to starvation, forced to eat raw mutton because of the lack of fuel. They kept on, driven by Rubruck's obsession to penetrate deep into this heathen wasteland and transform it into the new Eden. However, this proved more difficult than he had ever imagined – especially as his guide and interpreter, Omodeo, was more of a liability than an asset, having virtually none of the local languages.

Just before Christmas they arrived at Mongke's camp, a few miles west of Qaraqorum, and almost immediately the friars were granted an audience with the Great Khan. Once again the Mongols found it hard to swallow William's declaration that he simply wanted to live at court and preach the gospel. It seems that Mongke was untroubled by the lack of precious tribute and accepted that they were not royal emissaries from Louis. However, given the Mongols' own heavy reliance upon spies and informers, they were naturally suspicious of someone from Europe requesting permission to wander about the countryside. For the next two months William and his party were regularly interrogated by the Great Khan's ministers, who were never entirely satisfied with their explanations. Mongke, on the other hand, treated his guests with great courtesy. He granted them many audiences and listened intently to William's sermons.

Some of the eastern Christians at court even maintained that it was simply a matter of time before the Great Khan was baptized; after all, his mother, Sorghaghtani Beki, a niece of the Kereyid King Ong Khan, had been a Christian all her life. Be that as it may, Sorghaghtani had nevertheless always practised the traditional Mongol policy of religious impartiality, and had instilled these virtues in her son. Although a Christian, she was also remembered for having founded a richly endowed Muslim college in Bukhara.

Rubruck was sufficiently observant to notice that Mongke Khan paid equal attention to all the various foreign religions represented in his realm, making certain to attend all the important ceremonies. In a conversation with Rubruck, he was once reported to have explained his religious impartiality thus: 'We Mongols believe there is but one God, by Whom we live and by

Mongke Khan with his wives
and sons, from a manuscript
of Rashid al-Din.

Whom we die, and towards Him we have an upright heart. . . . But just as God gave different fingers to the hand so has He given different ways to men.' Despite Mongke's highly sophisticated views on religion, the fact is that he remained fundamentally a shamanist, dependent upon fortune-tellers who burnt the shoulder-blade of a sheep to divine the future.

At the beginning of April the Great Khan moved his court to Qaraqorum and Rubruck and his party followed, thus becoming the first Europeans ever to visit the capital of the largest empire that the world had ever seen. He was not impressed. After spending time in Batu's capital, he wrote: 'I was overcome with fear, for his own houses seemed like a great city stretching out a long way and crowded around on every side by peoples to a distance of three or four leagues.' Qaraqorum, on the other hand, had not flourished to quite the same degree, and Rubruck declared that he found it no bigger than the village of Saint Denis to the north of Paris. Nevertheless, he was impressed by the uniquely international population; there was not another city like it anywhere. According to Rubruck it was divided up into various quarters: one for artisans, one for clerics, another for builders and engineers, and so on. There was a 'European colony', which apparently comprised craftsmen, merchants and scribes from Germany, Poland, France and Hungary, and even an Englishman called Basil, all of whom mingled with artisans, scientists and builders from Persia and China. Within its confines there were no fewer than twelve Buddhist temples, two mosques and a church. Along the many highways that linked the far reaches of the empire with Qaraqorum there flowed an unlikely traffic of priests, ambassadors, mystics and charlatans, come to beg indulgences or to take advantage of the Mongols' legendary superstitious nature. In the midst of this cosmopolitan society Rubruck and his entourage set about preaching the gospel.

Even by his own account Rubruck found his mission something of a struggle. Part of his problem was his own over-zealous approach. His teaching was shackled with academic dogma, and his arguments often reduced to threats of hellfire. Eventually even the local Christian community began to tire of him, especially after he threatened the Great Khan himself with eternal damnation. It is reported that Mongke responded to Rubruck's haranguing with the wisdom of a sage:

> The nurse at first lets some drops of milk into the infant's mouth, so that by tasting its sweetness he may be enticed to suck; only then does she offer him her breast. In the same way you should persuade Us, whom you claim to be so totally unacquainted with this doctrine, in a simple and rational manner. Instead you immediately threaten Us with eternal punishments.

Rubruck succeeded in converting just one Nestorian to the Church of Rome, and baptized six children. He did, however, take part in a debate between all the religions at the court, presented before an amused Great Khan and his courtiers. In a remarkable atmosphere of religious freedom, the representative of each creed was expected to challenge the others while at the same time presenting a rational explanation of the virtues and benefits of his own doctrine. In any other regime it would have been an exercise fraught with dangers; at the Mongol court it was an event of some entertainment. As might be expected, William took up the spirit of the debate and immediately launched into an attack against the Buddhists. In the meantime the eastern Christians took on the Islamic representatives, who were not much interested in a debate and refused to respond; so the eastern Christians rounded on the Uighur Buddhists instead. The Taoists seemed to have escaped unscathed; however, the proceedings soon dissolved into a raucous carouse, leaving a disillusioned Rubruck to record that his arguments had captured not one single convert. With his Christian work a complete failure, Rubruck resigned himself to the secondary aspect of his mission – that of gathering intelligence on behalf of King Louis.

If he was not well suited to the role of evangelist, he was even less well equipped to be a spy. Apart from his valuable observations of Mongol life, which were never properly appreciated until they were rediscovered by scholars in the nineteenth century, Rubruck gleaned little of Mongol policies or plans that they were not willing for him to know. The most obvious development taking place throughout his stay at Qaraqorum was the preparations being made for a massive military undertaking. Rubruck learned that, at a *quriltai* held in 1252, Mongke Khan had set out the objectives of his reign: a campaign against the Sung in China and, at the same time, a separate and even larger expedition into Persia and Syria, 'as far as the borders of Egypt', which was to be led by his younger brother Hulegu.

PLANNING THE MIDDLE EASTERN CAMPAIGN

The decision to extend the empire deep into Persia would have tremendous political ramifications in western Asia. Ever since Genghis Khan had swept through Transoxania and Khurasan, the Mongols had maintained no more than a partial military presence. Under the first military commander, Chormaghun, the remnants of the Khwarazm Shah's empire had been swept away and with it all civil administration. During Batu's great expansion to the west the land between the Caspian and the Black Seas, Azerbaijan, came solidly under Mongol control; the next military governor of the area, Baiju,

pushed Mongol influence into Rum – now Turkey – and crushed the Seljuks. When Baiju was replaced by the devious Eljigidei there was talk of a campaign against Baghdad, but nothing came of it. With the accession of Mongke, Eljigidei was swept away with the old regime and Baiju was reinstated as governor. However, Baiju made no sign of any move upon Baghdad, being fully occupied quelling uprisings in Asia Minor and Georgia. Throughout this period there were no substantial Mongol forces garrisoned further south than Azerbaijan and the Araxes valley, so control remained sporadic and chaos reigned.

From the Mongol perspective, a campaign into Persia and Syria was the logical pursuit of their philosophy of world domination. But the essential point behind Mongke's objectives was that further expansion in the west was going to happen in the Middle East, not in Europe. For centuries the Mongols had been familiar with the great influence that Muslim merchants from Persia and the Gulf area enjoyed throughout Asia. More significant was the reputation of Persian scientists, astronomers, astrologers, mathematicians and technologists, who were without equal anywhere in the world. Apart from the sciences, there were also the arts: painting, carpetmaking, music and poetry. The Islamic Middle East was by any standards a vastly sophisticated, wealthy and advanced civilization, and the Mongols could hardly allow it to flourish outside of their sphere. Mongke's objectives were obvious: by invading both the Sung empire in southern China and Persia, he was attempting to place the two great civilizations of the era under Mongol control. It stands as one of the most grandiose plans for world domination ever conceived.

One obvious conclusion that can be drawn from Mongke's decision was that the Mongols appeared to have lost interest in Europe. Indeed, there is no evidence that after Batu's withdrawal from eastern Europe the Mongols ever saw Europe as a prize worthy of the effort it would have taken to conquer it. Although the pronouncements of the Great Khans continued to reiterate the conviction that it was the Mongols' God-given right to rule the world, and that all kings were obliged to offer tribute to the Great Khan, the reality was that in global terms Europe really did not matter that much.

Rubruck never imagined that the proposed expedition to the Middle East would benefit the cause of the crusaders in Palestine; on the other hand the eastern Christian community had become convinced that the Mongols were about to unleash a holy war against their ancient enemies, the Muslims. The Mongols' prime objective was the Caliph of Baghdad, but before confronting him they meant to eliminate the other major power in the region, the Ismailis or Assassins. They had emerged because of a schism in the Shia Muslim sect and established themselves in northern and eastern Persia by

A Persian drawing of Hulegu taking a drink;
though he still has hold of his bow and sword,
the artist has succeeded in creating a
very pastoral scene.

---

taking and controlling a series of mountain fortifications. Behind their walls they lived a contemplative life, producing beautifully wrought paintings and metalwork, but beyond their retreats they terrorized those civilizations they deemed heretical and so earned the enmity not just of the rest of the Islamic world but eventually of Europe. The local Ismaili leader had done little to enhance their reputation. Rather than confront his enemies in open combat he preferred to sponsor a campaign of political murder, usually executed with a dagger in the back, as the means to his end.

The Mongols had their own reasons for launching a campaign against the Assassins. First, they had received a plea of help from an Islamic judge in Qazwin, a town near the Assassins' stronghold at Alamut, who had complained that his fellow citizens were forced to wear armour all the time as protection from the Assassins' daggers. According to Rubruck, another reason that determined Mongol attitudes was the discovery of a plot to send

no fewer than 400 dagger-wielding Assassins in disguise to Qaraqorum with instructions to murder the Great Khan. The Assassins had encountered the Mongols once before, during Chormaghun's terror raids through northern Persia in 1237–8, which led them to send an envoy to Europe begging for help.

Gradually the new imperial army took shape. It would be the grandest expedition since Batu's invasion of Europe. Mongke Khan allocated one-fifth of the entire Mongol force to Hulegu's command. One thousand 'teams' of Chinese engineers were recruited to manufacture and operate the siege machines, while fifth-columnists were sent ahead to prepare the way. This meant appropriating vast tracts of grazing land for the herds, stockpiling reserves of flour, grain, wine and other stores, building roads and bridges and then organizing a massive round-up of the thousands of horses that grazed across the steppes of western Asia. In the spring of 1253 the first contingents left Mongolia, and in the autumn Hulegu rode out at the head of an enormous army which then moved gradually across central Asia to the outskirts of Samarqand, where it made ready for the final march.

As preparations continued throughout 1254 and 1255, the Eastern Christian community became ever more enthusiastic for a war they believed would soon return them to their original home, the lands of Mesopotamia, from which they had emigrated to escape persecution under the Muslims. Soon contingents of Eastern Christians arrived from Batu's Golden Horde; there were Georgians, Turks and Alans; all wanted to ride with Hulegu's *tumens*. It also happened that Hulegu's most senior commander, Ked-Buqa, was a Christian Naiman, while Hulegu's chief wife, Doquz-Khatun, was renowned for her Christian convictions. To a community that had suffered under the Muslims for centuries, Hulegu's campaign had all the hallmarks of a Christian holy war; however, Rubruck knew better. His observations of the Mongol court told him a religious war was as alien to the Mongol generals as were the concepts of mercy and forgiveness. Although the character of Hulegu's army was, in parts, heavily Christian, the commander himself was a Buddhist.

RUBRUCK'S RETURN

While the great army was encamped near Samarqand, Rubruck finally began his long journey home. Mongke gave the friar a letter for Louis in which the Great Khan repudiated the earlier diplomatic missives sent by Guyuk Khan and his regent Oghul-Ghaimish. He explained to Louis: 'How could that wicked woman, more vile than a dog, know about matters of war and affairs of peace?' Mongke goes on to describe his visions of a united world 'from

sunrise to sunset' under Mongol rule, and, although he urged Louis to send peace envoys, he did not make any demands for tribute. It was a far more conciliatory letter than previous communications, and one might speculate that perhaps Mongke could see some advantage in trying to win Europe's trust.

Rubruck delayed his departure as long as possible, in the hope that he might glean a clearer signal of Mongol attitudes towards Europe. He had heard that King Hayton, from Armenia, was travelling secretly to Qaraqorum in order to see the Great Khan in connection with the planned expedition, and Rubruck imagined he might learn more of the expedition's real objectives from a fellow Roman Christian. However, by the beginning of July he had tired of waiting and decided to leave. Friar Bartholomew remained behind. Too ill to travel, he remained in Qaraqorum; it is presumed that he died there, the first Italian to die in the Far East.

A few months after Rubruck's departure, King Hayton finally arrived at Qaraqorum. Having heard of the planned campaign, Hayton had immediately realized that an all-out war against the main Islamic powers would have tremendous advantages for Christian Asia. He was received by Mongke and eventually spent fifty days at the capital, during which time he convinced the Great Khan that the entire expedition would be assured of allies in Palestine if it was made clear that Hulegu's expedition was nothing less than a Christian Crusade. Hayton then returned with a *yarligh*, an edict that, in effect, enfranchised the Christian Churches throughout the empire – and in those areas not yet conquered. He returned to Armenia, and made preparations to join Hulegu's force.

Had Rubruck managed to encounter King Hayton, he might have delivered a completely different report to Louis. In the event, his was yet another depressing account of Mongol intransigence. His mission both as an evangelist and as a spy had been a failure. He brought no accounts of fabled monsters, nor of Prester John. He bitterly regretted not having managed very many conversions and railed against the 'pernicious influence' that the Church of the East, in preference to Rome, enjoyed at the Mongol court. He did, however, confirm that a massive army was currently advancing upon Persia and Syria, but he made no recommendation of an alliance – quite the opposite. He had become so disenchanted with the Mongols that he saw only one policy for Europe. 'Were it allowed me,' he wrote, 'I would to the utmost of my power to preach war against them throughout the whole world.' Rubruck's report had a tremendous influence, not just on the French King, but on the rest of the courts of Europe. It dealt another blow to the Prester John legend; but, perhaps more significantly, it was a great discouragement to those

who still imagined the possibility of an alliance with a great eastern Christian king against the Muslim nations.

ACROSS THE OXUS INTO PERSIA

On 1 January 1256 Hulegu's army crossed the Oxus River and brought into Persia the most formidable war machine ever seen. It possessed the very latest in siege engineering, gunpowder from China, catapults that would send balls of flaming naphtha into their enemy's cities, and divisions of rigorously trained mounted archers led by generals who had learnt their skills at the feet of Genghis Khan and Subedei. As news of Hulegu's army spread he was soon presented with a succession of sultans, emirs and atabaks from as far apart as Asia Minor and Herat, all come to pay homage. Its sheer presence brought to an end nearly forty years of rebellion and unrest in the old lands of Khwarazmia, but to the inhabitants of Persia and Syria it was the dawn of a new world order.

The Mongols made first for the Elburz Mountains, where the Assassins lay in wait behind what they believed to be their impregnable fortresses. With extraordinary ingenuity the Mongol generals and their Chinese engineers manoeuvred their artillery up the mountain slopes and set them up around the walls of the fortress of Alamut. But before the order was given to commence firing the Assassins' Grand Master, Rukn ad-Din, signalled that he wanted to negotiate. Hulegu countered that he must immediately order the destruction of his own fortifications; when Rukn ad-Din prevaricated, the bombardment commenced. Under the most devastatingly accurate artillery fire, the walls quickly tumbled and Rukn ad-Din surrendered. Hulegu took him prisoner, transported him to every Assassin castle they confronted, and paraded him before each garrison with the demand for an immediate surrender. Some obliged, as at Alamut; while others, like Gerdkuh, had to be taken by force. Today the spherical stone missiles fired by the artillery teams at the walls still litter the perimeter of the ruins. Whether each 'eagle's nest' surrendered or was taken, the Mongols put all the inhabitants to the sword – even the women in their homes and the babies in their cradles.

As this slaughter continued, Rukn ad-Din begged Hulegu to allow him to go to Qaraqorum where he would pay homage to the Great Khan and plead

These large pieces of stone ordinance were carried
by Hulegu's army up the mountain slopes, along with the catapults
which would fire them, to attack the walls of the Assassins' fortress
at Alamut, in what is now northern Iran.

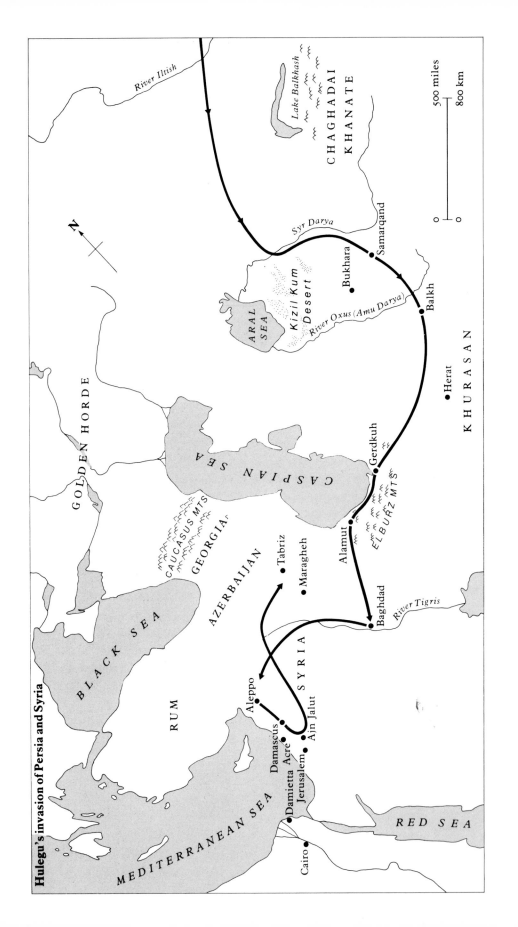

Hulegu's invasion of Persia and Syria

River Iltish

CHAGHADAI KHANATE

Lake Balkhash

500 miles
800 km

N

Syr Darya

Samarqand

Bukhara

Balkh

Kizil Kum Desert

ARAL SEA

River Oxus (Amu Darya)

KHURASAN

Herat

GOLDEN HORDE

CASPIAN SEA

Gerdkuh

CAUCASUS MTS

GEORGIA

ELBURZ MTS

AZERBAIJAN

Tabriz

Maragheh

Alamut

Baghdad

River Tigris

BLACK SEA

RUM

SYRIA

Aleppo

Ain Jalut

Damascus

Acre

Jerusalem

Damietta

Cairo

MEDITERRANEAN SEA

RED SEA

for clemency. Hulegu agreed, but when he got to Qaraqorum Mongke Khan refused to see him. It was effectively a sentence of death. On the journey back his Mongol escort turned on the Grand Master and his attendants, who were 'kicked to a pulp'. The Persian historian Juvaini commented that 'the world has been cleansed'. Five hundred years later Edward Gibbon echoed those sentiments, claiming that the Mongols' campaign 'may be considered as a service to mankind'. It took two years for the Mongols to dislodge over 200 'eagles' nests', but in the process they virtually expunged the Assassins from Persia.

THE DESTRUCTION OF BAGHDAD

In 1258, the first objective accomplished, Hulegu turned his army to the west into Mesopotamia and began the march on Baghdad. Since Hulegu had received the submission of all the petty warlords in Baiju's territory, the military governor was free to lead his *tumens* overland and link up with the main army. With further reinforcements from Christian Georgia, keen to be part of an attack upon Baghdad, Hulegu's force was virtually doubled. Demands for surrender were sent to the Caliph and refused.

The young man who currently reigned as the thirty-seventh commander of the faith was an unfortunately incompetent and cowardly individual by the name of Mustasim. His weaknesses were exploited by ruthless officials who had got used to running the city while Caliph Mustasim concentrated on spiritual affairs. As leader of the entire Sunni community he could have tried summoning Muslim armies from as far away as Morocco to defend Baghdad; instead he preferred the advice of his chief minister, Ibn al-Alkami, who assured him that the danger was not great and that the Baghdad defences were adequate. Ibn al-Alkami was at the same time sending secret messages to the approaching army, urging them to attack and describing the pitiless state of the Baghdad defences. Persian accounts of this treachery explain that the chief

Overleaf left: The standard bearers of the thirty-seventh
commander of the faith, Mustasim, the Caliph of Baghdad.
Always preoccupied with spiritual matters, he badly
neglected the defence of his city.

Overleaf right: The Mongols engaged in
the siege of a city, possibly Baghdad. Hulegu's army is
employing a pontoon bridge to cross the moat.
From a manuscript of Rashid al-Din.

وبكل الفضّ والجماله والفنّي والابله اتها لصغت على بالله فاضاعت بقض مذربجها
فنشد مذربجها فلما نسى وفربت بالرقعه دربهما وقطعه وقلت لها ان رغبت في المشوف المعلّم
واشرت الى الجّب دربهم موجى بالشّر المذهّم وان ابنا ان اترجى فى ذي القطعه واسبرجن

فالت الى اسطلاض البذر بالنّم والابلج الهم وقالت دع جد لك بنابعما بدلك فاسطع
طلع الشيخ لبلده والشّعر والشّغر وابيج بردته فقالت ان الشّيخ من اهل شروج وهو الذي وتى

minister, a Shia Muslim, had been motivated by his resentment of the Caliph's persecution of his Shia brethren. In the meantime ambassadors rode back and forth, offering to pay tribute to Hulegu but refusing to surrender, while behind the city walls there was growing fear and confusion.

When Mustasim finally gave the order that the city should be defended properly, the Mongols were just a day's march away. A contingent of some 20 000 of the city's garrison rode out to confront the enemy, but as they camped in the fields in sight of the city walls the Mongols surprised them by smashing the dams and dykes nearby and flooding the encampment. Those who did not drown were cut to pieces by the Mongol heavy cavalry.

Meanwhile Baiju's *tumens* had occupied the western suburbs which, once filled with vast warehouses, had been the great commercial heart of the city. On the opposite side, in the eastern Shia suburbs, Hulegu's engineers were constructing a ditch and a rampart that eventually surrounded the city. On 30 January the bombardment of Baghdad began. Events had moved so swiftly that the bullock carts bringing up ammunition, hewn from the Jebel Hamrin Mountains, were still three days away. So the artillery units improvised with stumps of palm trees and foundations from the occupied suburbs. Seven days later the Mongols stormed and took the east wall. There they remained, as gradually the city surrendered. As the garrison filed out, laying down their weapons, they were led away and slaughtered one by one. The Caliph eventually emerged with his family and 3000 courtiers. On 13 February, the sack of Baghdad began.

Though the city had lost its commercial importance, it remained an important cultural, spiritual and intellectual centre. Within the city's walls were magnificent mosques, vast libraries of Persian and Arabian literature, the greatest university in the world, plus numerous palaces belonging to the Caliph and his family and perhaps one of the greatest personal treasures to be found anywhere. It was the greatest city the Mongols conquered in the Middle East, and into this oasis of civilization they brought sword and torch. None of the invaders set about their task with more relish than the Christian contingent from Georgia. The Eastern Christian community hiding inside their churches were spared, but the Muslim population, Shia or Sunni, were ruthlessly dispatched. Most of the women and children were herded together and transported to Qaraqorum, as was the wealth of the Caliph's treasure house.

As the mosques and palaces burned and the cries from the street echoed into the night, the Caliph and his family were treated to a banquet with Hulegu. Afterwards they were sewn up in the customary Mongol carpet and then trampled to death under the hooves of Mongol horses, and so ended the dynasty of the Abbasid caliphs that had survived for 500 years. The treacher-

ous chief minister, Ibn al-Alkami, was rewarded by being allowed to retain his position under the Mongol rule. Persian accounts claim between 800 000 and 2 million killed within the city walls. At any rate, the stench from rotting corpses was so great that, not for the first time, the Mongols had to evacuate their campsites. Nevertheless, Persian historians tend to exaggerate the slaughter of Baghdad, for commercial evidence shows a thriving economy just two years later.

EXPEDITION TO SYRIA

Hulegu marched his army north-east towards Tabriz, where he planned to make his base in Persia. He paused briefly by the shores of Lake Urmiyeh and was impressed by the rugged beauty of a rocky island crag that loomed out of its waters. On Shai Island, a largely barren monolith heavily pock-marked with ancient rock tombs, Hulegu built a treasure house where he stored his portion of the spoils. He set up his encampment near Tabriz and waited as news of the fall of Baghdad swept through Syria and Palestine. It was one of the greatest catastrophes that had ever befallen the Islamic world. But the impact was felt far beyond Islam, for the virtual obliteration of one of the greatest cities of the world sent shock waves right across all civilization. The Mongols were again on the march.

Soon the eastern Christians who had lived under the Muslim yoke for five centuries were hailing Hulegu as a latter-day saviour, for the enemies of Christ were about to be thrown into the sea. An Armenian chronicler declared: 'During the time of Baghdad's supremacy like an insatiable bloodsucker she had swallowed up the whole world. Now she has been punished for all the blood she has spilled and the evil she has wrought, the measure of her iniquity being filled.'

As Hulegu marched into Syria, there appeared a long procession of princes come to offer rich tribute and their submission to their new lord. The Prince of Mosul presented Hulegu with a set of gold ear-rings, amongst other treasures, which he placed in the Mongol's ears himself. It was by way of a private joke between his ministers and himself, for he had once boasted that the Mongols would be no threat and that one day he would take the upstart

Overleaf: Hulegu's army was the most formidable force
ever to invade the Middle East. Alongside the traditional Mongol
skills of horsemanship, they brought with them
the very latest in siege equipment.

Hulegu by the ears. Another who came with gifts, Prince Kai-Kawus, presented Hulegu with a pair of slippers painted with the prince's own portrait on the soles, so that the Mongol might walk on his face.

In return the princes were being offered the privilege of becoming vassal lords to Hulegu and providing him with soldiers to augment his already massive host, and soon there was barely a single Muslim prince east of the Tigris who ruled without Mongol approval. There were exceptions, of course; the Prince of Mayyafarakin, Kamil Muhammad, had sworn allegiance to the Great Khan in Qaraqorum but had also provided soldiers to help defend the Caliph. When Hulegu learned of Kamil Muhammad's treachery, and that he had recently crucified a Christian priest travelling through his city on a Mongol passport, he commanded that the prince and all the inhabitants of Mayyafarakin be made an example of, a task he gave to some of the Christian contingents. King Hayton's 16 000 Armenians plus a large number of Georgians were despatched to take Mayyafarakin, which they did with some efficiency. The Christian commanders then dealt with Prince Kamil Muhammad with particular relish, first trussing the unfortunate victim like a chicken and then slicing off pieces of his flesh and feeding them to him until he was dead.

Before Hulegu set out to invade Syria the Sultan of that country, al-Nasir, sent his son to negotiate with the Mongol commander. He came claiming that his father wanted to make peace and to offer tribute to the Great Khan in Qaraqorum. Hulegu's reply, written in the most eloquent and flowing Persian prose, simply informed Sultan al-Nasir that he was 'doomed to fall'. Submission would not be enough; Hulegu meant to rule Syria. The Sultan's resources were in a terrible state since he had recently fought and lost a war with the Mamluks of Egypt, causing him to cede territory in Gaza and Jerusalem. Now the Mongols, with an army fast approaching a staggering 300 000, were demanding his immediate surrender – an act he knew would result in his execution. In desperation the Sultan turned to his erstwhile enemies in Cairo, thinking that as fellow Muslims they would come to his aid. In the meantime he had sent a suicidal letter, rejecting Hulegu's terms and defiantly demanding that the Mongols depart from his kingdom. But it all went terribly wrong when the Mamluks, who were just as intimidated by the Mongol presence, showed no interest in coming to the Sultan's defence.

Meanwhile, the mighty citadel at Aleppo had digested the news from Baghdad and defiantly prepared for the coming onslaught. On 12 September 1259, Hulegu swept across the Tigris, marching through Harran, Nasibin and Edessa. As news spread that they had crossed the Euphrates on a pontoon bridge at Manbij, the Church of the East hailed its imminent return to Jerusalem. Sultan al-Nasir had long since fled to Damascus, leaving the

Aleppo garrison in the hands of his elderly uncle, Turan Shah. The old man had reasoned that the best form of defence was attack and despatched a large contingent of his force to confront the Mongols in the open. As had happened at Baghdad, the defenders were ambushed and destroyed.

Outside Aleppo, the Mongols drew up a score of artillery teams to demolish the city walls. The bombardment lasted seven days, and on 20 January 1260 they occupied the city. Inside the great citadel the elderly Turan Shah and what remained of the garrison held out for another four weeks, while in the streets below Muslim men were being put to the sword and the women and children were herded out to be transported to Qaraqorum as slaves. Eventually the citadel surrendered. As a mark of respect for the way the old man had defended his post, the Mongols spared Turan Shah's life. When news reached Damascus that Aleppo had fallen, the Sultan abandoned that city too.

As al-Nasir made his way towards Egypt, the only sanctuary left to him, the great city of Damascus surrendered itself to the forces led by Ked-Buqa. His triumphant entry was made into an all-Christian affair, as Muslims were made to bow before the cross which was carried in procession through the streets. Behind it marched a unique Christian alliance: Ked-Buqa, a true eastern Christian; King Hayton of Armenia; and his father-in-law Count Bohemund, the veteran crusader from Antioch. To add insult to injury, a mosque was converted into a church in which was held a celebratory mass.

In the meantime Hulegu's patrols had been despatched to hunt down their quarry, the Sultan al-Nasir. He was pursued through Samaria and as far south as Gaza, where he was finally captured. As al-Nasir was being transported to Hulegu's camp, the Mongol had already sent a final threat to the last remaining Islamic force of any consequence – the Mamluks:

> You have heard how we have conquered a vast empire and have purified the earth of disorders which tainted it. It is for you to fly and for us to pursue, and whither will you fly, and by what road will you escape us? Our horses are swift, our arrows sharp, our swords like thunderbolts, our hearts as hard as the mountains, our soldiers as numerous as the sand. Fortresses will not detain us, nor arms stop us: your prayers to heaven will not avail against us.

Then he reminded them (as if they needed it): 'At present you are the only enemy against whom we have to march.'

Overleaf: The citadel at Aleppo. The Mongols were so impressed with the way in which the garrison defended its post that they spared the life of the commander Turan Shah.

The rapidly changing situation was giving some pause to the remaining crusader forces still entrenched behind their vast fortifications along the Mediterranean coast. Count Bohemund's loyalty during the campaign in Syria was rewarded when Hulegu bequeathed to him the lands between Aleppo and the narrow strip of coast he already occupied. It seemed as though Christendom's prayers were being answered. But even as this news reached Rome, it was followed by the report that Bohemund, under Hulegu's direction, had installed a Greek Orthodox bishop as patriarch of Antioch in place of a Catholic. To Rome this was a heresy; to Hulegu it was simply traditional Mongol impartiality towards all religions. Nevertheless it sent a confusing signal to the western Christian community, especially that small band of crusader states along the Palestinian coast who had become locked in a fierce debate about the Mongol invasion and what it meant to their future.

To everyone in the Middle East it was obvious that Islamic power stood at the precipice: one more significant Mongol victory, and Islam as a political power would be finished. The eastern Christian forces that had campaigned with the Mongols were convinced that the entire expedition was nothing less than a Christian Crusade to rid the Holy Land of Islam – or so they had believed since King Hayton's secret visit to Qaraqorum. So far the campaign had every appearance of having been Christian-inspired: Christians had been spared in Baghdad, Aleppo and Damascus; Christian churches were being repaired and the Mongols were giving every indication that they wanted an alliance with the crusader states in the next phase of their campaign. Hulegu, King Hayton and Count Bohemund were at that very moment planning the march on to Jerusalem and its long-awaited return to Christendom.

MONGOL RETRIBUTION IN POLAND

However, behind their crusader castle walls, from Krak des Chevaliers to Acre, the argument raged: should western Christendom throw its lot in with this new superpower, or stand back and remain impartial? Those crusaders like Anno von Sangherhausen, the Grand Master of the Teutonic Knights, who were more familiar with the eastern Christian community, were inclined to encourage an alliance. However, the signals from Rome itself were unequivocal: the Mongols were pagans and were not to be trusted. Whatever the views of the eastern Christians, they were of no consequence when the crusaders took their orders from Rome.

There was good reason for Rome's intransigence, for there had been a fresh Mongol incursion into Europe, rekindling old fears of another invasion. Four years after Mongke had come to the throne in Qaraqorum, Batu Khan

of the Golden Horde had died. Over the next three years the khanate passed from Batu's son to his grandson in quick succession, until in 1257 it finally rested with Batu's younger brother Berke. During this period of instability, and especially while much of the army was abroad with Hulegu in Syria, a number of Russian princes saw an opportunity to overthrow the Mongol yoke. Prince Daniel of Galicia, supported by Prince Mendovg of Lithuania, had driven out the Mongol outposts in Volhynia but failed to gain any further territory and retired their forces to the fortified cities of Galicia.

When Berke Khan finally came to power, he wasted no time in gathering together a force large enough to mete out the appropriate punishment. Burundai, the Mongol commander in charge of the exercise, swept through Volhynia and Galicia, forcing all the cities there to destroy their fortifications. In pursuit of the errant princes, and perhaps also to warn off any neighbouring state still harbouring similar ambitions, Burundai took his army into Poland. The destruction he left behind was far greater than that caused during the invasion of 1241. All the towns and villages of northern Poland were destroyed, as were the cities of Lublin, Sandomir and the hapless Cracow – which had hardly recovered from the last encounter. Thousands were slaughtered before Burundai rode back into Russia, having encountered virtually no opposition.

The new Pope, Alexander IV, had implored the neighbouring states to come to Poland's aid, but once again there was no response. In desperation he proclaimed yet another Crusade against the Mongols, which would have meant in effect an invasion of Russia; but there were no volunteers. The only significant act he could accomplish was to excommunicate Count Bohemund for having fought beside the pagan Easterners in Syria, and it was this which had the greatest influence upon the crusader states in Palestine. The news arrived just as the crusader lords were debating an alliance and virtually sealed the issue. At any rate, all the evidence suggested that the Mongol forces were about to deal the death blow, so crusader neutrality would be of no consequence.

AN UNLIKELY ALLIANCE LEADS TO VICTORY

Then, around February 1260, just as Hulegu and his generals were calculating the next stage of their campaign, the march on Jerusalem, a rider entered the Khan's camp with news from China. Since autumn the year before messengers had been making their way along the great Mongol *Yam*, the system of highways and staging posts that embraced the breadth of Asia, to bring the news to the farthest outposts of the empire. While engaged in the campaign

against the Sung, Mongke Khan had contracted dysentery and died. In an uncanny repetition of history, Mongke Khan's death saved Islam from certain extinction just as Ogedei Khan's demise had saved Europe from Batu's hordes, for upon hearing the news Hulegu immediately withdrew the bulk of his forces from Syria and regrouped around Maragheh, where he sat and pondered the situation.

With Hulegu's withdrawal the military landscape was transformed. He had left his redoubtable commander, Ked-Buqa, in Damascus with a small fragment of the once great army to stand at the frontier of his empire. The first to test the Mongols' strength were two crusader lords, Julian of Sidon and John of Beirut, who led raids into Mongol territory. Ked-Buqa's retaliation led to the sack of Sidon and the total destruction of an army of Templars led by John of Beirut. The crusaders reeled in fright. But the Mongol action had fully revealed their strength – or, more to the point, their weakness – and news soon spread. As the Mamluks were pondering Hulegu's demand for surrender, sent before his withdrawal from Syria, they learned that a much-depleted contingent was all that held the Mongol frontier. Having assumed they would soon have to defend their capital, the Mamluks now decided to throw caution to the wind and march out to meet the Mongols on their own territory. There would

Above: Two warriors practising their swordsmanship, from a Mamluk manual of cavalry tactics. The Mamluks were the only cavalry force that might have been a match for the Mongols.

Left: Krak des Chevaliers in Syria. The largest of the Crusader fortifications in the Middle East, it was abandoned when the Mamluks finally overran the rest of the Christian enclaves.

never be a better opportunity to throw back the invader, and they signalled their intentions by executing the Mongol envoys and impaling their heads on the spikes of one of Cairo's gates.

The Mamluk commander, Qutuz, had become fired with what he saw as his mission to save Islam and civilization. In an audacious move he sent emissaries to the crusaders, asking for an alliance against the Mongols. Barely able to believe this token from Islam, the crusaders struggled to produce a response. Despite the recent Mongol raids, there were still Christian voices arguing that an alliance with the Mongols was the best chance of ridding the Holy Land of Islam. Whether they realized it or not, as they debated the merits of an alliance with either the Mongols or the Muslims the crusaders were in fact weighing up the future of Christianity and Islam in the Middle east. In the event, the memories of Sidon were too fresh for the pro-Mongolists to have prevailed, and while the crusaders found it impossible actually to fight with the Mamluks, they did eventually send word to Qutuz that they would at least not impede his army's journey north into Syria. It was an absolutely crucial decision.

Qutuz led his army north through Gaza, where they encountered and destroyed a small Mongol force out on a long-range patrol. Encouraged, the Mamluks moved further north, passing through Christian-held territory where they received supplies and fresh horses. While Qutuz and his generals were enjoying crusader hospitality at Acre, Ked-Buqa led his two *tumens*, perhaps no more than 15 000 men, out of Damascus and headed south-west. Amongst his army was a large contingent of native Syrian conscripts. On 3 September 1260 Ked-Buqa crossed the River Jordan and began his final march towards the Mamluk army.

Qutuz in the meantime had also advanced, and the two forces drew up in the valley where legend held that David had slain Goliath. At Ayn Jalut, Goliath's spring, the Mongols finally encountered the Mamluk vanguard. Ked-Buqa ordered a charge, and the Mamluk vanguard turned and fled. But the Mongols had fallen for one of their own tactics, for they were led straight into the main Mamluk force spread thinly across the 6-km (4-mile)-wide valley. Accounts vary about the sizes of the two forces, but what is known is that at some point in the proceedings, possibly as the Mongols discovered they had charged into a trap, the Syrian contingent broke ranks and fled the field. From that moment the Mongols were at a great disadvantage.

Realizing that he was now committed to engaging the entire Mamluk force, Ked-Buqa ordered his ranks to charge the Mamluk flank. This they did, turning it and eventually destroying the Mamluk wing. Qutuz despaired at the lost advantage as the battle swung first one way, then the other. For either side

it was a fight to the death, and for most of the day the result might have gone either way. But then two events occurred that decisively turned the tide. As the Mamluk ranks appeared in danger of being routed, Qutuz is reported to have thrown his helmet to the ground and implored his troops to regroup and renew the fight. He reminded them that they were fighting not simply for their lives, but for the very future of Islam. Fired by his call, the Mamluks regrouped and charged the Mongols' ranks. At the same time, fortune struck against the Mongols as their commander Ked-Buqa fell in combat. There is a conflicting report that he was actually captured by the Mamluks and executed on the battlefield; but whatever the case, the result was the same. Against overwhelming odds the Mongol generals finally lost their nerve, turned the army and retreated. They were pursued for 12 km (8 miles) to the town of Beisan, where they drew up to face the Mamluk cavalry. But they had already lost the momentum, and the resulting clash decimated the Mongol ranks. Within days a Mamluk messenger, bearing Ked-Buqa's head on the end of a staff, returned to Cairo to spread the news. Qutuz was about to enter Damascus in triumph.

What had happened in the valley of Ayn Jalut was one of the most significant battles in world history. Although the battle itself was not conclusive – it did not sweep the Mongols from the Middle East – it nevertheless utterly smashed the myth of Mongol invincibility. They were just as fallible as any other army, and subject to the same twists of good and bad fortune. Ayn Jalut also marked the end of any concerted campaign by the Mongols to conquer that part of the world. After Damascus was taken by the Mamluks, and soon afterwards Aleppo, the Mongols sent contingents back into Syria to conduct revenge raids – but there was no sign of a co-ordinated reconquest. All this was not, however, due to Mamluk hegemony alone. The Mamluks had not encountered the full weight of the Mongol force, and never would. There were other reasons for Hulegu's reticence – reasons related to events that were unfolding on the other side of Asia.

KHUBILAI KHAN
AND CHINA

T THE DEATH OF EACH KHAN IT WAS Mongol custom for the widow to rule as regent until the question of his succession had been settled; this policy provided women with a brief opportunity to exercise some influence over the direction of the empire. Unfortunately, during the regencies of Toregene and Oghul-Ghaimish their energies were largely devoted to securing the succession of their favourite sons. However, by far the most influential woman at the Mongol court never actually reigned as regent.

Sorghaghtani Beki, Tolui's widow, bore him four sons before he died, probably of alcoholic poisoning, around 1233. Soon afterwards, Ogedei tried to get Sorghaghtani to marry his son Guyuk – a union between aunt and nephew – in the hope of uniting the two houses of Tolui and Ogedei; but the good widow declined. Her commitment to her children, she explained, prevented her from accepting the responsibility of marriage. One suspects it was more political than maternal instincts that obliged her to turn down the proposition.

As time passed, it became obvious that the qualities that distinguished the sons of Tolui were entirely the result of Sorghaghtani's influence. Throughout the reigns of Ogedei and Guyuk she emerged as easily the most accomplished, learned and certainly the wisest woman in the Mongol court, and as she aged so her importance grew. Rashid al-Din, the Persian historian, described her as 'extremely intelligent and able and towered above all the women in the world'. A poet of the age waxed even more lyrically: 'If I were

194

to see among the race of women another woman like this, I should say that the race of women was far superior to that of men!' One can only speculate how she might have directed the course of the empire had she, a lifelong Christian, managed to rule as regent. How differently might she have received the various papal envoys. But it was not to be.

Instead, Sorghaghtani devoted herself to the education and development of her four sons: Mongke, Khubilai, Hulegu and Ariq Boke. It was her shrewd and careful manoeuvring that forged an alliance with Batu Khan after Guyuk's death and ensured the election of her eldest son, Mongke, as Khan in 1251. Unfortunately the great woman died a year later, surviving only just long enough to share in her son's triumph and to see the empire once again striving to expand. Nevertheless, her influence was felt long afterwards through the actions of her children: a Great Khan who was to revitalize the empire; Hulegu, who conquered Persia, Mesopotamia and Syria; Ariq Boke, another great commander steeped in Mongol lore and tradition; and of course Khubilai, also a gifted warrior, arguably the most learned and most cultured, and easily the most sophisticated of the four.

CHINESE INFLUENCES

Sorghaghtani gave birth to her second son in 1215 at Chung-tu, while her husband and father-in-law were on campaign in northern China. Khubilai was brought up to ride and shoot, as every Mongol was, but Sorghaghtani was also at pains to ensure that he was literate and so from childhood he was attended by tutors who were either Uighurs or Chinese. His early life was spent on his mother's appanage in northern China, and when he was old enough he moved to his own large tract of territory in the Hopei region. Under his mother's tutelage Khubilai became deeply concerned with the administration of his lands, and in particular with the wellbeing of his peasants, who at that time were abandoning their farms and migrating elsewhere. Sorghaghtani taught him to appreciate that the peasantry were leaving because Mongol taxes were far too high, and that, unless something was done quickly, soon there would be no one left to tax. Khubilai dismissed the Mongol tax merchants and installed Chinese officials, who brought in a more affordable and productive tax regime. Soon the young Khubilai drew the attention of his contemporaries because both his attendants and advisers were mostly Chinese. It was not long before other Mongols complained that not only did he spend most of his time in China, hardly ever visiting Qaraqorum, but that he actually seemed to identify with his Chinese subjects.

Despite these complaints, when Mongke Khan set in motion the long-

overdue campaign against the Sung he gave his brother Khubilai command of an important part of the campaign: the capture of the kingdom of Ta-li, south of Szechwan Province at the eastern end of the Tibetan Plateau. It was a daunting objective. The kingdom of the Ta-li was strategically vital, coveted by both the Mongols and the Sung as it provided access from the khanate of the Great Khan to the western territories of the Sung empire, and to Burma and Thailand. Populated by a mixture of Tibetans, Central Asians and a heavy suffusion of Chinese, it remained vigorously independent. Khubilai's first obstacle was to march his army all the way from the northern plateau, down through Szechwan and into the mountains of the Tibetan Plateau. Having accomplished this, he and his generals successfully, and somewhat uncharacteristically, subdued the Ta-li with the minimum of bloodshed. It was a huge military success, placing Khubilai amongst the already long list of great Mongol commanders. Mongke Khan rewarded him with even more land to add to his already considerable *ulus* in northern China, to which he returned with his Chinese advisers to begin long-term plans.

The most significant decision he made after his return was to demonstrate his growing commitment to the lands he governed by ordering the construction of a capital. To the Chinese it seemed a perfectly reasonable act, but to the Mongols in Qaraqorum it was an extremely provocative decision. To avoid provoking too much outrage, Khubilai went to some trouble finding an appropriate location – roughly on the frontier between the steppe and the western edge of Chinese agrarian territory, north of the Luan River and about ten days' ride from the town of Chung-tu. However, his concern for Mongol sensibilities eluded him when it came to its construction, for what emerged was a classic Chinese imperial city in all but name.

He had turned to his most important Chinese adviser, Liu Ping-chung, to supervise the design of what was to be known as K'ai-p'ing. Liu created a walled city based on the Chinese principles of geomancy: a near-perfect square with each side facing one of the four points of the compass. There were in fact three separate walled compounds, one inside the other, containing the Outer City, the Imperial City and, in the very heart of the complex, the Palace City. However, it was in the design of the buildings, halls and temples that made up the Palace City that Liu's influence was most strongly felt. He had called for the construction of eight large Buddhist monasteries in the 'eight corners' of the city, that is at the four cardinal points of the compass and the midpoints in between. These eight points corresponded with the eight fundamental trigrams of the *Yi Jing* (*Book of Changes*), the Confucian book of divinations. It could not have been more Chinese. Against the northern wall stood the largest building, the Da'an Ge, a large central hall for audiences and

banquets. It was built by Chinese craftsmen and painters, including the famous artist Wang Zhenpeng who had joined Khubilai's employ.

Ten years after construction began Khubilai renamed the city, giving it the Chinese title Shang-tu (Upper Capital), and it was this that was described by Marco Polo as containing rivers and forests running with game, which the Great Khan hunted for sport. In his account Polo mistranslated Shang-tu, calling it Ciandu – which, of course, the poet Coleridge eventually transformed into Xanadu. The groves and fields, 'where Alph the sacred river ran', were laid out in the 6½ hectares (16 acres) that made up the Outer City. It was the Khan's hunting park, an artificial steppe environment that was Khubilai's token affirmation of his Mongol origins.

But long before Khubilai had renamed the city Shang-tu its mere existence aroused opposition at Qaraqorum. To the traditionalists Khubilai had gone native – he had more then identified with his subjects, and seemed utterly infatuated with the attractions of Chinese civilization. To have a prince of the empire building a city in China was bad enough, but when reports arrived that it rivalled Qaraqorum with its marbled halls and magnificent temples it was seen by Mongke Khan's advisers as a challenge to the traditional Mongol way of life. Soon the Khan was hearing that his brother had dispensed with fundamental Mongol taxation policies and was exercising Chinese laws. Inevitably there were charges of treason, and soon a rift developed between the two brothers that threatened to break out into open conflict. At one point plots were even laid to have the young upstart assassinated, but in the event the sibling bonds proved too strong and eventually there was a reconciliation.

It appeared, for a time, as though the conservatives in Qaraqorum had been silenced. Khubilai relinquished some of his tax-gathering powers, and in 1257 the two brothers resumed the campaign against the Sung; Khubilai was once again entrusted with a large contingent of the army. The campaign was an ingenious one, involving the co-ordination of two separate attacks: one from the north and the other, by Khubilai, from the west. Everything progressed well, with Khubilai having the best of the military encounters. But

Overleaf: Marco Polo and his brothers presenting
the Papal letters to Khubilai Khan. Khubilai so took to the Italian travellers
that he kept them in his service in the Far East for seventeen years.
From an English manuscript, *Le Livres du Graunt Caam*
(The Book of the Great Khan), c.1400.

then, with the Mongols on the path to victory, on 11 August 1259 Mongke Khan died of dysentery in the hills at Tiao-yu Shan.

CIVIL WAR OVER THE SUCCESSION TO THE KHANATE

As has been seen, the news brought Hulegu's breathtaking campaign in the Middle East to a juddering halt, with terrible consequences for the Mongol presence there. But Mongke Khan's untimely death had even more dire consequences: it exposed once again the chaotic and unwieldy process of succession and presented an opportunity for the disaffected elements in Qaraqorum to challenge Khubilai openly. Although none of the other great houses of Genghis – Ogedei, Chaghadai or Jochi – presented a serious challenge, the absence of Sorghaghtani's influence over her children meant that the question of succession degenerated into a violent dispute amongst siblings that eventually heaved the empire into civil war.

When news reached Khubilai of his brother's death, he had been leading his army southward in preparation for the co-ordinated attack and had just reached the northern banks of the Yangtze River. But instead of returning north to be present at a *quriltai*, Khubilai decided to press on with his part of the campaign. He was keenly aware of the opposition in Qaraqorum, and probably reasoned that if he secured a spectacular new victory against the Sung it would ensure his success. It was a crucial decision – and a bad one.

For the next two months he campaigned deeper into Sung territory, crossing the Yangtze and eventually laying siege to the heavily fortified town of O'chou. As the Mongols settled in for what looked like being a long siege, the Sung sent forth emissaries in the vain hope that a bribe might send the Mongols away – but times had changed. Khubilai spurned the offers and, thinking time was on his side, decided to sit and wait.

Unfortunately, in those precious months when he was camped outside the walls of O'chou, dramatic moves were taking place back in Mongolia. During all the years that Khubilai and Hulegu had been abroad in China and Persia their youngest brother, Ariq Boke, had remained in the Mongol heartland. His had been a far more parochial upbringing surrounded by a far more conservative nobility – and he had emerged as the representative of traditional Mongol values. To those at court who felt isolated from the new power centres and who despised Hulegu and Khubilai as having betrayed the Mongol ethic and succumbed to the soft life in the towns and cities, Ariq Boke became the champion to drag the empire back to its origins – by force if necessary. Powerful figures in Qaraqorum had flocked to Ariq Boke's side: the late Mongke Khan's sons; one of his widows; the grandchildren of Ogedei,

Chaghadai and Jochi; plus many important officials and advisers. They had secretly begun to raise an army, and by November were already marching on K'ai-p'ing and Chung-tu.

When word reached Khubilai he must have cursed the fates, for just as the first major Sung city was about to fall he had to abandon his campaign, and most of the lands he had conquered, to return to his own backyard. Having garrisoned K'ai-p'ing he cloistered himself with his advisers to plan the next move. They unanimously agreed that Khubilai must establish his authority as quickly as possible; so he called a *quriltai* and had himself elected Great Khan on 5 May 1260.

It was another wrong move. Instead of riding to Qaraqorum with his army, confronting his detractors and demanding a *quriltai*, he immediately laid himself open to charges of having usurped the position of Great Khan. His *quriltai* contained none of the major Mongol nobility, and moreover it had been convened on foreign soil. Everything about it was illegitimate. With Qaraqorum now in open revolt Khubilai's response was to appear even more Chinese than before, exhorting his Chinese subjects to come to his aid. In return he offered a reduction in taxes, food for the hungry and a promise to reunite the country. They were the words of a typical Chinese emperor; he could hardly have done a better job of inciting Qaraqorum, and what followed was four years of civil war.

In confronting the forces in Mongolia, Khubilai's strategy was to expose their fundamental weaknesses: their lack of indigenous supplies, especially of grain and manufactures. Qaraqorum had always been a city with little inherent reason for existence save the Great Khan's wish it be so. It survived only because of a massive and regular flow of food and other supplies from northern China and elsewhere. With that source cut off and Qaraqorum totally isolated, Ariq Boke became desperate. He turned to Central Asia, to the great fertile lands in the south-west that lay in the control of the Chaghadai khans. An opportunity to concoct an alliance arose when the incumbent khan suddenly died. Ariq Boke urged one of his entourage, Alghu – as it happens a grandson of Chaghadai – to lay claim to the khanate. Once Alghu had been duly elected, Ariq Boke would effectively extend his command over nearly a quarter of Asia.

On the other side of Asia, near the shores of Lake Urmiyeh, Hulegu watched with growing anxiety as the war between his brothers developed. Having declared his support for Khubilai, he had become somewhat anxious about his own position. Technically his entire campaign in Persia had been to extend Mongke Khan's lands in the West. Nevertheless, he clearly had ambitions to become a khan himself and to rule the lands he had just

conquered. But if Ariq Boke and the forces from the capital prevailed, he must expect to lose everything. The news that Ariq Boke had apparently extended his rule to the Chaghadai khanate, through his vassal Alghu, did not augur well.

An added complication was Berke, Khan of the Golden Horde. As a Muslim, Berke had been deeply pained by the destruction his cousin had wrought on Islamic civilization. The Mamluks, aware of Berke's sentiments, had sought to build an alliance with the Mongol Khan. By 1260 the Mamluks had a new leader in the form of Baybars, who had come to power after a coup d'état. It was he who had secretly sent ambassadors to Berke, urging him to join them in a holy war against Hulegu. Berke agreed, and set about putting together an army large enough to move on Hulegu.

Within two years the internal strains, petty jealousies, cultural divisions and craven greed of the various power groups were wrenching the empire apart. Not only were Mongols fighting Mongols in the very heartland of the empire, but now an alliance had been made by one Mongol ruler with non-Mongols against a fellow Mongol ruler. In the midst of this maelstrom Hulegu put aside his ambitions to reach the Mediterranean, concentrated on defending his territory from Berke's forces and sought allies wherever he could find them.

In 1262 Hulegu wrote to Louis IX, proposing that the King of the Franks join forces with him against the Mamluks. Unfortunately, there is no record of the King's response. These years proved to be Christendom's last gasp in Palestine. With solid Christian help Hulegu might have been able to sweep the Mamluks out of Syria and Palestine. But instead, having shattered two great myths about the Mongols – their invincibility, which lay buried in the sand at Ayn Jalut, and their solidarity, destroyed by the alliance with Berke Khan – the Mamluks now felt omnipotent and were determined to rid the whole of the Middle East of infidels. The first to go would be the last remaining crusader strongholds along the Mediterranean coast.

When Hulegu died in 1265, followed soon afterwards by his Christian wife Doquz-Khatun, the eastern Christian community mourned the death of a latter-day Constantine and Helena – their last hope of regaining Jerusalem. Nevertheless Hulegu's son, Abaqa, continued his father's policies with equal enthusiasm. He carried the war up to Berke and at the same time sent ambassadors to the Vatican, still hoping to enlist the Pope's support for an

Portrait of Khubilai Khan from
the National Palace Museum, Taipei.

alliance against the Mamluks. Abaqa believed absolutely, and perhaps naïvely, that Christendom would eventually realize that they shared the same objectives. But the Pope was not easily persuaded. The Christian community in both Palestine and Europe still nursed memories of innumerable Mongol attacks and were convinced that, if they assisted the Mongols in dealing with the Mamluks, it would only be a matter of time before the Mongols turned again upon Christendom. So Abaqa received no help from Europe, and the Mamluks were unimpeded in extending their influence up and down the Mediterranean coast.

Abaqa had no choice but to concentrate on the threat from Berke, which was precisely what the Mamluks had intended when they sought the alliance with the Golden Horde. Both khanates had amassed such enormous armies that at times it looked as though the empire was doomed to disappear in an almightly conflagration. At one point Berke led an army of more than 200 000 while Abaqa stood before another army almost as large. However, the holocaust failed to ignite because of the sudden death of Berke in 1267. His successor, Mongke-Temur, though also a Muslim, had no will to prosecute the war and he withdrew. By now the war in the Mongolian homeland had also been concluded.

Ariq Boke had begun the war with great optimism, but as it unfolded it became apparent that he had neither the wit nor the resources to defeat Khubilai. His great scheme to provide himself with supplies from the Chaghadai khanate failed because his erstwhile client, now Alghu Khan, proved a less than reliable ally. Having been promoted from retainer to khan almost overnight, the young man's ambition suddenly knew no bounds: taking advantage of Ariq Boke's vulnerability, Alghu Khan launched an attack against his former patron. Ariq Boke was soon waging a desperate and ever more hopeless campaign, bereft of supplies and with limited manpower. As the tide turned against him even his staunchest supporters melted away. So as Ariq Boke was trying to cope with this treacherous upstart on his western frontier, Khubilai advanced steadily from the east. By 1264 the young pretender was forced to accept defeat and make peace.

With hostilities at an end Khubilai had effectively become the most powerful man in Asia; but if he imagined he would soon be joined by the rest of the khans at a *quriltai* to be publicly and finally proclaimed Great Khan, he was mistaken. Although no one of any significance challenged his right to be elected, nor was anyone sufficiently moved to be present at his enthronement. The joints of the great empire had been more then stressed during nearly five years of war, and to the far-flung khanate courts the long journey across Asia to witness the making of a Great Khan no longer seemed as imperative as it had

for Ogedei or Mongke. In consequence, Khubilai was surrounded by a faint whiff of illegitimacy that remained for the rest of his reign.

REFORMS AND INNOVATIONS

The empire that emerged from these wars was greatly transformed from the one that had been led by Mongke Khan during the 1250s. There was no longer, in any practical sense, a real union of khanates all subordinate under the Great Khan. Each vast khanate was now set upon its own separate path and, although they all paid nodding tribute to Khubilai, there was never again any chance of the empire uniting behind the policies of one man. The great campaign led by Hulegu into Persia was the last imperial military expedition ever undertaken in the name of a Great Khan.

Nevertheless, Khubilai was slow to appreciate the change and for some years still expected his commands to reach to the far corners of the empire. He always managed to maintain strong links with the Ilkhan in Persia; but, whether he realized it or not, the Golden Horde and the Chaghadai khanate were now beyond his reach. But this situation rarely impinged upon the life at his court, for without question his enduring preoccupation was the governance of China.

Although Khubilai was surrounded by a vast entourage of extremely skilful Chinese administrators, perhaps the most influential figure in Khubilai's court was a Mongol, his senior wife Chabi. She was a woman blessed with many of the qualities that had graced her late mother-in-law, Sorghaghtani Beki. Like her, Chabi took a great interest in the way the land was governed, often over-ruling Mongol advisers when their policies threatened to destroy the traditional Chinese agrarian economy. Chabi had long understood how enormous wealth could be generated from agriculture – something many Mongols never came to appreciate. Her influence was felt everywhere, from the day-to-day running of the court to redesigning Mongol uniforms so that they were more practical. But what set her above most of Khubilai's advisers was the vision she shared with her husband of building a new and lasting dynasty that would rank with all the great periods in Chinese history. To this end she actively encouraged her husband to emulate the great Chinese emperor T'ang T'ai-tsung.

Even though Khubilai went to great efforts to emulate past Chinese emperors, to govern the country with the best interests of the Chinese in mind and to identify closely with his Chinese subjects, he always remembered that he was a Mongol and that he reigned as Khan of Khans. His approach towards the governance of China seemed to many of his compatriots anti-Mongol, yet

although he broke with many traditional Mongol precedents and made his ambition to be Emperor of China quite clear, he did not lose sight of his responsibilities to his Mongol inheritance.

In organising his government of China Khubilai appreciated that the old Mongol habit of carving up a conquered nation into appanages for the élite, as had been done after the fall of the Chin, was hopelessly impractical. A new centralized structure had to be created, but it had to be one that ensured the Mongols retained a firm grip on the reins of power. The Mongol population in China was probably a few hundred thousand, whereas the Chinese numbered tens of millions – a daunting prospect. Khubilai adopted a great many suggestions made by his Chinese advisers about the structure of his government, but he made sure that the key positions were invariably held by Mongols or other non Chinese. He did this by introducing a blatantly racial system of classification for his subjects. He devised three, and later four, separate social strata, the most important being Mongols. These were followed by Central Asians – those who were not Mongols but who were in the Mongol service; then came the northern Chinese; and finally the southern Chinese.

Superimposed on this was a new government structure made up of three large bureaux: the Secretariat, which was responsible for all civil matters; the Privy Council, responsible for military matters; and the Censorate, the most important of the three, which supervised and reported on all government officials throughout the land. All these government departments had representatives in every province, where they executed the major policy decisions made at court. Khubilai's primary objectives, which permeated down through all government departments, were to prevent the risk of local rebellions amongst his Chinese subjects, to ensure that government officials remained loyal and incorruptible, and to encourage the economy.

The China that Khubilai inherited, that is the northern part of it, was in a desperate condition, having still not fully recovered from the ravages of Genghis Khan's campaign during the 1220s and the wars of conquest that followed under Ogedei. It is impossible to produce a precise picture of the tragedy, but statistics help to create an outline. The discrepancy of 30 million between the population before Genghis's campaigns began and that left afterwards suggests that the Mongol campaigns were virtually genocidal in

Khubilai's wife Chabi wearing the
baqtaq, the Mongol married woman's
head-dress; from the National Palace
Museum, Taipei.

character, and, perhaps in response to that, the early records of Khubilai's reign suggest that he was much distressed by the state of his realm. It might be too much to claim that Khubilai had been motivated by regret for the way in which his grandfather had prosecuted his wars; nevertheless the records show that Khubilai devoted large resources to the relief of that beleaguered population. He granted tax exemptions to areas reported to be on the verge of collapse, reduced the taxes of peasants who produced silk because of the damage their industry had suffered during the wars, delivered grain to widows and orphans, and ordered his Mongol officers not to place excessive demands on those peasants engaged in turning land back to agriculture.

To encourage farmers to return to their lands he even established an Office for the Stimulation of Agriculture – quite an extraordinary concept for a Mongol. At the same time he ordered the building of hundreds of granaries, especially in the north where famine was a constant threat, and eventually managed to organize the peasant farmers into collectives called *she*. Each *she* would be responsible for reclaiming land, planting crops, stocking lakes and rivers with fish, irrigation and flood control. The *she* had an appointed leader who had authority to reward success and punish failure. The key element here was that these were tiny self-governing groups, structures which effectively gave ordinary Chinese peasants responsibility over their own lives. The *she* also became a useful structure for maintaining control, conducting censuses, educating the masses and passing information. Khubilai even passed laws that prevented his fellow countrymen from grazing their herds on land that was controlled by a local *she*.

The Khan also developed policies for the benefit of groups with whom the Mongols traditionally had good relations – artisans and merchants. By fostering a great number of vast civil projects, he ensured there was always work for artisans and craftsmen; at the same time he created laws that restricted the chance of corruption amongst the officials who supervised their work. But even more important to the economy was his encouragement of trade with the rest of Asia.

China had always been an extremely insular nation, self-sufficient in most raw materials and deeply uninterested in the outside world. Those merchants that did wash up on China's shores were regarded with great disdain by most Confucian officials: they were either charlatans or parasites, while trade itself was thought to be a somewhat disreputable profession.

Khubilai, being a Mongol, saw merchants in a completely different light and elevated them to a very high status. There already existed a very solid relationship between the Mongol aristocracy and merchant associations, known as *ortaghs*, which were usually set up with what might be described as

Mongol 'venture capital' and which operated large trading expeditions across Asia, bringing back exotic goods and a profit for the original investors. The *ortagh* also operated in reverse, lending to the Mongol courts, especially when new conquests were being planned. In China, Khubilai eventually established an office to formalize the relationship between the government and the *ortaghs*. He actively encouraged these associations to flourish within China, where he could control both the exchange of goods and money at the border. This relationship formed part of a grander scheme to manage and formalize the entire Chinese economy.

Upon entering Chinese territory all merchants were obliged to exchange their gold and silver for paper money, which was carefully issued and controlled by Khubilai's exchequer. In fact, throughout the domain the population was encouraged to exchange precious metals for paper currency, which became the foundation of Khubilai's remarkably sophisticated economic programme. The merchants accepted these terms for the new system allowed them access to the whole of the Chinese market and facilitated internal trade; in return the exchequer maintained a tight control on inflation and was therefore a ready source of capital for future military expeditions.

The Mongol court also elevated other social groups to a new and higher status, against Confucian traditions. Along with merchants and artisans, physicians were greatly valued: Khubilai's court invited learned practitioners from both India and the Muslim lands to travel to China and practise their skills. Hospitals were built and eventually a medical academy was

A Yuan currency note. Khubilai tried to maintain a tight control over the economy and was largely successful through the innovation of paper money.

Left: Persian astronomers making calculations. Their fame inspired Khubilai to bring the most talented of them to China to help establish the Institute of Muslim Astronomy.

Right: The Gaocheng Observatory in Henan Province, one of twenty-seven observatories established by Khubilai to recalculate the Chinese calendar in an effort to improve agricultural production.

established to regulate the training of physicians. Scientists too flourished under Khubilai, especially astronomers and mathematicians.

It was in Persia that the greatest advancements in astronomy and the calculation of calendars were being realized. Under Hulegu's direction a large observatory was built at Maragheh in 1263, and by the 1260s important new discoveries were pouring forth, news of which had travelled to China. In 1267 Khubilai brought the Persian astronomer Jamal al-Din to his capital and invited him to help Chinese astronomers build the same kind of instruments that had been developed in Persia. Out of this exchange between the Great Khan's domain and the Ilkhanate, Khubilai established the Institute of Muslim Astronomy where the Chinese astronomer Kuo Shou-ching produced his famous Calendar Delivering the Seasons – which survived as the fundamental Chinese calendar for nearly 400 years.

THE NEW GREAT CAPITAL

Long before Kuo Shou-ching's great work was complete, Khubilai set his seal upon Chinese life in a way that would endure even longer: the construction of what would become the great national capital. The grandson of the great destroyer would be remembered as the great builder. The new city was situated near the old Chin capital of Chung-tu, in the most prosperous and populous part of northern China. Work on Ta-tu (Great Capital) was begun in 1266, and it was to be constructed on traditional Confucian lines, for it was Khubilai's wish that the city would eventually win the hearts and minds of the Chinese intelligentsia.

It was surrounded by a vast rammed earth wall nearly 30 km (some 20 miles) in circumference. As with K'ai-p'ing, his city at the edge of the steppe, inside the outer wall were two compounds that housed separate sections of the city. The innermost of these enclosed the Imperial City where Khubilai and his entourage lived, while beyond that wall were the various ranks of civil servants and other government officials. Beyond the outer wall, outside the city proper, lived ordinary Chinese and Central Asians.

In those respects the city was a model Chinese capital, yet it was not wholly Chinese. The chief architect, Yeh-hei-tieh-erh, was a Muslim from Central Asia and the craftsmen who worked on the site came from the four corners of the empire. Khubilai's sleeping quarters inside the palace were hung with carpets, silk screens and rugs like the inside of a typical Mongol *ger*. Although the city was laid out with traditional lakes, bridges and gardens, those gardens were dotted with Mongol *gers* where members of the royal family were expected to live. It differed from a traditional Chinese city in other aspects too.

For a start the site was chosen so that it could be well defended and would enjoy good communications with the outside world. Look-out towers were constructed at the major gates, and provision was made for a good water supply and sufficient store houses for grain.

With a workforce of nearly 30000 men the city took shape remarkably quickly. By 1271 work had already begun on the palaces and temples of the Imperial City, where Khubilai took up residence in 1274. As Ta-tu took shape, K'ai-p'ing was renamed Shang-tu (Upper Capital) and was relegated to the status of an extensive hunting residence to which the Khan would retreat during the oppressive humidity of Ta-tu's summer.

A little time after work on the city was completed Khubilai instigated the extension of the Grand Canal, an even larger project that was designed to allow the shipment of grain from the prosperous south up to the new capital. Using a staggering 3 million labourers, 218 km (136 miles) of canal were dug from Ch'ing-ning to Lin-ch'ing, allowing continuous water transportation from the Yangtze River to Ta-tu. There, by all accounts, the magnificent new city grew richer and more glorious as Khubilai's reign proceeded. It became not only the heart of Khubilai's own personal domain, but with time the capital of all China – for as work on Ta-tu progressed apace, Khubilai was putting into motion his greatest legacy.

A MIGHTY NAVAL POWER CONQUERS THE SUNG

Although Khubilai was deeply influenced by Chinese civilization, as were a large proportion of the Mongol élite who had gravitated to the new capital, he remained fundamentally a Mongol. Nowhere was that more telling than in his attitude towards expanding the empire. Since his withdrawal from Sung territory at the start of the civil war, he had attempted to induce the Sung into accepting him as their universal ruler in return for a certain degree of self-government. Although this non-belligerent approach was supported with a long list of concessions, like the release of Sung prisoners, there was no mistaking that behind Khubilai's entreaties lay the tacit threat of the Mongol's awesome military power. But the Sung could never conceive of relinquishing their sovereignty and eventually hostilities broke out again, finally exploding in 1265 when a Sung army was defeated at the coastal town of Tiao-yu shan. At that battle, Khubilai's forces captured more than 140 of the enemy's ships and in the process transformed the Mongol empire itself into a major naval power.

However uncharacteristic it may seem for a cavalry-led war-machine to fight on the sea, the Mongols nevertheless took to naval warfare just as they had

taken up other foreign fighting techniques like artillery, siege machines and gunpowder. The influence of a prominent Sung defector, Liu Cheng, was strong: he had convinced Khubilai and his generals that they would never defeat the Sung without a navy. So even before the great victory in 1265 Khubilai had been gathering together an armada, either by confiscating Sung vessels or having the Koreans build them for him. By 1268 he had put together a navy made up of four separate fleets. With this he set about the longest and, thanks to Marco Polo's account, the most famous campaign of the war.

The cities of Hsiang-yang and Fan-ch'eng lay on opposite banks of the Han River, and were effectively the final defensive positions guarding access to the Yangtze River basin – and in turn the heart of the Sung empire. Hsiang-yang was massively fortified; Rashid al-Din claimed it had a 'strong castle, a stout wall and a deep moat'. The Mongols began their campaign by laying siege to the fortress, but this proved a waste of time as the Sung were readily getting supplies by boat up the Yangtze. Khubilai's generals called for the construction of 500 boats with which to patrol the waters of the Han River, while troops moved on neighbouring Fan-ch'eng.

As the Mongol forces grew in size the Sung defenders panicked and tried to break out. Those that managed to get beyond the gates were captured and executed. The Sung then attempted to run the blockade, and sent a fleet of no fewer than 3000 ships up the Han; however, these were met and defeated by Khubilai's Korean sailors and fifty Sung vessels were captured.

Gradually the military situation developed into a stalemate. Hsiang-yang was utterly impregnable and the Sung could not be induced to surrender. They had sufficient essential supplies for a prolonged siege, and occasionally supplies managed to get through the blockade as well. The Mongols gradually succeeded in isolating the two cities from the rest of the Sung empire, but they could not actually take them. The siege rolled on, year after year, and Khubilai became more and more impatient.

Desperate for some means of breaking through, he sought help from Hulegu's son Abaqa, for it was known that the Persians had great siege engineers. In 1272, two such experts arrived at Khubilai's court and were sent on to the battle zone. These two engineers, Isma'il and Ala al-Din, surveyed the Sung fortifications and then set about designing and building a number of very large machines, a mangonel and catapult, that would hurl the most enormous missiles at the walls. According to an account of Marco Polo's visit to China, 'When the machinery went off the noise shook heaven and earth; everything that [it] hit was smashed and destroyed.' In December Fan-ch'eng fell after only a few days of shelling. New machines were constructed for Hsiang-yang, and that city fell in March the following year.

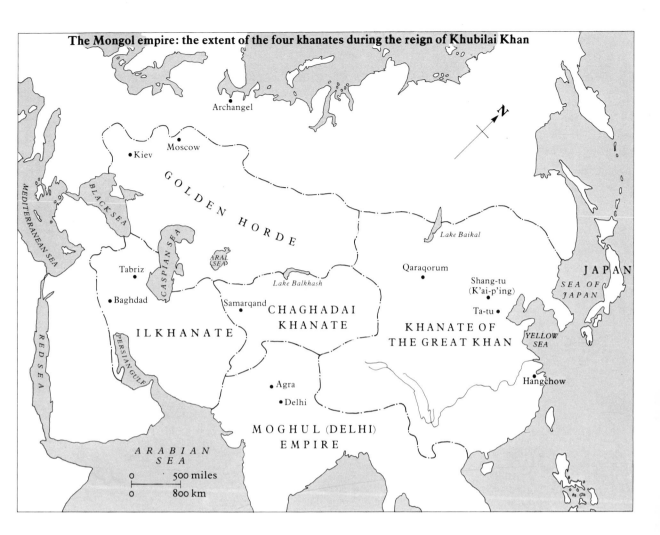

The Mongol empire: the extent of the four khanates during the reign of Khubilai Khan

Led by General Bayan, a veteran of Hulegu's campaign in Persia, the Mongol forces moved irresistibly forward towards the Sung capital of Hangchow. He crossed the Yangtze at the beginning of 1275, encountering on the far bank a huge Sung force that was routed. Tens of thousands were killed, and the main force retreated. In March 1276 Bayan encountered the Sung commander at Ting-chia chou, and again the Mongols proved unstoppable. The superior artillery and cohesiveness of their army was too much for the terrified Sung, who soon broke ranks and fled the field. In the Sung court at Hangchow there was growing consternation. Two years earlier the young emperor Tu-tsung had suddenly died, leaving heirs who were still children. His successor, Hsien, was just four years old. Actual power resided with the late emperor's mother, the Empress Dowager Hsieh. She was by now an ill old woman, growing more anxious with each piece of bad news. When Bayan's army was on the approach road to Hangchow, the Empress Dowager refused to desert the city and sent a messenger to the Mongol camp offering tribute if

215

they would abandon the war. But Bayan dismissed the offer and continued down the road.

As the pressure mounted the Empress Dowager continued to procrastinate, but eventually it all became too much for her and she conceded defeat. When the Mongol armies entered her city, instead of putting the place to the torch and slaughtering the inhabitants they behaved, for once, like a typical conquering army and set about making a survey of the city's wealth and facilities. Bayan returned to Shang-tu with the Sung royal court, where they were presented to Khubilai. Still conscious that he needed to win the support of the most highly populated country on earth, Khubilai, under very pertinent advice from his wife Chabi, treated the Sung royalty with great respect, providing them with most of their accustomed luxuries.

However, not all the Sung royal family had been transported to Shang-tu. Before Bayan's arrival at Hangchow, two half-brothers of the child emperor had escaped. En route to sanctuary the elder of the two had been crowned emperor, and he immediately became the focus of renewed Sung resistance. But in every practical sense the Sung had already been crushed, and the skirmishes that continued for the next three years were an irritating delay to the extension of Khubilai's rule over all of China. That came finally in 1279, when in a sea battle off the coast of Yai-shan the last Sung emperor was lost overboard while the Mongol fleet was inflicting another crushing defeat.

CULTURAL FLOWERING UNDER THE NEW YUAN DYNASTY

As has already been seen, long before the conquest of the Sung was complete Khubilai had already put in place a political structure that would eventually govern the whole of China. However the crowning glory of this plan, enthusiastically encouraged by Chabi, was to establish a new dynasty which would survive long after his own death. In selecting a name, Khubilai was keen that it be seen by his Chinese subjects as belonging to the long tradition of Confucian emperors – so something Chinese was essential. The choice of the word Yuan, which meant 'origin', also recalled the famous Confucian *Book of Changes*, where the term refers to the 'primal force' or the very 'origins of the universe'. In declaring his Yuan Dynasty, Khubilai was consciously employing references from classical Chinese literature to allude not only to his own pre-eminence, but to the fact that his dynasty marked the beginning of a new and politically unified China. It would remain so right up to the present.

The reign of Khubilai Khan was probably the most productive and beneficial of all the reigns of the Great Khans. Its over-riding contribution was to unite the nation and to lay the foundations for an unprecedented era of

peace and prosperity. Under Khubilai, trading links were forged with Persia and eventually Europe. Trade flourished across the great continent as it had never done in the past, not just by land but also by sea. Khubilai constructed a large merchant fleet that plied all the major ports of south-east Asia, India and the Persian Gulf. European merchants, Genoese and Venetian in particular, began to visit China – the Polos being the obvious name that springs to mind. They loom large in our image of Khubilai Khan because of Marco's account of his time in Cathay and the somewhat exaggerated claims he made about the official functions he is supposed to have carried out there. Yuan records, however, fail to register one jot of information about any of the Polos, and it would appear they were no more significant than any of the hundreds of other merchant travellers who made the arduous journey across Asia to the Great Khan's court. No one really knows how many Europeans did make that journey, but whatever the number it was nothing compared with the thousands of merchants from the Middle East and south-east Asia.

Few commodities required by the Chinese could not be provided from within their own borders. But on the other hand they produced a great deal of merchandise that found a ready market abroad. Chief amongst these, of course, was silk – an industry which the Mongols soon monopolized. No Mongol needed to be told the value of Chinese manufactures in foreign markets, and Khubilai took many measures to encourage the export of indigenous crafts. Next to silk, the most valuable commodity was ceramics. Khubilai decreed that all kilns within the country had to be licensed, regulated and taxed. At the same time his envoys promoted a thriving trade with the countries of south-east Asia and the Persian Gulf. The industry boomed, and Yuan ceramics were exported in prodigious quantities.

Khubilai also contributed to the ceramics industry in a creative way. The somewhat tedious artistic restrictions that had been imposed by previous regimes were abolished and potters were free to use their imaginations. Some breathtaking creations appeared as a result, including the famous blue-and-white porcelains which later characterized Ming work.

What happened in the potting kilns up and down the country was mirrored in many other spheres of the arts and crafts, for Khubilai's very business-minded court was also deeply devoted to the arts. Khubilai took on the patronage of a number of artists, adding greatly to the large Imperial Painting Collection that he had captured from the Sung. This had been transported to Ta-tu, where Khubilai built a special gallery to house it. As his own collection grew it soon became apparent to him and the scholars he employed that a distinctive Yuan school of painting had developed, and that examples of this style had to be preserved. Some recent scholars have even

Above: Khubilai's patronage led to a great flourishing of the visual arts.
The Mongols' favourite subject was horses, and here the painter
Liu Kuan-tao shows Khubilai himself on a hunt.

Left: Yuan Dynasty porcelain vase, 1320–50.
Knowing that Chinese ceramics were potentially a valuable export,
Khubilai encouraged potteries to open up across the country.
Artists were allowed a free hand to develop new styles and
some wonderful work was produced.

referred to a 'revolution' in Chinese painting. Again it was a question of Mongol sensibilities not having been schooled in the Chinese classics and being prepared to allow greater freedom and innovation.

When these policies were applied to the theatre, again they produced new and original works – especially as money was available to build theatres in the growing cities and to sponsor new companies. More than 160 Yuan plays have survived, plus the titles of another 500. What emerged from this canon was a range of subjects that had never been tackled on the stage before; unfettered by imperial censors, Chinese drama shed the stiff, formalized style of an earlier era and became more relaxed and accessible.

Khubilai's patronage of the arts was not simply an attempt to banish his 'barbarian' heritage; it had a political aspect to it as well. The construction of galleries, the collection of art and the production of drama all fostered a cultural atmosphere in Ta-tu which was attractive to the wealthy Sung families whom Khubilai needed to attract to his court if his reign was to have real credibility throughout the country. Having removed the barrier of the frontier, Khubilai made it not only possible but attractive for southerners to mix once again with their northern cousins. By encouraging this migration of Sung gentry up to his court, he strengthened the ties with the south and with it the legitimacy of his reign.

ILL-FATED INCURSIONS INTO JAPAN

Had Khubilai concentrated on nothing else but governing his realm, his glory and that of his dynasty might have shone longer and more brightly than it did. But as the man aged he became distracted by a need to reaffirm his Mongol origins, and so he launched a number of ill-fated military campaigns which both tarnished his reputation and almost bankrupted the country. The most famous of these were the two invasions of Japan: the first in 1274 in the midst of the Sung campaign, and the second in 1281. These expeditions were motivated by the urge to expand the empire in the great Mongol tradition. Apart from India there was precious little land in Asia that was not under Mongol rule, so the Japanese islands were the obvious solution.

Following the 'insolent' reply that the Japanese sent to his demand that they submit, Khubilai prepared for war. The recalcitrant Koreans were pressganged into providing the fleet and sailors that would carry some 20000 troops – more than sufficient to deal with the disorganized and poorly equipped Japanese. On 19 November 1274, the Mongols landed and made easy progress against the Japanese forces. But as night fell a great storm blew up; the Korean sailors insisted that the fleet put to the open sea – otherwise it

would be dashed against the rocks and their only means of retreat lost. The Mongols reluctantly withdrew from their positions and climbed back on board their vessels. What happened next is history. The ships were scattered, hundreds foundered and more than 13000 lives were lost. The invasion had to be abandoned.

In 1280, after the Sung had been defeated, Khubilai set about his revenge. Over 900 ships were gathered to carry 40000 troops from northern China, while a further 100000 Chinese would depart from the south. When they landed at Nokonshima Bay on the island of Kyushu, the Mongols found that the Japanese had built a defensive wall along the coast. For two months they battled away against the Japanese defences, when suddenly the fates intervened once again. Another typhoon blew up, and the Koreans again tried to get their fleet back out to sea. In the ensuing panic more than 60000 of Khubilai's army drowned or were slaughtered trying to get off the shore. To the Japanese this second storm served as proof that they inhabited a land that was precious to the Gods and that the storms had been 'divine winds' (*kamikaze*) sent to sweep away the invader.

Further military expeditions were despatched in the years to come, into Burma and by sea down to the island of Java, but met with little success. The triumphs that had crowned Khubilai's youth eluded him in later years, and more and more his expeditions to far-off island kingdoms seemed to lack the logic that had driven previous Mongol campaigns. As his life became filled with disappointments, especially after the deaths of Chabi in 1281 and his son Chen-chin in 1285, the great man became a recluse and withdrew from the world. He gave up hunting, became devoted to food and drink and soon became extremely overweight. He eventually died, a sad and miserable figure, in February 1294. His body was carried across to Mongolia where it was buried in what is now Hentiy province. As with his grandfather before him, no tomb was constructed above ground. The site of his burial is now lost to eternity.

Overleaf: A painting from the Japanese Imperial Collection
showing Khubilai's ill-fated invasion of Japan. A typhoon
struck the invading fleet and one third of
Khubilai's army was drowned.

221

9

DECLINE
AND FALL

ESPITE ALL THE CIVIL WARS, military setbacks and other digressions that plagued the various khanates, the reign of Khubilai Khan was nevertheless the apogee of the empire's history. He exercised nominal supremacy over the greatest land-based empire in history, and while his writ may not have extended over all the empire's subjects in central and western Asia, his supremacy was at least acknowledged by the Khans of the Golden Horde – and of course by the Mongols in Persia who remained his loyal and obedient servants. There the descendants of Hulegu had adopted the title of Ilkhans, meaning amicable or subordinate khans to the Great Khan, and at their capital in Maragheh and later in Tabriz Khubilai's viceroy maintained an imperial presence, applying Khubilai's seal to all state documents. In the words of Marco Polo, he was 'the greatest lord that ever was born in the world or that now is'.

A VAST TRADE NETWORK

Though the end of Khubilai's reign was clouded by military and personal disappointments, his singular success in reuniting China would alone have guaranteed his position as one of the great figures in world history. However, it might also be argued that by continuing the policies of his grandfather to their logical conclusion – by internationalizing the empire – Khubilai made an even greater contribution to world history. The Mongols' conviction that they

had been granted a divine mandate to rule the world presupposed that the world extended far beyond the physical reach of the Mongol armies, and Khubilai did everything he could to extend contact to the limits of the civilized world – to south-east Asia and Europe. Chinese insularity was swept aside by a flood of foreign visitors come to the seat of the Great Khan. Khubilai's merchant fleet developed important markets in India, Sri Lanka, Malaya and Java; and, because of the close links with the Ilkhanate, it also ventured as far west as the Persian Gulf, contributing to the growth of the new port of Ormuz.

Arab dhows also sailed east and became regular visitors at the ports of Hangchow, Quinsay and Zaiton, and with the construction of the Grand Canal ocean-going vessels regularly called at Ta-tu, making it one of the busiest inland ports anywhere. More than 200 000 ships navigated up and down the Yangtze each year. Silk, rice, sugar, ceramics, pearls and other precious stones were exported in return for exotic medicines, herbs, ivory and other luxuries. Chinese manufactures reached everywhere under the custody of Mongol world dominance, and for the first time in human history Europe had direct contact with Cathay, through trade. Merchants travelled the vast Mongol highways from the Crimea, through the land of the Golden Horde to Sarai and Utrar, across the Altai Mountains and into the empire of the Great Khan, to Ta-tu. Others travelled from the cities along the Yangtze across the empty steppes to Besh-balik, through the Chaghadai Khanate to Samarqand and Bukhara, and down to the cities of Persia.

APPEALS TO EUROPE

There was also an increase in diplomatic traffic between the empire and Europe, particularly to and from the Ilkhanate. This took on a more urgent character after 1260, a year in which many historians claim the serious fracturing of Mongol unity began. Before that date, most contacts had been instigated by the Pope and were devised to appease the Mongols and perhaps even effect a conversion. However, after the humiliation at Ayn Jalut the traffic was reversed; the Mongols began making serious appeals for an alliance with the Christian forces in Palestine, if that would mean the swift elimination of Muslim resistance. Following Hulegu's now famous letter to Louis IX, written in 1262, many attempts were made by both sides to establish good relations. Letters passed back and forth between the respective courts as first Abaqa, Hulegu's successor, and then in turn his successors, tried to nail down an alliance with Christendom. Europe's response was always favourable (especially if there was a prospect of some large-scale conversions), though ineffectual. No European power actually ever despatched an army, but the

Mongols were nothing if not persistent and by the time of the fourth Ilkhan, Arghun, their appeals to Europe had reached a new pitch.

In 1287 Arghun sent an emissary to Rome, an Eastern Christian monk by the name of Rabban Sauma who had travelled to the Middle East on pilgrimage from Ta-tu. Unable to reach the Holy Land because of the conflicts in Syria, Rabban Sauma was commissioned by Arghun to impress the crowned heads of Europe with how well Christianity had flourished under the empire. The envoy did just that: in Rome he took part in long theological discussions with cardinals, in Paris he was received by Philip IV 'the Fair' in the glorious Ste-Chapelle, and in Gascony he so impressed Edward I of England that he was allowed to conduct a mass and give holy communion to the King. On his return through Rome he conducted further masses during Holy Week and Easter, this time in the presence of the Pope himself, after which the cardinals rejoiced, declaring: 'the language is different but the use is the same.'

Rabban Sauma returned with an extremely positive response from Philip IV, who proposed: 'If the armies of the Ilkhan go to war against Egypt [the Mamluks], we too shall set out to go to war and to attack in common operation.' To which Arghun replied:

> . . . we decided, after consulting heaven, to mount our horses in the last month of winter in the Year of the Tiger [1290] and to dismount outside of Damascus on the 15th of the first month of spring [1291]. Now, We make it known to you that in accordance with Our honest word, we shall send Our armies [to arrive] at the [time and place] agreed, and, if by the authority of heaven, We conquer these people, We shall give you Jerusalem.

It was a time when Christianity enjoyed unprecedented acceptance right across the empire – not just in Persia, but in Mongolia and China, where Khubilai encouraged its spread as a way of improving his contacts with Europeans and so proving to his Chinese subjects that he was indeed the Great Khan of the world. Following Rabban Sauma's visit to Rome, during which he had reaffirmed the willingness of the Church of the East to accept the Pope's supremacy, a bishopric was eventually established at Sultaniyya, a new city being constructed by the Ilkhans in Persia, and another in Ta-tu itself.

The fall of Acre in 1291. Once the Mongols had withdrawn from Syria, the Mamluks were able to establish themselves as the dominant military force and they set about eliminating the Crusader presence in the Middle East.

Comment le roy saint loys en auldint retorner a dumete fut
prins. le voyn. chapre.   le filz du souldan mort. dont
pres ceste desconfitu   des parties dorient z auuia
re ainsi faitte sur   a la massore. et le receurent
les sarrazins ne   les egyptiens a grande reue
demoura gueres apres que   rence z honneur comme seur

During Arghun's reign, relations with the Pope were so strong that it must have seemed possible that the Ilkhanate might convert to Christianity. How that might have affected the course of Middle Eastern history is open to speculation, but needless to say it did not come about. The Mamluks had by March 1291 already stormed the crusader fortress at Acre, the last Christian outpost in Palestine, and within a few days Arghun had died of a long illness. His successor, Geikhatu, devoted his short life to drink and the pursuit of young boys, and never once showed the slightest interest in either war or alliances.

THE PERSIAN ILKHANATE

So for the first forty years of Mongol rule, Persia was forced to accept the demotion of Islam as the pre-eminent religion of the area. To the locals' great distress, in all the great towns and cities Buddhist temples were constructed in even greater abundance than the new Christian churches. Although some of the Ilkhans showed distinct leanings towards either Buddhism or Christianity, in the main they were fairly impartial – that is until the reign of Ghazan the 'Reformer', who became Ilkhan in 1295.

The year before, in faraway China, the great Khubilai Khan had died. Although all the other khans accepted his successor, Temur Oljeitu, as Great Khan in name, he did not enjoy anything like the same authority as his father. There would never be another universal khan at the head of the empire, and the next generation of Ilkhans never felt they had to demonstrate the same deference as had their forefathers. By the 1290s the Ilkhanate was going through a period of great internal unrest: the economy had virtually collapsed, foreign debts were not being met, and the cities were torn by riots and the threat of insurrection. This had largely been brought about by a combination of Geikhatu's heady excesses, a haphazard and somewhat ruthless form of tax collection and an ill-judged attempt to cure these ills through the forced introduction of Chinese-like paper currency to an economy that had been based upon gold and silver for more than 2000 years.

When the throne became vacant in 1295, the new pretender, Ghazan the 'Reformer', was advised that if he wanted to be khan he had better find some way of forging a link with the already restive populace, who were by now tired of being ruled by pagans. As there was no longer any need to seek Ta-tu's approval for the election of a local khan, Ghazan split with Mongol tradition and embraced Islam, as did most of his Mongol generals.

Ghazan had other changes in mind too. According to the Persian historian Rashid al-Din, who was also his chief minister, when the new Ilkhan

argued with the Mongol élite about reforming the Ilkhanate administration, he explained himself in the following words: 'If you insult the peasant, take his oxen and seed, and trample his crops into the ground – what will you do in the future?' Just like Khubilai, thirty years before, the Mongol khan had begun to identify with his subjects. Their wellbeing was equated with the wellbeing of the state. He went on: 'You must think, too, when you beat and torture their wives and children, that just as our wives and children are dear to our hearts, so are theirs to them. They are human beings, just as we are.' The influence of civilization had again prevailed over the instincts of the nomad.

Under Ghazan's firm and pragmatic government, the economy gradually improved. The system of taxation was reformed, as was the judiciary, and incentives were offered to the peasantry to return to the land. Most importantly Mesopotamia and Persia were returned to the bosom of Islam, where they have remained ever since.

Ghazan's brother, Oljeitu, was the next Ilkhan, and he too adopted the Muslim faith and continued the process of reform. However his greatest monument was built in stone: the lavish embellishment of the new city of Sultaniyya with its domed and octagonal buildings, many of which were architectural masterpieces – none more so than his own tomb, constructed in 1313. Just as Khubilai had wanted to prove himself a great builder as well as conqueror, so the Ilkhans were keen to demonstrate their wealth with lavish constructions.

The Mausoleum of Oljeitu is one of the great Islamic landmarks; its cupola stands over 75 m (nearly 250 feet) above the ground and is decorated with the most dazzling blue ceramic tiles. The windows are made of intricate cast iron, while the interior walls are decorated with typically ornate stonework. When it was built it was the largest domed cupola anywhere in the world – a breathtaking engineering breakthrough, and a milestone in Islamic architecture. It was a resoundingly pro-Islamic statement and underscores how the Mongol aristocracy in this part of the world had absorbed the Islamic culture.

This was also an era of great artistic expression in general, fostered by the Ilkhan's patronage. Poetry, painting and ceramics, but above all architecture, all flourished under the Mongols. Oljeitu's son, Abu Sa'id, who in 1316 became the first Ilkhan with an Islamic name, ruled during what was described as the 'best period of the domination of the Mongols'. The economy boomed, a treaty was negotiated with the Mamluks and Persia looked forward to peace and prosperity.

The only thing that Abu Sa'id failed to produce was an heir, and when he died in 1335 so did the house of Hulegu. There was no one to take up the

Above: The funeral procession of Ghazan
the 'Reformer'. He was the first Ilkhan to embrace Islam.
Right: Chu Yuan-chang, the first Ming Emperor.
He led the peasant revolt that turned into a united uprising
which finally overthrew the Yuan Dynasty and brought
to an end the Mongol presence in China.

reins of power, and the line of the Ilkhans abruptly ceased. The majority of the Mongol élite who had not embraced Islam had emigrated, while those who had assimilated were simply absorbed into the population. Mongol control over Persia ceased and the Ilkhanate itself disappeared. Meanwhile, Persia drifted without a unified government until another Turko-Mongol warrior, Timur the Lame, rode out of Samarqand thirty years later.

NATURAL CATASTROPHE AND REBELLION

The Ilkhanate was the first Mongol nation to collapse. The next was China. Under Khubilai's successors China, and the empire as a whole, enjoyed thirty years of stability and peace. However, following the assassination of the fifth Yuan emperor in 1323 there erupted more than ten years of factional fighting between various branches of the Mongol aristocracy. Altogether five separate descendants of Khubilai were made emperor by different warring factions. In 1333 Toghon Temur, the eleventh Yuan emperor, was crowned; and although he ruled uninterrupted for the next thirty-five years, he did so over a dynasty that was already in terminal decline.

Before his enthronement, while the Yuan factions were still squabbling amongst themselves, southern China had been racked by a series of peasant rebellions. These were not proto-nationalist movements, but uprisings born out of simple poverty. In earlier times they would have been promptly crushed, but the Mongol garrisons were no longer led by seasoned campaigners and many of the officers in charge had never actually been to war. Gradually the rebellions turned into a contagious infection of guerrilla movements that spread north until by the 1330s open civil war had become established in central China. As the Yuan authorities seemed helpless against the rebels, the local Chinese gentry raised their own private militia, thus increasing the numbers of armed soldiery in the country.

In the midst of this rising sea of troubles, a number of natural disasters struck which would have tried the strengths of even the most resilient administration. First there was an earthquake, followed by the great flood of 1352 when the Yellow River burst its banks and inundated vast tracts of countryside, bringing with it both disease and famine. To cope with the great damage the Yuan authorities set about conscripting a vast army of labourers to repair the dykes and dams. This was frustrated by yet another disaster in the following year, when a terrible pestilence swept through the country and killed enormous numbers. According to traditional Chinese superstitions, nature was no longer in harmony with the ruling dynasty, and this did not augur well for its future. Because of labour shortages work on the flood control became

haphazard. Conditions were harsh and the pay low, which led to further rebellions. Out of these new insurrections emerged a number of bandit leaders who began to attract to their cause people from different classes. Soon landowners, master artisans and even the clergy began flocking to what became a massive, yet wholly disorganized national rebellion. It had become a great popular movement against the Emperor's utterly ineffectual attempts at dealing with the various natural disasters.

By 1356 a single leader had emerged from amongst the rebel forces: Chu Yuan-chang. Under his charismatic leadership the rebellion became more focused, and soon the gentry were also flocking to his banner, now they could sense a real opportunity to be rid of the foreign dynasty once and for all. Chu Yuan-chang's forces, augmented by the numerous militia armies, marched north and eventually captured Nanking, thus cutting off supplies to the north and creating a rallying-centre for other rebel groups. With the support of the gentry his cause had acquired a degree of legitimacy, but before he confronted Yuan authority head-on he was urged to form an alternative government – and for the third time in history a peasant became the founder of a Chinese dynasty.

He chose the name Ming Hung-wu, and the motif for the new Ming Dynasty would be 'Rule Like the T'ang and the Sung'; a return to traditional Chinese values. As the Ming forces grew in strength, the Mongols lost sight of the danger they were in and became embroiled in another brief civil war, once again between the houses of Ogedei and Tolui. While the Mongols were at each other's throats, the Ming forces consolidated their hold on the south and effectively eliminated Yuan authority anywhere south of the Yangtze River. By 1368, Chu Yuan-chang was ready to march on Ta-tu, which he did virtually unopposed. By the time the Ming army had breached the city walls the last Yuan Emperor, Toghon Temur, had fled to Qaraqorum where he died in 1370.

It is no coincidence that the first khanates to collapse, the Persian and Chinese, also happened to be the most urbanized and sophisticated. In both cases the Mongol rulers were effectively overwhelmed by the difficulties of governing large sedentary societies. Though China had indeed become too much for the Mongols to cope with, their brief reign brought that society closer

Overleaf: In the sixteenth century, the Ming forces
built these defences, creating what became known as the Great Wall.
They were determined that a Mongol invasion would never again
trouble the people of northern China.

to the rest of the world than it had ever been in its entire history. Persian merchants plied their wares in its markets, designed its irrigation systems and sometimes even governed its cities. Nevertheless, most Chinese chroniclers saw the Mongol dynasty as a most disagreeable period of their history and dismissed the benefits of contact with the rest of the world as an unfortunate infection that was eventually cauterized.

The physical manifestation of their determination to keep the Mongols out was of course the construction of the Great Wall, which the new Ming Dynasty undertook in the sixteenth century. Though the Mongol empire had brought Europe into contact with China, the influences flowed almost exclusively in one direction: despite the foreign religions, merchant houses and even architecture, China remained the most culturally self-sufficient of civilizations. Most Christian and Islamic presence withered after the death of Khubilai, the last emperor with truly international ambitions. The Chinese took very little notice of Persian culture, though the Persians were influenced especially in the areas of painting and ceramics. But it was Europe that benefited and learned the most. Its knowledge of Asia expanded enormously and led directly to the great Age of Discovery. When Christopher Columbus set sail in 1492 he did so in search of the sea route to Cathay, the land of the Great Khan.

THE GOLDEN HORDE

In contrast with Persia and China, the Mongols in central Asia and Russia put down very deep roots. After the great campaign through Poland and Hungary in 1242, Batu made his base in the lower Volga region and eventually laid the foundations of the city of Sarai, situated on the banks of the Akhtuba River. From here he maintained control over the Russian princes and watched the traffic of merchants and envoys that proceeded from Europe across the steppe to Qaraqorum and China. With the rich tribute he extracted from the Russian states, the Golden Horde – as the Russians came to call Batu's khanate – grew fabulously rich.

However it was Batu's younger brother, Berke Khan, elected in 1257, who finally determined the territory of the Golden Horde. Its heart lay in the lower Volga and extended to the steppes around the rivers Don and Dnieper, the Crimean peninsula, the northern slopes of the Caucasus Mountains and even into Bulgaria and Thrace. If anything Berke strengthened Mongol control, ruthlessly crushing the slightest hint of a rebellion amongst the Russians. He might also have launched another invasion of Europe had he not been diverted by Hulegu's savage campaign against Islam.

Being a Muslim himself, Berke had been appalled by the destruction that had been wrought upon Baghdad and the eventual quarrel that erupted between the Ilkhanate and the Golden Horde not only shelved his ambitions towards Europe, it also guaranteed the survival of the new Mamluk kingdom that had emerged from Cairo.

The next Khan, Mongke-Temur, who was a son of Batu's, led the Golden Horde into an era of great prosperity from which it emerged a real world power. Peace was agreed with the Ilkhanate, after Khubilai's insistence, while relations were maintained with the Mamluks in Egypt. Trade flourished between Egypt and Russia, and north of Batu's capital a new city was eventually constructed called Berke Sarai (New Sarai), where many of the mosques and palaces were built by Egyptian architects. But under Mongke-Temur's successors the Golden Horde never shone quite as brightly. New campaigns were launched into Poland and Hungary, but this time the Mongols were defeated and turned back; there was no Subedei to lead the armies.

In the early fourteenth century, under Ozbeg Khan, the Golden Horde officially adopted Islam as the state religion and throughout the Middle East the Muslim states rejoiced. Nevertheless, good relations were maintained with the Christian West and the Genoese strengthened their foothold at Kaffa on the Black Sea. After Ozbeg the Golden Horde seemed to wither somewhat, especially when the line of Jochi-Batu finally came to an end in 1359. Other Mongol pretenders from the Chaghadai khanate attempted to place puppet khans on the throne at Sarai, but none of these enjoyed proper power or distinction. In 1371, with the khanate appearing to disintegrate, the Russian princes refused to make their annual journey to Sarai to pay tribute, and when a Mongol army was sent to persuade them it was defeated by the Grand Duke of Moscow at Kulikovo Pole. However Russian freedom was still just a dream, for there had emerged a new power out of Transoxania that would wreak havoc throughout Central Asia.

Timur the Lame, or Tamerlane in Western literature, had been born around 1330 near Samarqand. He progressed from banditry to international conqueror in much the same way as Genghis Khan. Although he was descended from the Mongols he was in fact a Turkic Muslim, and his youth had been spent in the cities of Transoxania, not the empty steppe. He had developed a massive army, modelled along Mongol lines, and with it set out on a campaign of destruction that, by all accounts, was even worse than Genghis's excesses.

Timur's campaigns were really more like plundering raids which ex-tended throughout Khwarazmia, Transoxania and eventually, through one of

his protégés, up into Russia. Toktamish, a nephew of an earlier khan, was granted by Timur the lordships of a number of Transoxanian cities and, through Timur's patronage, was eventually made Khan of the Golden Horde in 1377. In 1381, Toktamish led an army furnished by Timur up into Russia as a punishment for the defeat at Kulikovo Pole. He left countless cities and towns in absolute ruin, pillaged Moscow and put thousands of its inhabitants to the sword. The Russian states were back to where they had been under Batu.

Later a war developed between Toktamish and his patron, which shattered the Golden Horde and left Toktamish a penniless refugee wandering the Central Asian steppe. Timur sacked Sarai, but never bothered to annex the lands of the Golden Horde. He made one determined plunge north towards Moscow, but turned back and instead set his sights on conquering China. He was on his way there in 1405 when he died. Timur had left neither government nor successors and the Golden Horde, mortally wounded, staggered on until 1419. By this time it had fragmented into a number of separate power centres, at Astrakhan, Kazan and notably in the Crimea, which survived until it was annexed by Catherine the Great. Russian independence only finally emerged under Ivan II 'The Terrible', who refused to kiss the stirrup of the Khan in 1502. No Mongol army appeared strong enough to force the Muscovites into submission, and 265 years after Batu's campaign into the West the Golden Horde finally disappeared.

THE BLACK DEATH: A GIFT FROM CENTRAL ASIA

One final legacy that the Mongols bequeathed to Europe, albeit unwittingly, sailed from the city of Kaffa, on the Black Sea, in 1346. The year before, an army of Kipchaks in the service of Janibeg Khan, the penultimate Khan of the Golden Horde, were besieging the city when a dreadful pestilence swept through their ranks. As the disease took so many casualties, the Mongol commander decided to bring the siege to a quick end before his army was itself decimated. In what must be the first recorded instance of biological warfare, the Mongol commander had the diseased corpses catapulted over the city walls and then waited for the pestilence to do the rest. From Kaffa it travelled, via Genoese merchants, along the sea routes to the Mediterranean ports of

A bust of Timur the Lame (Tamerlane)
made from his exhumed skull. This bandit from Samarqand
tried to enhance his reputation by
marrying into the Genghis dynasty.

---

southern Europe. Then it swept up through Spain and France, east into Germany, and across the English Channel to the British Isles. Even in the depth of winter it continued relentlessly into Scandinavia and even reached as far as Greenland. The Black Death, as it came to be known, was the most devastating catastrophe in European history – killing one in three of the population. Nothing ever perpetrated by Genghis, or any of his offspring, compared with the death toll caused by the arrival of this disease. It is assumed that the opening up of the trade routes from Central Asia allowed the Black Death to be transmitted to both western and eastern Asia; for just five years later, it is assumed that the same pestilence struck China during the last years of the Yuan Dynasty.

THE MOGHULS

The Chaghadai Khanate survived well into the sixteenth century, though the house of Chaghadai kept its influence far longer. The name of Genghis Khan retained an enormous reputation throughout Central Asia and helped perpetuate Mongol control in the absence of any other power. In fact, the prestige attached to the name was so great that when Timur set about his career he concocted a number of ways of either marrying into the house of Genghis, or at the very least maintaining members of the family as puppets. A hundred years after Timur's death, the name Genghis still carried significance throughout Asia. In the early sixteenth century a prince of Transoxania named Babur, who was a descendant both of Timur and Genghis Khan himself, fled south to Afghanistan and eventually to India to escape the Ozbeg Turks.

Babur took up his Mongol heritage by carving out an empire for himself in northern India, where he established the great Moghul Dynasty (Moghul being the Persian pronunciation of Mongol). He conducted a campaign against the ruling Lodi Dynasty, and captured their capital, Agra, in 1526. Following the defeat of Sikandar Lodi, Babur sent his son to Agra to secure the Lodi treasury. There the son is said to have discovered the Maharani of Gwalior cowering with her family. According to legend, she apparently offered him a huge diamond if he would spare her and her family; it was the famous Koh-i-noor, now among the British crown jewels.

Babur spent the last years of his life at Agra, where he constructed a wonderful garden, one of four famous Moghul *char baghs*, in Agra. The Moghuls went on to construct some of the most magnificent palaces and fortresses in India, but their crowning glory was the mausoleum built for the Mumtaz Mahal, wife of the fifth emperor, Shah Jahan. The great Taj Mahal, the jewel of India, is a most unlikely legacy of the Mongols, those great

destroyers who first swept out of the eastern steppe. Yet there it stands on the banks of the Yamuna River, the very antithesis of its barbaric heritage.

CHINA AND MONGOLIA IN THE WAKE OF GENGHIS KHAN

Following the establishment of the Ming Dynasty in China the Mongols made a series of attempts, under various tribal leaders, to return to China and reclaim their lost power. However, they had only sporadic success; they lacked both the military and political leadership, though their armies had lost none of their fighting skills. Their most serious problem was their lack of unity, for Mongolia itself had become split between two major tribal groups, the Oirats in the west and the Khalkhas in the east, and these became the rivals for the remains of the old empire. Nevertheless Mongol raids continued into China, and in the mid-fifteenth century the Oirats succeeded in capturing the Ming Emperor. However, they lacked the leadership to take up any kind of campaign of conquest and settled for ransom.

In the seventeenth century the new Manchu Dynasty came to an accommodation with the Khalkha people in eastern Mongolia, who agreed to a loose Chinese rule in preference to accepting the supremacy of the Oirats. The western tribe had turned its attention to Central Asia, which they dominated for more than a hundred years until they were finally defeated by a Manchu army in 1758. This led to the Mongol nation undergoing an even greater division, for the rise of the Manchus coincided with the expansion of the Russian empire from out of the west. Those people in the north around Lake Baikal came under Russian control, while those south of the Gobi Desert were dominated by China. This situation continued right into the twentieth century. In 1924 Sukhe Bator led the Communist take-over of northern Mongolia and created, with Soviet agreement, the People's Republic of Mongolia; and following the creation of the People's Republic of China in 1949, an Inner Mongolian Autonomous Region was created out of the other half of the old nation.

Chinese control over Inner Mongolia remains as strong today as it was under the Manchus, and although there is a certain degree of tolerance for the

Overleaf left: Babur, a descendant of both Timur and Genghis Khan and founder of the Moghul Empire in India. He is depicted receiving envoys in the garden he built at Agra.
Overleaf right: The Taj Mahal. Built by the fifth Moghul Emperor Shah Jahan for his wife Mumtaz Mahal, it is the very antithesis of its barbaric origins.

observance of traditional Mongol rituals, there is at present no sign that the population will be allowed to unite with their brethren across the border. To the north-west, Mongolia, until recently a vassal state of the Soviet empire, is at present trying to find its feet now that it is free of Communist dogma. For the moment, the only sheet anchor that binds together the entire population is the ever-powerful figure of their once-great Genghis Khan. On the labels of vodka bottles, on coins, on carpets, at rock concerts and at political rallies – in almost every facet of contemporary Mongol life – the face of Genghis has become the most potent national symbol. It is a shibboleth for a people whose ancestors once ruled an empire that stretched from the Korean peninsula to the River Danube.

DYNASTIC TABLE

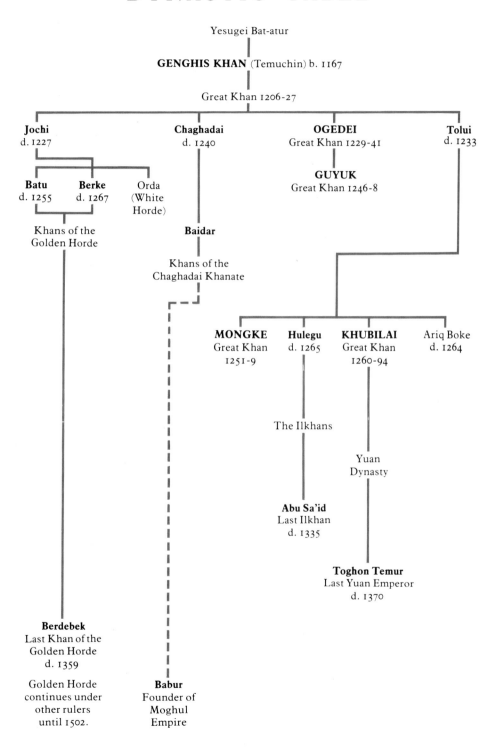

Yesugei Bat-atur

GENGHIS KHAN (Temuchin) b. 1167

Great Khan 1206-27

Jochi
d. 1227

Chaghadai
d. 1240

OGEDEI
Great Khan 1229-41

Tolui
d. 1233

GUYUK
Great Khan 1246-8

Batu
d. 1255

Berke
d. 1267

Orda
(White
Horde)

Khans of the
Golden Horde

Baidar

Khans of the
Chaghadai Khanate

MONGKE
Great Khan
1251-9

Hulegu
d. 1265

KHUBILAI
Great Khan
1260-94

Ariq Boke
d. 1264

The Ilkhans

Yuan
Dynasty

Abu Sa'id
Last Ilkhan
d. 1335

Toghon Temur
Last Yuan Emperor
d. 1370

Berdebek
Last Khan of the
Golden Horde
d. 1359

Golden Horde
continues under
other rulers
until 1502.

Babur
Founder of
Moghul
Empire

Although the communist regime introduced village settlements,
the majority of Mongolians still prefer to live a nomadic life,
sleeping in *gers* and tending their herds.

CHRONOLOGY

?1167	Birth of Genghis Khan
1200	Accession of 'Ala' al-Din Muhammad II, Khwarazm Shah
1206	Genghis Khan proclaimed supreme ruler of the tribes at *quriltai* in Mongolia
1209	Mongols invade Hsi-Hsia
1211	Mongols invade Chin empire of north China
1215	Chung-tu falls to Mongols
1218	Mongol troops occupy Qara Khitai empire
1219	Genghis Khan invades empire of the Khwarazm Shah
1221	Death of Khwarazm Shah
1221–3	Journey of Ch'ang Ch'un from China to Genghis's camp
1223	Genghis Khan returns to Mongolia
1227	Death of Genghis Khan. Definitive conquest of Hsi-Hsia
1229	Election of Ogedei as Great Khan
1234	End of Chin resistance to Mongols
1235	Ogedei builds Qaraqorum, Mongol capital
1237–42	Batu's campaigns in Russia and eastern Europe
1240	Kiev falls to Mongols
1241	Battles of Liegnitz and River Sajo. Death of Ogedei
1245–7	Journey of John of Plano Carpini to Mongolia
1246	Election of Guyuk as Great Khan
1248	Death of Guyuk
1250	Mamluks seize power in Egypt
1251	Election of Mongke as Great Khan
1252	Conquest of Sung empire begins
1253–5	Journey of William of Rubruck to Mongolia

1253	Hulegu's forces set off for Persia
1255	Death of Batu, first Khan of Golden Horde
1256	Hulegu takes Assassin castles in north Persia
1257	Accession of Berke, Khan of Golden Horde
1258	Fall of Baghdad to Hulegu. Death of last Abbasid Caliph
1259	Death of Mongke
1260	Hulegu invades Syria, then withdraws. Battle of Ayn Jalut. Rival *quriltais* elect Kubilai and Ariq Boke as Great Khan: civil war ensues
1261–2	Civil war between Hulegu and Berke
1264	Kubilai victorious over Ariq Boke
1265	Death of Hulegu, first Ilkhan. Accession of Abaqa
1266	Building begins at new Mongol capital of China, Ta-tu (Peking)
1267	Death of Berke, Khan of Golden Horde
1272	Kubilai adopts Chinese dynastic title, Yuan
1274	First Mongol expedition against Japan
1276	Hang-chou, capital of Sung empire, falls to Mongols
1279	Sung empire defeated
1281	Second Mongol expedition against Japan
1287	Rabban Sauma sent to Europe by Ilkhan Arghun
1294	Death of Kubilai
1295	Accession of Ghazan as Ilkhan. Mongols in Persia become Muslim
1304	Death of Ilkhan Ghazan. Accession of Oljeitu
1313	Accession of Ozbeg, under whose rule Golden Horde becomes Muslim
1335	Death of Abu Sa'id, last Ilkhan of line of Hulegu
1346	Outbreak of Black Death in Mongol force besieging Kaffa, in the Crimea: from there it spreads to Europe
1353–4	Major outbreak of the disease in China
1368	Mongols driven from China by Ming forces
1370	Death in Qaraqorum of Toghon Temur, last Yuan emperor

BIBLIOGRAPHY

BARFIELD, THOMAS J., *The Perilous Frontier: Nomadic Empires and China*, Basil Blackwell Inc., Cambridge, Mass., and Oxford, 1989

BRYER, ANTHONY, 'Edward I and the Mongols', in *History Today* XIV/10, October 1964

CHAMBERS, JAMES, *The Devil's Horsemen: The Mongol Invasion of Europe*, Weidenfeld & Nicholson, London, 1979, and Cassell, London, 1988

CLEAVES, FRANCIS WOODMAN, *The Secret History of the Mongols*, Vols. 1 & 2, Harvard University Press, Cambridge, Mass., 1982

CROSS, F. L. and LIVINGSTONE, E. A., (eds), *The Oxford Dictionary of the Christian Church*, Oxford University Press, London, 1974

EDWARDS, E. H., *Horses: Their Role in the History of Man*, Willow Books, London, 1987

FULLER, J. F. C., *Decisive Battles of the Western World*, Eyre and Spottiswoode, London, 1954

GILES, J. A., *Matthew Paris's English History*, Henry G. Bohn, London, 1852

GRIFFITHS, JOHN C., *Afghanistan: Key to a Continent*, Andre Deutsch, London, 1981

HARTOG, LEO DE, *Genghis Khan, Conqueror of the World*, I. B. Tauris & Co Ltd., London, 1989. Originally published as *Djenghis Khan's Werelds Grootste Veroveraar*, by Elsevier, Amsterdam, 1971

JACKSON, PETER, (trans.) and MORGAN, DAVID, *The Mission of Friar William of Rubruck: His Journey to the Court of the Great Khan Mongke, 1253–1255*, Hakluyt Society, London, 1990

JANKOVICH, MIKLOS, *They Rode into Europe* (trans. Dent, A.), George G. Harrap, London, 1971

JUVAINI, ALA-AD-DIN ATA MALIK, *The History of the World Conqueror* (trans. BOYLE, JOHN ANDREW), Manchester University Press, Manchester, 1958

LAMB, HAROLD, *Genghis Khan: The Emperor of All Men*, Robert McBride, New York, 1928

LIDDELL HART, B. H., *Great Captains Unveiled*, Cedric Chivers Ltd, Bath, 1971

MATHESON, SYLVIA A., *Persia: An Archaeological Guide*, Faber & Faber, London, 1972

MARTIN, H. DESMOND, *The Rise of Chingis Khan and his Conquest of North China*, The Johns Hopkins Press, Baltimore, 1950

McNIELL, WILLIAM H., *Plagues and People*, Doubleday and Anchor, New York, 1977

MITCHELL, ROBERT AND FORBES, NEVILLE (trans.), *The Chronicle of Novgorod, 1017–1471*, Camden Society, London, 1914

MORGAN, DAVID, *The Mongols*, Basil Blackwell, Oxford, 1986

RACHEWILTZ, I. DE, *Papal Envoys to the Great Khans*, Faber & Faber, London, 1971

RATCHNEVSKY, PAUL, *Genghis Khan, His Life and Legacy* (trans. HAINING, THOMAS NIVISON), Basil Blackwell Ltd., Cambridge, Mass., and Oxford, 1991. Originally published as *Cinggis-Khan: Sein Leben und Wirken*, Franz Steiner Verlag, GMBH, 1983

ROSSABI, MORRIS, *Khubilai Khan, His Life and Times*, University of California Press, Berkeley, 1988

SHATZMAN STEINHARDT, NANCY, *Chinese Imperial City Planning*, University of Hawaii Press, Honolulu, 1990

SAUNDERS, J. J., *The History of the Mongol Conquests*, Routledge & Kegan Paul Ltd., London, 1971

SEVERIN, TIM, *In Search of Genghis Khan*, Hutchinson, London, 1991

SHEPPARD, CAPT. E. W., 'Military Methods of the Mongols', *The Army Quarterly*, Vol. 18, 1929, pp. 305–15

SPULER, BERNHARD, *History of the Mongols Based on Eastern and Western Accounts of the Thirteenth and Fourteenth Century* (trans. H. and S. DRUMMOND), Routledge & Kegan Paul Ltd., London, 1972

WILBER, DONALD N., *The Architecture of Islamic Iran*, Princeton University Press, New Jersey, 1955

YOUNG, JOHN M. L., *By Foot to China: Missions of the Church of the East, to 1400*, Young, Japan, 1984

YULE, HENRY (trans.), *The Book of Ser Marco Polo, the Venetian, Concerning the Kingdoms and Marvels of the East by Henri Cordier*, John Murray, London, 1903